Part 2 of 180 Days of Communing with God Daily Devotional

JULY THROUGH DECEMBER 31ST

By LaRose A. Richardson

REJOICE
Essential Publishing

LaRose Angela Richardson/Rejoice Essential Publishing

PO BOX 512

Effingham, SC 29541

www.republishing.org

Part 2 of 180 days of Communing with God Daily Devotional/ LaRose Angela Richardson

ISBN-13: 978-1-956775-31-0

Contents

Acknowledgments

I WOULD LIKE TO THANK God, who is the head of my life, for giving me the ability to write my 4th book, "Part 2 of 180 days (about 6 months) of Communing with God Daily Devotional." I must be obedient to what God is telling me concerning the 2nd part of this book by writing and publishing it. So, many people will get a chance for the next 6 months of the year to commune with God on a deeper level.

I welcome the fire of God to saturate every page of this book so the one that is reading it can feel God's presence in their lives like never before in Jesus' name.

Lord, send Your Rauch wind to saturate their homes and lives so they will know without any doubt that You are real. It is so important to walk through our journey empowered with the Word of God in our lives. Also, it is so important not only to hear the Word, but to be doers of the Word of God. This is the last 6 months of the year that will take you on a journey with the Most High, so you can get to know Him intimately.

On this journey with Jesus, you will get to know Jesus from an intimate place. You will learn how to lean and depend on Jesus for everything that you will ever need in your life.

Jesus is our Helper, and He has sent the Holy Ghost and He lives on the inside of our spirit to lead and guide us in all truth.

The Holy Ghost is our teacher, so we will have to walk in humility, be teachable, and allow the Holy Spirit to keep us in proper alignment with God.

I would like to thank my husband, Richard Richardson, for being a man after God's own heart. I thank him for his total support of every endeavor that I have ever journeyed on. I thank him for helping to market and sell my books for me when he goes on a carpet cleaning assignment.

I thank him for being my number one fan and supporting me from day one with my book writing which is a part of the ministry that God has given me.

I want to thank my Pastors for the encouragement that they have spoken over my life and for being obedient to God when they have set me and my husband aside to be on the ministry team at the church, Becoming One Outreach Ministries in Vidalia, GA. I want to thank Pastor Carmella for all the classes that have shown me how to market my business and ministry. I would like to thank both of my leaders for being successful entrepreneurs and teaching us to be the same in our businesses because they want the whole membership to be successful in business.

I want to thank Prophetess Kimberly Moses for being obedient to God to offer certain classes and for God giving me the go ahead and taking these classes so I could learn what I needed to know for what season I am in at the time. I want to thank her for seeing the potential in me and helping pull me out of my comfort zone so I can move forward in the destiny that is on my life.

I would like to thank God for the additional people that He has placed in my life to get me to my next level in Him.

Introduction

THE DEFINITION OF DEVOTIONAL by Merriam-Webster is of or used in religious worship.[1] The Greek word for devotional is "Proskartereo," and the meaning is to attend constantly.[2] So, this is a 180 daily devotional designed to help you contact God daily. It will also help you get more of the Word into your heart to use it when the enemy comes at you like a flood. You will use the Word of God as a standard. All days will end with the prayer of faith or declarations based on the Word of God.

Each subject will help you understand the Word daily and God and get you deeper in the Word. God wants all His children to be victorious in our walk with Him. But many times, we need to continue to have the Word before our eyes and in our hearts to stay encouraged in the Lord.

You will find scriptures in part 2 from a particular book so you can get a deeper understanding of what is being said in

1. Devotional Merriam-Webster.com 2019. https://www.Merriam-Webster.com accessed June 2021
2. "Proskartereo" The Greek word for devotional https://www.biblehub.com accessed June 2021

each chapter for greater understanding. Knowledge is power and the more we know about Jesus and who we are in Christ, the better off we will be. Let us embark on the journey for the last 6 months of the year so we can continue to keep our hearts free from anything that tries to hold us hostage.

We must change our thoughts and change our speech to line up with the Word of God for our lives so we can walk in the victory that is part of our inheritance.

God does not wink at ignorance any longer. He has provided so many ways for us to become knowledgeable in our walk with Him. So, every chance we get, we should be reading, speaking, and living the Word of God so God's plans for our lives can start to fall into place for us.

God wants all of His children to be prosperous in every area of our lives, never lacking anything but we always must do our part in the plan that He has for our lives.

So doing your part will be studying, reading, practicing what you are reading, and speaking things that line up with the Word of God. The more Word you have in you, the stronger you are in the spiritual realm. More Word equals more power. The less Word equals less power.

Come on, let's enjoy the last 6 months of the year in the presence of God. This book will be a great teaching tool to teach Bible studies and show our children they need to know God as well. Our children need to know Him at a very young age because the enemy is trying to draw them younger and younger to serve him. God has given parents a mandate to teach their children and grandchildren about Him before they get introduced to the demonic realm. The Word of God states to *train up a child in the way that they should go, when they get old, they shall not depart (Proverbs 22:6)*. This book will be a great tool to give them the Word before they go off to school so they will know how to handle different situations that may come their way.

July 1st

*A*CTS 1:8 (NKJV), "*BUT you shall receive power when the Holy Spirit has come upon you; and you shall be witnesses to Me in Jerusalem, and in all Judea and Samaria, and to the end of the earth.*"

Power in Merriam Webster Dictionary is defined as the ability to do something or act in a particular way.[3] The Greek word for Power is "Dunamis" meaning the strength, power, and power for performing miracles.[4]

This verse has red font in the Bible because Jesus is talking. Jesus told his disciples to wait in Jerusalem in the Upper Room until the fire of the Holy Ghost would descend upon them. They needed the power of the Holy Ghost to be able to speak the Word effectively so yokes could be broken off people while the Word was going forth. Also, they needed the Holy Ghost to be able to heal the sick, open blind eyes, and cast out devils. No one was able to do these things in their own strength, but with

3. Power Merriam-Webster.com 2019. https://www.Merriam-Webster.com Accessed June 2021
4. "Dumanis" The Greek Word for Power https://www.biblehub.com Accessed June 2021

the Holy Ghost all these things are possible. We are supposed to be walking in the same power that raised Jesus from the dead. So, that is "Dunamis" (dynamite) power. When Jesus walked this earth, He operated in this "Dunamis" power and everyone that Jesus met; He healed, delivered, and set them free from all oppressions. As the body of Christ, we are supposed to be walking in the same demonstration that Jesus walked in. Jesus said in His Word that we would do greater things in our ministry here on earth. The only way that we can walk like Jesus walked and do the things that Jesus did is to be full of the Holy Ghost and fire.

PRAYER

Father God, in the name of Jesus, I come before You today asking You to give me another filling of Your Holy Ghost and fire so that I can walk in demonstration like You did when You walked this earth over 2,000 years ago. Lord, forgive me of any sin, knowingly and unknowingly, that I am not aware of so nothing will hold me back from receiving Your Dunamis power in Jesus' name. Lord, Your Word declares that we are to lay hands on the sick and they shall recover. Your Word declares that we are to cast out demons, devils, and anything that has Your people oppressed. Lord, Your Word declares that we will become witnesses for You in Jerusalem (in our hometown, family), Judea (in the state, country that you live in), Samaria (your region), and the other most parts of the world (in other countries). Lord, fill us up until we overflow with Your Dunamis power from this day forward. We will go into the highways and byways, letting people know that they need a Savior. When they give their lives to Christ to start living a holy and righteous lifestyle and being led by the Holy Ghost, sign, wonders, and miracles will follow them that believe according to Your Word God in Jesus' name. Amen.

July 2nd

*A*CTS *2:2-3 (NKJV), "²AND suddenly there came a sound from heaven, as of a rushing mighty wind, and it filled the whole house where they were sitting. ³ Then there appeared to them divided tongues, as of fire, and one sat upon each of them."*

Wind in the Merriam Webster Dictionary is defined as a natural movement of air of any velocity.[5] The Greek word for wind is "Pneuma," meaning wind, spirit, or breath.[6]

There suddenly came a sound as a mighty rushing wind (the breath of God) filled the room where they were praying. Everyone there was on one accord with the same mind because they were seeking the empowerment that Jesus had promised them. Jesus told them to wait on the promise of the Holy Ghost so they would be endued with power from on high because they needed the Holy Ghost before they could be effective in ministry. The Holy Ghost would no longer live on them, but He

---

5. Wind Merrian-Webster.com 2019. https://www.Merriam-Webster.com Accessed June 2021
6. "Pnuema" The Greek word for Wind https://www.biblehub.com Accessed June 2021

would now live inside of their spirits to lead and guide them. They were so hungry and waited to be filled. So, when the wind of God came into the room, everyone knew it and could feel the presence of God on them. They began to speak in other languages as the Spirit gave them utterance. The people that were visiting Jerusalem at the time all heard the Gospel of Jesus in their own language and 3,000 souls were added to the Kingdom of God that day.

So, just like it was in those days, it is important for each of us naming the name of Christ to have the baptism of the Holy Ghost living on the inside of us. He is our comforter and guide. He will lead you into all truth. God gave Him to us so we can walk in our calling, empowered from on high. It is impossible to do effective ministry without the leading of the Holy Ghost. The Holy Ghost will show you things and people who you need to be praying and interceding for. He will speak to you in a still, small voice and tell you many things that you need to know in your walk with Him.

DECLARATIONS

I decree and declare that I will walk in freedom being led by the Holy Spirit.

Lord, give me another filling of Your Holy Spirit and fire so I can be refreshed in Jesus' name.

Lord, I surrender everything to You so I can be led by the Holy Spirit in every area of my life.

Lord, fill me up until I overflow with Your Dunamis presence.

I will pray in tongues on a regular basis so I can be built up my Spirit man.

I decree and declare that the Spirit of the Lord will rest upon me and in me.

I decree and declare that the Spirit of wisdom and understanding shall rest upon me and in me.

I decree and declare that the Spirit of counsel and might shall rest upon and in me.

I decree and declare that the Spirit of knowledge shall rest upon me and in me.

I decree and declare that the fear of the Lord shall rest upon me and in me in Jesus' name.

July 3rd

*A*CTS *3:2,6,7 (NKJV),* "*²AND a certain man lame from his mother's womb was carried, whom they laid daily at the gate of the temple, which is called Beautiful, to ask alms from those who entered the temple. ⁶ Then Peter said, "Silver and gold I do not have, but what I do have I give you: In the name of Jesus Christ of Nazareth, rise and walk. ⁷ And he took him by the right hand and lifted him up, and immediately his feet and ankle bones received strength."*

Strength in the Merriam Webster Dictionary is defined as the quality or state of being strong or endurance.[7] The Greek word for strength is "Ischus," meaning might, power, force, ability.[8]

There was a man at the gate called beautiful asking for alms from everyone who passed him. He had been lamed from birth and he would sit out there to get money because of his inability to work. On this day, Peter and John were going into the temple

---

7. Strength Merriam-Webster.com 2019 https://www.Merriam-Webster.com Accessed June 2021
8. "Ischus" The Greek word for Strength https://www.biblehub.com Accessed June 2021

at the hour of prayer. The lame man asked them for money and Peter told him that he did not have any money, but he was endued with the Holy Spirit. The only thing that he could offer him was healing.

The man sitting there was expecting alms (money), but Peter gave him something even greater. He gave him the use of his legs to be able to walk and to start earning money now for himself instead of asking for alms at the gate called Beautiful. When you read a little further in the text, you will see that the man was able to get up leaping, walking, and praising God for his healing and he went into the temple with them. His legs and ankles were strengthened by just speaking the Word.

God wants to strengthen us as well. If you are dealing with something now in your body and you feel like there is no cure for it, I am here to tell you that God is a healer, and He wants you well.

PRAYER

Father God, in the name of Jesus, I come before You today, lifting the person up who is reading this prayer on today. Lord, I pray that You will touch them in their bodies and minds right now. I decree that they will rise and walk into whatever door that You have opened up before them in Jesus' name. Lord, we bind the spirit of depression and fear off their lives and loose hope into their lives in Jesus' name. Lord, I speak to that fear that is trying to hold them back and down and command it to go back to the abyss, never to return anymore in Jesus' name.

Lord, Your Word declares that we will not have the spirit of fear but of power and love and a sound mind in Jesus' name. Lord, we know that You love us so much and we do not have anything to fear because You are fighting for us in Jesus' name. Lord, we thank You for Your unconditional love, grace, and mercy that empowers us to continue to move forward in You, God, in Jesus' name. Amen.

July 4th

*A*CTS 4:29,30,31 (NKJV) "*29.* Now, Lord, look on their threats, and grant to Your servants that with all boldness they may speak Your word." *30.* "By stretching out Your hand to heal, and that sign and wonders may be done through the name of Your holy Servant Jesus." *31.* "And when they had prayed, the place where they assembled together was shaken; and they were filled with the Holy Spirit, and they spoke the word of God with boldness."

Shaken in Merriam Webster Dictionary is defined as vibrating, especially due to a blow or shock.[9] The Greek word for shaken is "Saleuo," meaning to shake, cast down, or stir up.[10]

God can protect us from our enemies. He can tie the hands of the enemy or turn their hearts. He sees all the threats that have been made against you. He will grant us more boldness so that we can speak the Word. Signs, wonders, and miracles may be done through the name of Jesus. Everything that we will do

---

9. Shaking Merriam-Webster.com 2019 https://www.Merriam-Webster.com June 2021
10. Saleuo" The Greek word for shaking https://www.biblehub.com Accessed June 2021

will be done through the Holy Spirit. Lord, give us grace to go into our work and not be afraid. Those sent on God's errands ought to deliver their message with boldness, not doubting what they say. The threatening of our enemies should stir us up to have more courage because when they are fighting against us, they are indeed fighting against Christ.

God will give us the power to work miracles for the confirmation of the doctrine that is preached. Nothing gives us confidence more than having the presence of God with us. Signs, wonders and miracles can only be done by the name of Jesus. There is no other name that a person can be saved, healed, delivered, or set free only through Jesus.

The shaking of the place was designed to raise their expectations and the reason was for them to fear God more and man less. The place was shaken so their faith might be established and be unshaken. God gave them a greater degree of His Spirit. Their prayer was accepted by God because it was answered by Him. The Holy Spirit taught them not only what to speak, but how to speak. Their prayer was for them to be filled with the Holy Spirit. Gifts and talents must be exercised for God so they can get stronger and be improved.[11]

DECLARATIONS

I decree and declare that I will use the gifts and talents that God has given me for His glory in Jesus' name.

---

11. Matthew Henry's Concise Commentary. Volume 1 Zondervan Accessed June 2021

I decree that God just didn't give me a gift for myself, but He gave it to me to be used for other people.

I decree and declare that signs, wonders, and miracles will follow me because I am a servant of God.

I decree and declare that my faith is getting stronger, and I can do what God wants me to do without doubting.

I decree and declare that I will walk closely with the Holy Spirit, so I can be led by Him.

I decree and declare I will speak God's Word with boldness and confidence in Jesus' name.

I decree and declare that I will cooperate with the Holy Spirit and let Him teach me what to say, how to do it, and when to say it.

July 5th

*A*CTS 5:29 (NKJV), "BUT *Peter and the other Apostles answered and said: "We ought to obey God rather than men."*

Obey in Merriam Webster Dictionary is defined as following commands or guidance of.[12] The Greek word for Obey is "hupakoe," meaning obedience, submission, or compliance.[13]

In this scripture, the Chief Priests came to Peter and the other Apostles and told them not to teach or preach about Jesus. But Peter and John said to them that they could not listen to them, but they could only do what Jesus was telling them to do. They told the chief priests that they could only speak what they had seen and heard. The chief priests had them thrown in jail, but at night an angel of the Lord came to them and released them and told them to stand in the temple and speak to the people. The council kept commanding them to stop teaching about Jesus. Peter and the other Apostles told them that they

12. Obey Merriam-Webster.com 2019 https://www.Merriam-Webster.com Accessed June 2021
13. "Hypakoe" The Greek Word for Obey https://www.biblehub.com Accessed June 2021

would only do what God told them to do and not what man told them to do.

This is what we must do today if anyone tries to get us to shut up and keep threatening us with bodily harm. We cannot stop but we must continue to do like the early Apostles and speak and teach this dying world about Jesus. So, they can have the opportunity to hear the Gospel and give their lives to Christ if they desire to do so.

We are to always obey God. The angels were on assignment from God, speaking to them in prison. They obeyed the voice of God and taught in the middle of the temple regardless of the threats from the chief priests and council. God's authority is always superior to man's authority.

The Word of God states that if we are willing and obedient (to God) that we will eat the good of the land. We will never have anything to worry about because God has our backs. He is going to keep us protected from any types of harm that the enemy sends against us or our families.

<u>PRAYER</u>

Father God, in the name of Jesus, I come before You today asking that You cover all the seasoned laborers that You have sent out into the world to preach and teach about Jesus. Lord, I pray that You would cover each of them with Your precious blood in Jesus's name. Lord, give them wisdom and knowledge on how to handle themselves as they go out into the highways and byways, compelling men and women to give their lives to You, God. I decree and declare that they will all walk in the boldness of God right now in Jesus' name. They will not worry what man can do to them, but they will know that if they are pleasing You, they will be well taken care of in Jesus' name. Lord, remove the spirit of fear off their lives so they can walk in the confidence of who You have called them to be in Jesus' name. Lord, help us all to be obedient to what You are calling and telling us to do for Your kingdom in Jesus' name. We will proclaim Your name in every country, state, city, and neighborhood, so people will know that they need a Savior. They will know that salvation and victory can only come through accepting the finished works of Jesus in Jesus' name. Amen.

July 6th

*A*CTS 9:33-35 (NKJV), *"³³ There he found a certain man named Aeneas who had been bedridden eight years and was paralyzed. ³⁴ And Peter said to him, "Aeneas, Jesus the Christ heals you, Arise and make your bed. Then he arose immediately. ³⁵ So all who dwelt at Lydda, and Sharon saw him and turned to the Lord.*

Paralyzed in Merriam Webster Dictionary is defined as making powerless or ineffective.[14] The Greek word for paralyzed is "Paraluo," meaning feeble, paralytic, to weakened, or disable.[15]

In this scripture, Peter went through all parts of the country preaching and teaching Jesus and healing all manners of illnesses and diseases. He had come to the saints in Lydda and found a man who had been crippled for eight years. Peter spoke the Word of God in boldness and authority and the man Aeneas was healed of the paralysis that he had been experiencing for all those years.

14. Paralyzed Merriam-Webster.com 2019 https://www.Merriam-Webster.com Accessed June 2021
15. "Paraluo" The Greek word for Paralyzed https://www.biblehub.com Accessed June 2021

Many of God's people have been paralyzed in fear for many years, but if you are reading this today, Jesus wants to heal you and set you free. In Jesus' name, be healed and delivered from fear. Get out of the place called 'stuck' and move forward into your destiny right now in Jesus' name. No longer will you be stuck in between two opinions. God is calling you deeper and to another place in Him. It does not matter who does not want to go with you, nor does it matter who does not agree with the calling on your life.

Just like this man, Aeneas, Arise and make your bed because God needs you. Don't miss the call waiting on confirmation after confirmation, especially when God has already told you to move forward. Signs, wonders, and miracles follow the Word of God because the Word itself is life and it can give life to the hearers.

God will use you to heal the sick, open blinded eyes, cast out demons and devils. He is going to use you for His glory. When you are preaching and teaching the Word and it is followed by demonstration, people will know that you are sent by God and that He is with you. It is your job to preach, teach, lay hands, or speak the Word and it is God's job to make it happen.

DECLARATIONS

I decree and declare that just like Aeneas, I am going to arise and make up my bed.

I decree and declare that I will let nothing stop me from moving forward in God.

I decree and declare that I will not continue to make excuses about moving forward in my calling.

I decree and declare that I am one that has been called by God to speak the Word of God.

I decree and declare along with the Holy Spirit, I will lay hands on the sick or speak the Word and they shall recover in Jesus' name.

I break the spirit of fear off of my life and I will no longer be paralyzed in fear.

I decree and declare that I will speak the Word as the Holy Spirit leads me to and people will be delivered and set free.

July 7th

*A*CTS 16:25-26 (NKJV), *"²⁵ But at midnight Paul and Silas were praying and singing hymns to God, and the prisoners were listening to them. ²⁶·* *"Suddenly there was a great earthquake, so that the foundations of the prison were shaken; and immediately all the doors were opened, and everyone's chain were loosed."*

Suddenly in Merriam Webster Dictionary is defined as happening or coming unexpectedly.[16] The Greek word for Suddenly is "Exaiphnes," meaning suddenly or unexpected.[17]

Paul and Silas were beaten and thrown in jail because the girl with the spirit of divination could no longer make money for her masters. Paul commanded the demonic spirit to come out of her in Jesus' name, and the spirit came out of her. Her masters brought them to the magistrates claiming that they were troubling the city. They were beaten and thrown into the in-

16. Suddenly Merriam-Webster.com 2019 https://www.Merriam-Webster.com Accessed June 2021
17. "Exaiphnes" The Greek Word for Suddenly https://www.biblehub.com Accessed June 2021

ner prison and fastened their feet with stocks so they couldn't move.

But regardless of that fact, they had a prayer meeting in the jail where they were. They didn't let their circumstances determine their praise. God answered their praise and worship with a great earthquake that shook the whole jail. When the jailer awoke and saw these doors open, he assumed that they were gone. But Paul called out to him to let them know that they were still there. It shook up the jailer so that he wanted to know what he must do to be saved.

This goes back to walking in demonstration that even during praise and worship, the Spirit of God is moving. Just like Paul and Silas prayed and sang songs, we must do the same thing. It does not require a pretty voice to contact God. God heard their prayers and worship and loosed their bands. God is not a respecter of persons; He is waiting on us to pray and sing songs to Him. God can do mighty things in our lives, but we have to be willing to do our part. Paul and Silas just spoke the Word in faith and authority and the girl was cured of the demonic spirit.

We have the same power dwelling on the inside of us today. All we have to do is speak in faith that God will move on our behalf in a situation. It is our job to pray and worship, but it is God's job to heal.

PRAYER

Father God, in the name of Jesus, I come before You today to ask that You be amid my worship as I worship You in Spirit and truth in Jesus' name. Lord, forgive me of any sin, knowingly and unknowingly, that I may have done that may have separated me from Your presence in Jesus' name. I repent so that I can get back into right standing with You on today. I do not want anything hindering my prayers or my worship to You. Lord, just like You came suddenly to Paul's and Silas's rescue; I know that You can come to my rescue too. Lord, I need You to intervene on my behalf today because the enemy is trying to hem me in on every side. Lord, I need a way of escape from the enemy on today in Jesus' name. Lord, hide me in the secret place and keep me covered under Your wings in Jesus' name. Lord, I believe but help my unbelief so that I can believe You for the impossible in my life on today in Jesus' name. Lord, I speak to my storm and command it to move out of my life right now in Jesus' name. Lord, let the storm be replaced with Your peace that passes all understanding in Jesus' name. Lord, thank You for moving on my behalf today in Jesus' name. Amen.

July 8th

*R*OMANS 1:16 (NKJV), "FOR I am not ashamed of the gospel of Christ, for it is the power of God to salvation for everyone who believes, for the Jew first and also for the Greek."

Ashamed in Merriam Webster Dictionary is defined as feeling shame, guilt or disgrace, and unworthy.[18] The Greek word for Ashamed is "Aischune," meaning shame, shamefaced, or shameful deeds.[19]

In Matthew Henry's Commentary Book Volume One, Paul states that he is not ashamed of the Gospel of Jesus Christ. Paul may have been considered a Christian. Indeed that is neither shame of the Gospel or a shame to it.[20]

Paul had done many things before His name was changed to Paul. When his name was Saul, he arrested and locked up

18. Ashamed Merriam-Webster.com 2019 https://www.Merriam-Webster.com Accessed June 2021
19. "Aischune" The Greek Word for Ashamed https://www.biblehub.com Accessed June 2021
20. Matthew Henry's Concise Commentary book @1960 Zondervan Accessed June 2021

Christians all the time because he thought he was helping God out by doing so. Since he was fighting against Jesus, he had to have that Damascus Road experience so he could realize that Jesus was real and that he needed a Savior regardless of what he knew of the scriptures because he really didn't know Jesus.

Today, we need to know Christ as our personal Savior and not think that we are okay without knowing Him. Jesus is the answer that many of us have been seeking for years, we know something is missing, but we cannot always put our finger on what is missing in our lives. Jesus is the only person in our life that will make us feel whole and complete. Because without Jesus, we are not really living our lives. We are just existing. But when we accept Christ in our lives, that is only when the true living begins in our lives. All we have to do is accept the finished works of Jesus by giving our lives to Him and making Him Lord of our lives.

When God accepts us into the fold, we are made alive by His Holy Spirit, and He will lead and guide us in all truth. God will take us through a process to get to the destiny that He has laid out before us. We will have to stay rooted and grounded in God and allow Him to use us for His glory. So, many of the things that we used to do before Christ will start to fall away from our lives over a period as we continue to grow in God.

We can be like Saul after his name was changed to Paul. We can tell people about Jesus and offer them a new way of life through Him. We should never be ashamed of the Gospel of Jesus Christ, nor should we make Him ashamed by our actions or how we carry ourselves once we are taught the way to walk with the Lord.

DECLARATIONS

I decree and declare that I will not be ashamed of the Gospel of Jesus Christ.

I decree and declare that I will not make Jesus a shame of me.

I decree and declare that I will love God with all my heart, mind, and soul.

I decree and declare that I will not let fear stop me from telling someone about the goodness of the Lord.

I decree and declare that I will remain teachable, grow, and learn more about Christ.

I decree and declare that I will read my Bible to learn about Jesus's ministry while He walked this earth.

July 9th

❋

*A*CTS 4:12 *(KJV)*, *"N*EITHER *is their salvation in any other: for there is none other name under heaven given among men, whereby we must be saved."*

Salvation in the Merriam Webster Dictionary is defined as the deliverance from the power and effects of sin.[21] The Greek word for Salvation is "Sozo," meaning deliverance, salvation, safety, or prosperity.[22]

Jesus is the only name by which we all can be saved. We can't get to God unless we come through Jesus and accept the work that He has done on the Cross.

Matthew Henry's Commentary Book Volume One states that it is absolutely necessary that people believe in His name and call upon it. Jesus is the stone that the church is supposed to be built around. Jesus is the Head Cornerstone. All of our

21. Salvation Merriam-Webster.com 2019 https://www.Merriam-Webster.com Accessed June 2021
22. "Sozo" The Greek Word for salvation https://www.biblehub.com Accessed June 2021

teaching should be built upon Jesus. There is no salvation in any other person known in this world or in the other world.

There is no other name by which diseased bodies can be healed, nor is there any other name by which sinful souls can be saved. Jesus is the doorway to God. Jesus is the doorway to eternal life. Jesus is the doorway to abundant life here on earth. All other ways to God are a dead end. Our salvation is not in our own ability because we cannot save ourselves, but we need Jesus' shed blood to be saved.

God has appointed Jesus to be head over everything. We cannot find favor with God unless we accept Christ as our Lord and Savior.[23] So if you desire to be saved today, repeat the bottom prayer and believe it in your heart and you can be saved.

<u>PRAYER</u>

Father God, in the name of Jesus, I come before You today ready to give my whole life to You. Lord, I am tired of running from the calling on my life right now in Jesus' name. Lord, Your Word declares in *Romans 10:9-10 (NKJV), "That if you confess with your mouth the Lord Jesus and believe in your heart that God has raised Him from the dead, you will be saved. For with the heart one believes unto righteousness, and with the mouth, confession is made unto salvation."* Lord, come inside of my heart and make a new creature out of me from this day forward in Jesus' name. Lord, fill me with Your Holy Ghost and fire in Jesus' name. Amen.

---

23. Matthew Henry's Concise Commentary Book Volume 1 @ 1960 Zondervan Accessed June 2021

July 10th

*A*CTS 5:38-39 (NKJV) "*38 And now I say to you, keep away from these men and let them alone; for if this plan or this work is of me, it will come to nothing. *39*. "But if it is of God, you cannot overthrow it—lest you even be found to fight against God."*

Away in the Merriam Webster Dictionary is defined as in another direction or on the way.[24] The Greek word for Away is "Apo," meaning away from, or from.[25]

The High Priest and the Sadducees were filled with indignation at the Apostles because they preached Jesus in the temple. They plotted to kill them because of their teachings and especially being told to their faces about what they had done to Jesus.

One of the council members stood up and told them to put the Apostles outside the room for a while. He addressed the Council and told them, "Men of Israel, take heed to yourselves,

24. Away Merriam-Webster.com 2019 https://www.Merriam-Webster.com Accessed June 2021.
25. "Apo" The Greek Word for Away https://www.biblehub.com Accessed June 2021

what you attend to do regarding these men." He told them to keep away from these men because they would be fighting against God if they did any harm to them.

This applies to us today: those that are living for God and doing the work of the Lord. The enemy will send people to come up against us and try to harm or hurt us. When they think they are fighting against us, they are really fighting against God because we are spirit beings that have the Holy Ghost on the inside of us. Our true self is our spirits that are filled with the Holy Spirit and being led by Him. When the enemy comes against us like a flood, God will raise up a standard against the enemy and he must flee seven ways.

So just like with the Apostles in those days, the enemy will use anybody who lets him use them to come against God's elect. We have God as our refuge, and we have Him fighting for us and we have nothing to fear from the enemy. Continue to be on fire for the LORD regardless of the warfare that you are going through. We are covered under the shadow of the Almighty God, and nothing can hurt us.

PRAYER

Oh, precious Father, we come before You today to ask that You keep us covered under Your blood from every fiery darts of the enemy against our lives in Jesus' name. Lord, cover us from the top of our heads to the soles of our feet in Jesus' name. Lord, we put on the full armor of God so we can fight against the enemy and come out victorious in You Jesus. Lord, we cover our families, businesses, homes, and everything that we own and are connected to under Your blood in Jesus' name. Lord, we apply the blood of Jesus over the eyes of every monitoring spirit in Jesus' name. Lord, we cancel and veto every threat from the enemy on our lives in Jesus' name. Lord, release Your warring angels on our behalf right now in Jesus' name. So, they can go to bat for us and keep us protected from anything that is evil sent to destroy us in Jesus' name. Amen.

July 11th

ROMANS 4:20-21(KJV), "²⁰ HE *staggered not at the promise of God through unbelief but was strong in faith, giving glory to God." ²¹· "And being fully persuaded, that what he had promised, he was able also to perform it."*

Persuaded in the Merriam Webster Dictionary is defined as position, course of action, to plead with, or urge.[26] The Greek word for Persuaded is "Peitho," which means to persuade and have confidence.[27]

Abraham believed that God was going to open Sarah's womb so that she could have the promised child, Isaac. Abraham knew that his body was dead and that Sarah's womb was dead. So, it had to be God's doing because they could not do it on their own. They didn't have a choice but to believe God for Isaac. God had told Abraham that he would be the father of many nations, so the seed would have to come through him. Abra-

26. Persuaded Merriam-Webster.com https://www.Merriam-Webster.com Accessed June 2021
27. "Peitho" The Greek word for Persuaded https://www.biblehub.com Accessed June 2021

ham had great faith to believe God at His Word concerning the promised child.

We need to do the same thing and believe God at His Word instead of doubting that He can do it. He would do what He has promised in your life. All we have to do is have faith and continue to speak faith regardless of what we are seeing with our natural eyes. We are spirit beings. When we pray about the problem, God starts to work the answers out to our prayers. Prayers are answered in the spiritual realm before manifesting into the natural realm. Just keep praying and reminding God of His Word concerning your situation.

DECLARATIONS

I decree and declare that I will have great faith in God to work things out for me.

I decree and declare that my faith can move mountains in my life.

I decree and declare that I will speak what the Word of God declares over my life, family, ministry, and marriage in Jesus' name.

I decree and declare that healing and deliverance are in my mouth in Jesus' name.

I decree and declare that I can have what I say according to Your Word, God.

Your Word declares, "According to my faith," be it unto me.

I decree and declare that I will read, study the Word, and speak it aloud so that my faith can grow in Jesus' name.

July 12th

ROMANS 3:3-4 (NKJV), "*³ For what is some did not believe? Will their unbelief make the faithfulness of God without effect? ⁴ "Certainly not! Indeed, let God be true but every man a liar. As it is written: "That You may be justified in Your words and may overcome when You are judged."*

Unbelief in the Merriam Webster Dictionary is defined as incredulity or skepticism especially in matters of religious faith, disbelief, or nonbelief.[28] The Greek word for Unbelief is "Apistia," which means unbelief, unfaithfulness, or distrust.[29]

According to Matthew Henry Commentary Volume One, the scriptures are the oracles of God: they are a divine revelation. Salvation first came to the Jews, God's chosen people, who rejected Him. The Jews were entrusted with the sacred treasure for their own use and benefit in the first place. After the Jews

28. Unbelief Merriam-Webster.com https://www.Merriam-Webster.com Accessed June 2021
29. "Apistia" The Greek word for Unbelief https://www.biblehub.com Accessed June 2021

rejected Jesus, salvation was offered to the Gentiles so that we could have a right to the tree of life.

Many Jewish people today are still strangers to Christ. They have rejected Him, but God has a plan to bring the gospel of Jesus back to the Jews. Their unbelief does not affect the Gospel of Jesus Christ. It is still valid as it was when Jesus walked the earth. God's Word was accomplished despite their unbelief. Let God's Word be true and every man a liar, meaning that God is true to every Word that He has spoken. He cannot lie. All men are liars compared with God.[30]

This is true for us today. God's offer for salvation is the same. God loves us and He wants everyone to come to repentance, but He will not force Himself on anyone. It has to be your choice, and He is standing with His arms wide open, welcoming you into the fold. People only reject what they do not understand, and many have read the scriptures without a true understanding. The reason is that you need the Holy Spirit living on the inside of you to understand the Word of God. A carnal mind cannot comprehend the spiritual things of God. You have to be born again to understand what God is saying through His Word.

But you do not have to keep standing in the window looking in. God has offered salvation to you as well and all you have to do is surrender your whole life over to Him and start living a life that is pleasing unto Him. Get into a Bible preaching church that is preaching about Jesus and leading people to Jesus. Study

30. Matthew Henry's Concise Commentary Volume 1 @1960 Zondervan Accessed June 2021

your Word and go to Bible Study to be taught more about Jesus and what salvation means to you now that you are saved. You must continue to grow more in God daily, and as you mature in Him, God will begin to use you for His glory. This is what God wants for each of us and of course now we have eternal life and heaven is our home when we leave this earth.

<u>PRAYER</u>

Father God, in the name of Jesus, I come before You today to thank You for sending Your Son Jesus so that I can have a right to the tree of life in Jesus' name. Lord, forgive me of every sin that I have committed up until this present time in Jesus' name. Your Word declares in *Romans 10:9 (NKJV)*, *"That if I confess with my mouth the Lord Jesus and believe in my heart that God has raised Him from the dead, I will be saved in Jesus' name.* Lord, save me and fill me with Your Holy Ghost and fire with the evidence of speaking in tongues. Lord, I do not want to walk in carnality any longer. I want to read and understand the scriptures through the leading of the Holy Spirit in Jesus' name. Lord, I thank You for making a new creature out of me and getting rid of the old man in Jesus' name. Lord, thank You for loving and caring about me so much that You do not want to see me lost in Jesus' name. Amen.

July 13th

*R*OMANS 6:1-2 (NKJV), *"¹WHAT shall we say then? Shall we continue in sin that grace may abound? ²· "Certainly not! How shall we who died to sin live any longer in it?"*

Grace in Merriam Webster Dictionary is defined as unmerited divine assistance given to humans for their regeneration or sanctification.[31] The Greek word for Grace is "Charis," which means grace as a gift, or blessing brought to many by Jesus Christ, favor, or thanks.[32]

According to Matthew Henry Commentary Volume One, we must die to sin and start living a holy and righteous lifestyle. We have to put off the old man with its deeds and put on the new man. Yet there are none that live without sin. Yet there are those that do not live in sin. We must not only cease from the acts of sin, but we must get the vicious habits and inclinations weakened and destroyed. We must be dead to sin, practicing habitual sin and using grace as an excuse to stay in the sin. We

31. Grace Merriam-Webster.com https://www.Merriam-Webster.com Accessed June 2021
32. "Charis" the Greek word for Grace https://www.biblehub.com Accessed June 2021

must not fulfill its will no more in our lives. We must die to ourselves so that the Holy Ghost can get stronger in our lives. We must not yield our flesh or bodies to sin.[33]

DECLARATIONS

I decree and declare that I will not sin against You, God.

I decree and declare that I will take up my cross and follow Christ.

I decree and declare that I will put off the old man and put on the new man.

I decree and declare that I will utilize the grace that You have given me and continue to move forward in righteousness and holiness.

I decree and declare that I am the righteousness of God in Christ Jesus.

I decree and declare that my body is the temple of the Holy Ghost, and I will not sin against God.

I decree and declare that I will not use grace as a crutch to continue to grieve the Holy Spirit in me.

---

33. Matthew Henry's Concise Commentary Volume 1 Zondervan @ 1960 Accessed June 2021

July 14th

*R*OMANS 8: 1-2 (NKJV), *"¹There is therefore now no condemnation to those who are in Christ Jesus, who do not walk according to the flesh, but according to the Spirit.* ²· *"For the law of Spirit of life in Christ Jesus has made me free from the law of sin and death."*

Condemnation in the Merriam Webster Dictionary is defined as to declare to be reprehensible, wrong, or evil usually after weighing evidence or without reservation.[34] The Greek word for Condemnation is "Katakrima," which means penalty, disapproval, blame, or judgment.[35]

Matthew Henry's Commentary Volume One states that there are unspeakable privileges to those in Christ Jesus because there is no condemnation to them. There is no accusation against them. The accusation has been thrown out. There is nothing in them that deserves condemnation. Through our communion with Him, our faith has been secured. Those in

34. Condemnation Merriam-Webster.com https://www.Merriam-Webster.com Accessed June 2021
35. "G2631 - katakrima - Strong's Greek Lexicon (kjv)." Blue Letter Bible. Accessed 6 Jun, 2022. https://www.blueletterbible.org/lexicon/g2631/kjv/tr/0-1/

Christ will not walk after the flesh, but after the Spirit (Holy Spirit). We come to justification (just as if I never sin) through Jesus's finished work on the cross. We had to accept Jesus' finished work to receive salvation from our sin. Jesus is the only way to salvation, justification, redemption, and eternal life in this life.[36]

If you feel any type of condemnation in your heart, it comes from the enemy and not God. Once you ask God to forgive you, He throws your sin in the sea of forgetfulness, never to remember it anymore. So, the enemy is trying to make you feel guilty and not God. It is a trick of the enemy against your life to get you to back down and not serve a merciful and gracious God. One of the ways to give the devil a black eye is to tell your testimonies and when you do, he cannot hold you hostage any longer about your past. We all have a past. We need not to feel ashamed and let people know what God has delivered us from. Many people are waiting to hear your story. God has placed so much in you to help people get delivered from their pasts too.

PRAYER

Father God, in the name of Jesus, we come to You today to thank you for sending Jesus to suffer, bled, and die for us, but He rose on the third day with all power in the palm of His hand. Because through His finished work on the cross, and through His sacrifice for our sins, now I can have the gift of salvation. Lord, I know now that once I have given my life to You, the sin of my past is no longer a threat to me because it is covered under the blood of Jesus. Lord, I know that all of my past sins

36. Matthew Henry's Concise Commentary @ 1960 Zondervan Accessed June 2021

is covered under the blood of Jesus, and I am no longer the old man. I am a new creature in Christ Jesus because I am redeemed by His blood in Jesus' name. Lord, I thank You for giving me a new lease on life from this day forward in Jesus' name. I will not let sin have dominion over me in Jesus' name. Amen.

July 15th

*R*OMANS 8:6-8 (NKJV), *"⁶ For to be carnally minded is death, but to be spiritually minded is life and peace.⁷ "Because the carnal mind is enmity against God; for it is not subject to the law of God, nor indeed can be. ⁸ "So then, those who are in the flesh cannot please God."*

Carnal mind in the Merriam Webster Dictionary means to have a worldly mind, giving into the pleasures and appetites of the world.[37] The Greek word for Carnal mind is "Sarkikos," pertaining to the flesh, carnal, fleshly, or earthly.[38]

Spiritual mind in the Merriam Webster Dictionary is relating to, consisting of, or affecting the spirit, religious values.[39] The Greek word for Spiritual mind is "Pneumatikos," which means spiritual, Holy Spirit, or relating to the realm of the Spirit.[40]

37. Carnal mind Merriam-Webster.com https://www.Merriam-Webster.com Accessed June 2021
38. "Sarkikos" the Greek word for carnal mind. https://www.biblehub.com Accessed June 2021
39. Spiritual Mind Merriam-Webster.com https://www.Merriam-Webster.com Accessed June 2021
40. "Pneumatikos" the Greek Word for Spiritual mind https://www.biblehub.com Accessed June 2021

Prayers that Availeth Much by LaRose A. Richardson states that lukewarm Christians care more about the world instead of taking care of God's business. Many of these Christians are still cursing (foul language) and twisting Scriptures to justify their behavior. A true man or woman of God has no business cussing. If this is happening, they have not truly been born again because bitter and sweet water cannot come out of the same mouth. Our speech must be always seasoned with salt. The grace of God is here to help us do what we can't do on our own. The world should be able to look at the people of God and see a difference in their lifestyles. Many Christians are trying to blend in with the world when God has mandated that we are to be set apart from it. We are living in the world, but there must be a difference between clean and unclean in our lives. Every day, we should be striving to become more like Jesus in our walk on this earth.[41]

DECLARATIONS

I decree and declare that I will guard my mouth so that nothing evil comes out of it.

I decree and declare that I will represent God in all I do on this earth.

I decree and declare that I will not compromise the Word for the sake of blending in with the world.

41. Prayers that Availeth Much by LasRose A Richardson @2019 Accessed June 2021

Lord, we repent for operating in the lust of the flesh, the lust of the eyes, and the boastful pride of life because it is not from the Father but of the world.

I will not be conformed to this world, but be transformed by the renewing of my mind, so you may prove what the will of God is.

I will set my mind to be governed by the Spirit and not by my flesh in Jesus' name.

I decree and declare that the Kingdom of God is not meat and drink, but righteousness, and peace, and joy in the Holy Ghost in Jesus' name.

July 16th

*R*OMANS 8:14-15 (NKJV), *"¹⁴ For as many as are led by the Spirit of God, these are the sons of God."* ¹⁵. *"For you did not receive the spirit of bondage again to fear, but you received the Spirit of adoption by whom we cry out, "Abba, Father."*

Adoption in Merriam Webster Dictionary is defined as the act of adopting: state of being adopted, welcoming into the family.[42] The Greek word for Adoption is "Huiothesia," meaning adoption as a son into the divine family or sonship.[43]

All believers are children of God, for all have been born from above into the family of God. One day all believers will be conformed into the likeness and image of the Lord Jesus Christ. As we grow and mature in the Spirit, we grow in grace and the knowledge of the Lord Jesus. We begin to learn the lessons the Spirit wants to teach us so we can grow into adulthood in Christ. Everyone who is led by the Spirit of God are the sons of

---

42. Adoption Merriam-Webster.com https://www.Merriam-Webster.com Accessed June 2021
43 . "Huiothesia" the Greek word for Adoption https://www.biblehub.com Accessed June 2021

God![44] When an unbeliever makes the choice to give their lives to Christ and start believing in Him, they are now on their way to learning more and Christ and their walk with Him as their guide.

When we are no longer led by our flesh but now led by the Holy Spirit, it shows a sign of maturing in God. We are servants of God to be used for the ministry to spread the Gospel of Jesus Christ to a hurting and dying world.

We have nothing to fear because we have been received into the Body of Christ by just accepting Jesus as our Lord and Savior. We are Sons of God meaning, that He can now trust us to do what is right in God's eyesight. We are to call evil, evil and good, good, and not vice versa, because we are to hate what God hates and love what God loves.

PRAYER

Father God, in the name of Jesus, I come before You today, surrendering my will so that I can be led by the Holy Spirit in all that I do for You and in my life as well. Lord, help me not to walk as the world walks or think as the world thinks, but Lord, help me think spiritual minded from this day forward in Jesus' name. Lord, forgive me for the times I thought carnally when I should have kept my mind stayed on You all times in Jesus' name. Lord, help me to do what is always right in Your eyesight and shun any evil. I will not walk in carnality but will walk in the Spirit. I will set my mind on things above and not on things on this earth in Jesus' name. Lord, I will submit to the pruning

44. https://www.dailyverse.kniwingjesus.com accessed June 2021

that You are doing in my life so I can reach full maturity in You in Jesus' name. Lord, thank You for Your grace to help me do what I can't do on my own in Jesus' name. Amen.

July 17th

ROMANS 8:24-25 (NKJV), "²⁴ FOR WE are saved in this hope, but hope that is seen is not hope; for why does one still hope for what he sees? ²⁵. "But if we hope for we hope for what we do not see, we eagerly wait for it with perseverance.

Perseverance in the Merriam Webster Dictionary is defined as a continued effort to do or achieve something despite difficulties, failure or opposition, and steadfastness.[45] The Greek word for Perseverance is "Hupomone," meaning a remaining behind, a patient enduring, steadfastness, or patiently waiting.[46]

Matthew Henry's Commentary Volume One states that happiness is not in our present possessions. We are saved by hope (faith). Our reward is out of sight. Those that deal with God must deal upon trust. Faith respects the promise and hope for the thing that is promised. Faith is the evidence and hope of the expectation of things not seen. Faith is the mother of hope.

45. Perseverance Merriam-Webster.com https://www.biblehub.com Accessed June 2021
46. "Hupomone" The Greek word for Perseverance https://www.biblehub.com Accessed June 2021

I am hoping for this glory. We need to be patient. Though the promise tarry, we have to wait for it to manifest.[47]

We got to have faith because without faith, it is impossible to please God. The Kingdom of God is built upon faith. When we got saved, we had to use faith to believe that Jesus is the Son of God to be saved. The enemy comes to make you doubt God and weaken your faith. The Word of God states that faith comes by hearing and hearing by the Word of God. So, we need to start reading our Word aloud and speak to our situations with the Word of God. No more speaking what we are seeing with our natural eyes, but we need to be looking into the eyes of the spirit and speaking from that realm.

What we are praying for starts manifesting in the spiritual realm before it shows up in the natural realm. We also can listen to other people's testimonies and gain faith from them as well. We know that God is no respecter of persons. What He has done for one person, He can do for the next one. We need to have hope in God and trust Him at His Word concerning our lives.

DECLARATIONS

I decree and declare that I will walk out in faith and believe God at His Word.

I decree and declare that I will get up every morning with expectation in my heart.

47. Matthew Henry's Concise Commentary @1960 Zondervan accessed June 2021

I decree and declare that expectation is the breeding ground for miracles in my life.

I decree and declare that my faith is increasing the more I read the Word of God.

I decree and declare that I will have the faith of Abraham, and God is not slack in answering His promises.

I decree and declare that I continue to move forward in endurance and expectation.

I decree and declare that I will have the faith the size of a mustard seed in Jesus' name.

July 18th

*R*OMANS 8:26-27 (NKJV), *"²⁶ Likewise the Spirit also helps in our weaknesses. For we do not know what we should pray for as we ought, but the Spirit Himself makes intercession for us with groanings which cannot be uttered. ²⁷. "Now He who searches the hearts knows what the mind of the Spirit is, because He makes intercession for the saints according to the will of God."*

Intercession in the Merriam Webster Dictionary is defined as the act of interceding, prayer, or petition.[48] The Greek word for Intercession is "Huperentugchano," meaning to intercede or to make petition for.[49]

Matthew Henry's Commentary Volume One states that the infirmities of Christians are many and great. We would be overpowered if it were left to ourselves. The Holy Spirit supports them. The Spirit is an enlightening Spirit that teaches us what to pray for and as a sanctifying Spirit, works and stirs up pray-

48. Intercesssion Merriam-Webster.com https://www.Merriam-Webster.com Accessed June 2021
49. "Huperentugchano" the Greek word for Intercession https://www.biblehub.com Accessed June 2021

ing graces; as a comforting Spirit, it silences our fears, and helps us over all discouragements.

The Holy Spirit is the spring of all desires toward God, which are often more than words can utter. The Spirit who searches the heart, can perceive the mind, and advocates His cause. The Spirit makes intercession to God, and the enemy prevails not.[50] The Holy Spirit dwells in us and strengthens us as we continue to pray in tongues regularly. Praying in tongues will build you up in your most holy faith.

An article on www.kcm.org talks about the Five benefits of Praying in Tongues. Praying in tongues is a powerful gift that every believer should desire.

1. Praying in tongues allows you to speak directly to God. — 1 Corinthians 14:2
2. Praying in tongues keep you in tune with the Holy Spirit. — Acts 2
3. Praying in tongues strengthens your spirit. — 1 Corinthians 14:4
4. Praying in tongues allows you to pray even when you don't know what to pray for. — Romans 8:26
5. Praying in tongues is a weapon against the enemy. — Mark 16:15-18.

The Word of God declares that we are to pray without ceasing.[51]

---

50. Matthew Henry's Concise Commentary Volume 1 @1960 Zondervan Accessed June 2021

51. https://www.kcm.org 5 benefits of speaking in tongues. Accessed June 2021

PRAYER

-

Father God, in the name of Jesus, I come before You today to ask that You fill me with the Holy Spirit with the evidence of speaking and praying in tongues. Lord, I realize that this is a gift that is given to the believers who want it. So, Lord I am asking to be filled up with Your Holy Spirit so that I can pray in tongues to help build me up in the holiest of faith in Jesus' name. Lord, I realize I need tongues to be able to pray directly to You in the language that the enemy cannot understand in Jesus' name. Lord, I need strengthening in my spirit man today and every day of my life in Jesus' name. Lord, teach me how to be led by the Holy Spirit in all areas of my life right now in Jesus' name. Lord, I need the weapon of tongues to foil the trick, plots, and plans of the enemy over my life. Lord, I receive the gift of the Holy Spirit now by faith with the evidence of speaking and praying in tongues in Jesus' name. Lord, I open my mouth and say what I hear my spirit saying in the Spirit in Jesus' name. Amen.

July 19th

*R*OMANS 11:29 (NKJV), "FOR *the gifts and the callings of God are irrevocable."*

Callings in the Merriam Webster Dictionary is defined as a strong inner impulse toward a particular course of action, especially when accompanied by conviction of divine influence.[52] The Greek word for Callings is "Klesis," meaning a calling, invitation, or always of a divine call.[53]

God has given every one of us gifts and talents and He will not take them back from us regardless if we serve Him or not. If we serve Him now, we have the Holy Spirit to help us mature that gift or talent so we can produce more fruit from it. Some use the gifts that God has given them for evil purposes and God is not pleased with this at all, but He will not take their gifts from them. He had planned our destinies before the world began and how He wanted our lives to be. It is a personal choice by the person if they will live for God or stay with the

---

52. Callings Merrian-Webster.com https://www.Merriam-Webster.com Accessed June 2021
53. "Klesis" the Greek word for Calling Https://www.biblehub.com Accessed June 2021

enemy. When we were born, we were born in sin and shaped in iniquity, so we were born sinners. The only way that we can be redeemed is through Jesus' shed blood and accepting Him as our Lord and Savior.

DECLARATIONS

I decree and declare that I will use my gifts and callings for God and Him alone.

I decree and declare that every gift that has been placed on the inside of me will grow in grace.

I decree and declare that the gifts and calling of God are irrevocable.

I decree and declare that I will not be led by a familiar spirit but by the Holy Spirit.

I decree and declare that I will give all of my gifts and talents back to God right now in Jesus' name.

July 20th

❋

ROMANS 12:19 (NKJV), "BELOVED, do not avenge yourselves, but give place to wrath; for it is written. "Vengeance is Mine, I will repay," said the Lord."

Vengeance in the Merriam Webster Dictionary is defined as with great force or vehemence, to an extreme or excessive degree.[54] The Greek word for Vengeance is "Ekdikesis," meaning vengeance, vindication, a defense, or full complete punishment.[55]

This scripture tells us not to repay evil with evil, meaning do not try to get people back who have mistreated you or talked about you. God said in His Word that we are to treat people kind regardless of how they treat us. We are to show the love of God to people regardless of what they are doing to us because we can draw them to God by showing the love of God to people who are worldly or carnal minded.

54. Vengeance Merriam-Webster.com https://www.Merriam-Webster.com Accessed June 2021
55. "Ekidikesis" the Greek word for Vengeance https://www.biblehub.com Accessed June 2021

Sometimes it may seem hard not to retaliate but we must turn the other cheek or fight back through prayer and let God deal with the people in His own unique way. God can change the heart of the most hard-hearted person there is. So, give them the same grace that God has given to you, and pray for them to be saved, delivered, and set free from the influence of the enemy.

<u>PRAYER</u>

Father God, in the name of Jesus, I come before You today to ask that You help me to turn the other cheek when someone has mistreated me. Lord, help me to not hold grudges against the person who has tried to hurt me. Lord, help me to walk in forgiveness toward them because if they do not have the Holy Spirit, they do not have anything to stop them from being carnal or worldly in Jesus' name. Lord, help me to show Your love with dealing with difficult and wicked people in Jesus' name. Lord, I pray for those that hate me without a cause because of who I represent. Lord, I pray that You would send Your Holy Ghost fire to saturate their hearts and save them and make new creatures out of them. Lord, I pray that You would send a Holy Ghost bomb fire to consume them in their hearts right now in Jesus' name. Lord, remove their hearts of stone and give them a heart of flesh from this day forward in Jesus' name. Lord, help them realize that they need a Savior, and His name is Jesus. Lord, create in them a clean heart and renew a right Spirit in them in Jesus' name. Amen.

July 21st

ROMANS 15:13 (NKJV), "NOW may the God of hope fill you with all joy and peace in believing that you may abound in hope by the power of the Holy Spirit."

Abound in the Merriam Webster Dictionary is defined as to be present in large numbers or in great quantity, to be prevalent.[56] The Greek word for Abound is "Huperperisseuo," which means to abound more exceedingly, or overflow.[57]

This was a prayer that Paul prayed for the Corinthians, and it is often used today in churches as a benediction. It is a powerful statement about what God can do in the heart and mind of every Christian. Paul makes this request for the God of hope, another beautiful name for God. He is the only lasting source of hope we have in meaning in this life and for the life beyond. Paul asks that the God of hope fill all of these believers with all joy and peace in believing in Him. Also, as they trust in Him,

56. Abound Merrian-Webster.com https://www.Merriam-Webster.com Accessed June 2021
57. "Huperperisseuo" The Greek word for Abound https://www.bibleheub.com Accessed June 2021

Paul is asking that these believers will trust in God and their faith will bring joy and peace into their hearts. God will help them to keep believing so that they can experience joy and peace in their lives. Paul is asking God to give them more than regular human hopefulness. He is asking for supernatural, Holy Spirit powered hopefulness.[58]

This will be a great prayer to pray for ourselves and other people so that God will give us a supernatural dose of joy and peace in our lives. This prayer could be prayed daily by the believer even after joy and peace shows up in their lives. Mark this scripture in your Bibles so that when you are praying, just start praying this scripture each day.

DECLARATIONS

I decree and declare that I will start praying the scriptures back to God until Joy and peace shows up in my life.

I decree and declare that all of my hope can be found in Jesus.

I decree and declare Romans 15:13 over me on a daily in Jesus' name.

I decree and declare that I will put my whole trust in God to supply my every need.

I decree and declare a Supernatural Holy Spirt Powered of hopefulness over my family, marriage, business, spouse, etc.

58. www.bibleref.com https://www.bibleref.com June 2021

I decree and declare that I can have hope because Jesus is Hope in Jesus' name.

July 22nd

1 Corinthians 1:10 (NKJV), "Now I plead with you, brethren, by the name of our Lord Jesus Christ, that you will speak the same thing, and that there be no divisions among you, but that you be perfectly joined together in the same mind and in the same judgment."

Speak in the Merriam Webster Dictionary means to express thoughts, opinions, or feeling, and confession.[59] The Greek word for Speak is "Homologeo," which is to say the same thing as another, or to agree with.[60]

Matthew Henry's Commentary states that Paul extorts them to unity and brotherly love and reproves them for their divisions. He told them to be perfectly joined together in the same mind speaking the same things. He stated that pride laid at the bottom of these contentions that were going on within them. He asked them if Christ was divided. No, there is but one

---

59. Speak Merriam-Webster.com https://www.Merriam-Webster.com Accessed June 2021

60. "Homologeo" the Greek for saying the same thing https://www.biblestudytool.com Accessed June 2021

Christ. And therefore, Christians should be of one heart and not divided among themselves.[61]

There is no division in Christ. When the spirit of division is stirred up, this spirit comes from the enemy. We must not fall for the tricks of the enemy, especially if we are following God and being humble before the Lord. Every time pride gets in the way, it causes major problems, but no one is the end all be all. We all need Jesus to do anything effective in this earth. God can raise up another and bring down another. No one is irreplaceable. We are to speak the same thing as long as it lines up with the Word of God.

We can get more done in this world when we are on one accord. We can be just like the Apostles in the Bible days, turning the parts of the world that God has called us to upside down by spreading the Good News of Jesus Christ to a lost and dying world.

PRAYER

Father God, in the name of Jesus, I come before You today to ask that You send peace amid a storm in Jesus' name. Lord, help us all to remain humble before You and to not cause confusions and contentions by speaking other doctrine that is contrary to Yours right now in Jesus' name. Lord, help us to keep our hearts and minds pure and continue to walk in love toward each other. Help us to live a life that is pleasing to You, so when the world looks at us, they will see You and not us in Jesus' name. Lord, help us to walk in love and be love instead of just talking about

61. Matthew Henry's Concise Commentary @1960 Zondervan Accessed June 2021

it and not showing it in Jesus' name. Lord, help us to walk in unity because we can do more together on one accord than separated in our cliques. Lord, we veto and cancel every prideful spirit, cast it out, and send it back to the pits of hell from where it came from in Jesus' name. We will walk by faith and walk together as one in Christ in Jesus' name. Amen.

July 23rd

*J*EREMIAH 23:29 (KJV), "ISN'T my word like
fire? Says the Lord. And like a hammer that breaks
the rock (whatever that is coming against you) you
into pieces."

Hammer in the Merriam Webster Dictionary is defined as
a hand tool consisting of a solid head set crosswise on a handle and used for pounding.[62] The Greek word for Hammer is
Maqqebeth.[63]

No longer will we be afraid of the enemy and his schemes,
but we will open our mouths and war with the Hammer of God
(Word of God) over our lives. We will use what God has given
us to use against the enemy and it is the Word of God. The
Word is full of so many weapons to combat the enemy with
and if we do not know what they all are, then do a study on it.
So, you can find out the right tools to use to defeat the enemy.
We have the whole armor of God that we can put on every day,

---

62. Hammer Merriam-Webster.com https://www.Merriam-Webster.com Accessed
June 2021
63. "Maqqebeth" the Greek word for Hammer https://www.biblehub.com Accessed
June 2021

and it will protect us from head to toe against the attacks of the wicked one. There are many more nuggets in the Word of God that you can pray and put your name in the scripture to make it personal. I pray many of those scriptures and put my name in these scriptures. God is steadily answering my prayers concerning these scriptures. You cannot go wrong praying the Word of God because God is only obligated in honoring His Word. He is listening to hear His Word coming from our mouths, so He can hasten to perform them.

When a hammer hits a rock repeatedly, it keeps chipping pieces away until finally the rock has either been broken into small pieces or it has been shattered into dust before our eyes. The Word of God is alive and sharper than any two-edged sword. The Word is sent to cut and correct, and it does not feel good sometimes, but it is needed.

DECLARATIONS ABOUT THE HAMMER OF GOD

We activate the Hammer of God to break up and crush the spirit of fear, every terrorizing spirit, all sickness, and all illnesses that have been sent by the enemy to wreak havoc in our lives in Jesus' name.

We apply the Hammer of God (Word of God) to our minds, bodies, lives, and homes right now in Jesus' name.

I decree and declare that every oppressor and stronghold of the enemy will be broken off our lives right now in Jesus' name.

I decree and declare that every attack against my destiny will be crushed by the Hammer of God from my life and destiny in Jesus' name.

I decree and declare that the Hammer of God will destroy every tormenting spirit that is sent to keep me awake at night.

I decree and declare that from this day forward, I will have sweet sleep and I will sleep through the night so I can be well rested in the morning.

More of the declarations can be found on my blog at www.ministerrich0628.blogspot.com

July 24th

1CORINTHIANS 2:9 (KJV), "BUT as it is written, Eye hath not seen, nor ear heard, neither have entered the heart of man, the things which God hath prepared for them that love him."

Prepared in the Merriam Webster Dictionary is defined as to work out the details of a plan.[64] The Greek word for Prepared is "Katartizo," which means to fit together, compact together, or bring into its proper condition.[65]

Matthew Henry's Commentary states that waiting upon God is evidence of our love for Him. God has put His mysteries in the Word of God for us to read and discover the mysteries that He wants to reveal to each of us. God wants to give us revelation on the things that we are reading in His Word so we can get a better understanding of it. With a better understanding, we can apply the revelation that God has given us to our lives

---

64. Prepared Merriam-Webster.com https://www.Merriam-Webster.com Accessed June 2021
65. "Katartizo" The Greek Word for Prepared https://www.biblehub.com Accessed June 2021

as well as help someone else that is dealing with that issue as well.[66]

God has prepared so many things for His people. That is why it is so important to read the Word of God and pray before we start reading it and God will give us a revelation of what we are studying. You will have a light bulb moment where everything that you have learned will start to make sense to you. God has so many nuggets that He wants to get to us, so we can live the abundant life in Him. When we study to show ourselves approved, we can rightly divide the Word of God and apply it in our lives. We will be able to walk out in holiness and righteousness and be better servants for God to use for His glory. God wants to give us financial nuggets so we can walk in the good of the land. God has many answers to the questions that you have been asking Him that pertain to His Word, and He wants you to be able to get everything that you need to go further in the Kingdom of God.

PRAYER

Father God, in the name of Jesus, I come before You today to ask that You would open my eyes so I can see the mysteries that You have placed inside of Your Word that I need to see in Jesus' name. Lord, I want to grow in that area and any other area that You want me to go in or grow in so You can get the glory out of it in Jesus' name. Lord, I ask that You open my eyes to see into the spiritual realm right now in Jesus' name. Lord, open my ears to hear Your voice clearer than ever before right

66. Matthew Henry's Concise Commentary @1960 Zondervan Volume 1 Accessed June 2021

now in Jesus' name. Lord, help me as I study Your Word to get every nugget that You have placed in the Word of God for me to be able to get everything that pertains to my walk with You. Lord, I ask that You reveal them to me as I study Your Word in Jesus' name. Lord, help me know what to release and what to keep in Jesus' name. Amen.

July 25th

1 CORINTHIANS 4:20 (KJV), "*FOR the kingdom of God is not in word, but in power.*"

Kingdom in the Merriam Webster Dictionary is defined as the eternal kingship of God or the realm in which God's will is fulfilled.[67] The Greek word for Kingdom is "Basileia," which means kingship, sovereignty, royal power, rule, especially of God.[68]

Matthew Henry's Commentary states that whenever the gospel is effectual, it comes not in word only but through power, by the Holy Spirit quickening dead sinners, delivering people from the slavery of sin and Satan. Renewing them both inwardly and outwardly, comforting, strengthening, and establishing the saints which cannot be done by the persuasive language of men, only by the power of God.[69]

67. Kingdom Merriam-Webster.com https://www.Merriam-Webster.com Accessed June 2021
68. "Basileia" The Greek word for Kingdom https://www.biblehub.com Accessed June 2021
69. Matthew Henry's Concise Commentary Volume 1 @1960 Accessed June 2021

The kingdom is by demonstration and not just words. We need to be able to demonstrate what we have learned from reading the Word of God and by receiving impartations from other leaders as well as getting them from the Holy Ghost. We have the same power living within us that raised Jesus from the dead, so we should be able to operate that power. *John14:12 (NLT), "I tell you the truth, anyone who believes in me will do the same works I have done, and even greater works, because I am going to be with the Father."* Jesus was all about demonstrating the Kingdom by healing those that were sick, opening blinded eyes, healing bodies from oppression, and resurrecting the dead. Yes, Jesus, demonstrated the kingdom wherever He went. So, we should be demonstrating the Kingdom of God every chance we get by praying for people. We are to pray and lay hands on them and the Holy Ghost will heal their bodies, hearts, and minds like only He can. Sometimes we do not even have to lay hands. We can just speak the Word of God over them, and they will be healed in their bodies.

DECLARATIONS

I decree and declare that I will be a demonstrator of the Kingdom like Jesus was.

I decree and declare that I will pray the prayer of faith over someone so they can be healed, delivered, and set-free.

I decree and declare that the same power that raised Jesus from the dead lives on the inside of me.

I decree and declare that I have the mind of Christ.

I decree and declare that I can speak life in any dead situation, and it will be resurrected in Jesus' name.

I decree and declare that the Kingdom suffers violence and the violent take it by force.

I decree that the strongholds of oppression and depression are broken off the lives of Your people in Jesus' name.

July 26th

CORINTHIANS 6:17 (KJV), "*BUT he that is joined unto the Lord is one Spirit.*"

Joined in the Merriam Webster Dictionary is defined as to put or bring together so as to form a unit.[70] The Greek word for Joined is "Suzeugnumi," meaning to yoke together or unite (as man and wife).[71]

Matthew Henry's Commentary states that our bodies have been redeemed from deserved condemnation and hopeless slavery by the atoning sacrifice of Christ. We are to be clean, as vessels fitted for our Master's use. Being united to Christ as one spirit, and bought with a price of unspeakable value, the believer should consider himself as wholly the Lord's by the strongest ties. May we make it our business, to the latest day and hour of our lives, to glorify God with our bodies, and with our spirits which are His.[72]

---

70. Joined Merriam-Webster.com https://www.Merriam-Webster.com Accessed June 2021
71. "Suzeugnumi" The Greek word for Joined https://www.biblehub.com Accessed June 2021
72. Matthew Henry's Concise Commentary Volume 1 @1960 Zondervan Accessed June 2021

We know that the unrighteous shall not inherit the kingdom of God. The Word declares in *1 Corinthians 6:9-10 (KJV) who is not going to inherit the kingdom of God. "⁹ Be not deceived neither fornicators, nor idolaters, nor adulterers, nor effeminate, nor abusers of themselves with mankind. ¹⁰· "Nor thieves, nor covetous, nor drunkards, nor revilers, nor extortioners shall inherit the kingdom of God."* According to verse 11, the only people that can enter the kingdom of God are those that have been washed and sanctified, justified in the name of the Lord Jesus and by the Spirit of our God.

This is a question that we must ask ourselves. Where do we stand in all of this? If we are operating in any of these that are listed with unrepented sin in our hearts, then the Word says that we would not inherit the kingdom of God. According to these scriptures, the only way that we can inherit the kingdom of God is through being washed, sanctified, and justified by Jesus and by the Spirit of the Holy Spirit.

PRAYER

Father God, in the name of Jesus, I come before You today to ask that You would forgive me for every sin that I have committed knowingly and unknowingly, in thought and deed, omission and commission right now in Jesus' name. Lord, I thank You for forgiving me and putting me back into right standing with You in Jesus' name. Lord, help me not to walk in any unrepentant sin no matter what it is. Lord, help me to keep short accounts with You so nothing is blocking my prayers from getting to You in Jesus' name. Lord, I ask for more of Your grace so that I will have Your divine power to help me overcome the things that are displeasing to You in Jesus' name. Lord, remove the people from around me that help promote this type of behavior in Jesus' name. Lord, I give my life totally to You and wash me and sanctify me and justify by Your precious blood so I can be led by the Holy Spirit from this day forward in Jesus' name. Amen.

July 27th

1Corinthians 12:26 (KJV), "And whether one member suffer, all the members suffer with it; or one member be honored all the other members rejoice with it."

Suffer in the Merriam Webster Dictionary is defined as to submit to or be forced to endure.[73] The Greek word for Suffer is "Pascho," which means to suffer, to be acted on, or experience ill treatment.[74] Rejoice in the Merriam Webster Dictionary means to feel joy or great delight.[75] The Greek word for Rejoice is "Sugchairo," meaning to rejoice with or congratulations.[76]

Matthew Henry's Commentary Volume One states the members of the natural body are made to have a care and concern for each other. So should the whole Body of Christ be with each other. Christian sympathy is a great branch of Christian duty. When someone we know is suffering and going through,

73. Suffer Merriam-Webster.com https://www.Merriam-Webster.com Accessed June 2021

74 "Pascho" The Greek word for Suffer https://www.biblehub.com Accessed June 2021

75. Rejoice Merriam-Webster.com https://www.Merriam-Webster.com Accessed June 2021.

76. "Sugchairo" Greek word for Rejoice https://www.biblehub.com accessed June 2021.

we are to help them if we can and pray for them to overcome their trials.[77]

Even if they are rejoicing after completing classes or something else that is joyous to them, we should be happy for each other and never jealous toward one another because God wants to bless every one of us in His own timing. If I am compassionate when someone else is suffering, God will send someone to help me when I need it. The same thing goes for the ones that are rejoicing. I will celebrate with them for whatever accomplishment that God has given them. If I keep my heart pure, then the next time will be my time.

DECLARATIONS

I decree and declare that I will rejoice with those that rejoice in Jesus' name.

I decree and declare that I will be sympathetic and show compassion to those that are going through suffering.

I decree and declare that I will help them out in any way that I can.

I decree and declare that I will come into agreement with them in prayer for God to move on their behalf.

I decree and declare that every member of the church has a purpose and function in it.

77. Matthew Henry's Concise Commentary Volume 1 @1960 Zondervan Accessed June 2021

I decree and declare that I will be genuinely happy for my fellow church member when God is blessing them abundantly.

July 28th

*N*EHEMIAH 4:14 (KJV), *"AND I looked, and rose up, and said unto the nobles, and to the rulers, and to the rest of the people, be not ye afraid of them: remember the LORD, which is great and terrible, and fight for your brethren, your sons, and your daughters, your wives, and your houses."*

Fight in the Merriam Webster Dictionary is defined as taking part in a violent struggle involving the exchange of physical blows or use of weapons.[78] The Greek word for fight is "Agonizomai," which means to contend with an adversary or struggle.[79]

Matthew Henry's Commentary Volume One states that Nehemiah looked up, prayed to God, and put himself and his cause under divine protection. He made his prayer unto God. He laid all of his cares, fears, and griefs over to God and after he prayed. It made him at peace knowing that God was protecting

78. Fight Merriam-Webster.com https://www.Merriam-Webster.com Accessed June 2021
79. "Agonizomai" the Greek word for Fight https://www.biblehub.com Accessed June 2021

them from the enemy. Nehemiah set a watch against them after he had prayed. God gives us the same instructions while we are going through spiritual warfare. We must watch and pray as Nehemiah did while he was building the wall. We cannot secure ourselves by prayer only, but we must watch and pray. We cannot be slothful and tempt God. Without prayer, we are proud and slight God. If we do either of these things, we forfeit His protection.[80]

Nehemiah set the guards in strategic positions around the wall to watch as they built the wall. God had brought the plan of the enemy to naught because God had told Nehemiah what to do to foil the attacks of the enemy. God has done the same with us today. He has given us His word to use against the snares, pitfalls, tricks, and ploys of the enemy. We must have an active prayer life to get into the throne of grace and hide in the secret place with God.

PRAYER

Father God, in the name of Jesus, we come before You today, asking that You protect us from the snares, plots, and plans of the enemy against our lives and ministries in Jesus' name. Lord, cover me under Your precious blood right now in Jesus' name. Lord, we hush the mouth of the accuser off our lives and send it back to the pits of hell from where it came from in Jesus' name. Lord, we will do like *Philippians 4:6 (KJV)*, *"Be careful of nothing; but in everything by prayer and supplication with thanksgiving let your requests be made know unto God."* Lord, we will continue

80. Matthew Henry's Concise Commentary Volume 1 @1960 Zondervan Accessed June 2021

to pray until the tricks of the enemy are broken off our lives and families in Jesus' name. Lord, we pray Psalm 91, a prayer of protection around everyone in our circle right now in Jesus' name. Lord, we will not be afraid of the enemy and his devices because You are with me, leading and ordering my steps daily in Jesus' name. Amen.

July 29th

ISAIAH 11:2 (KJV), "AND the spirit of the LORD shall rest upon him, the spirit of wisdom and understanding, the spirit of counsel and might, the spirit of knowledge and of the fear of the LORD."

Spirit in the Merriam Webster Dictionary is defined as a supernatural being or essence.[81] The Greek word for Spirit is "Pneuma," meaning wind, spirit, or breath.[82]

God wants us to start making the scriptures personal by putting our names inside of them and speaking to them aloud over ourselves. Faith comes by hearing and hearing by the Word of God. Here is an example of how you would do this scripture.

Isaiah 11:2 (KJV) "And the spirit of Lord shall rest upon (your name)_____, the spirit of wisdom and understanding shall rest upon (your name)_____, the spirit of counsel and might shall rest upon(Your name)_____,

81. Spirit Merriam-Webster.com https://www.Merriam-Webster.com Accessed June 2021
82. "Pneuma" The Greek Word for Spirit https://www.biblehub.com Accessed June 2021

the spirit of knowledge shall rest upon (your name)_____ and the fear of the Lord shall rest upon(your name)_____.

This will make the scripture personal to you and now as you continue to say this scripture daily, the more it will start to manifest in your life, and you will start walking in the confidence that God declares that we should walk in. You can do this with any of the scriptures in the Bible. Especially the ones that you are having issues with and the next thing you know, you will be healed in that area.

God wants to heal us of all our oppressions, depressions, and anything else that is plaquing us. He wants us to walk in total freedom in every area of our lives. He will give us His grace to be able to overcome any obstacles that we may be facing or will face later in life.

DECLARATIONS

I decree and declare that the Spirit of the Lord will rest upon me and in me in Jesus' name.

I decree and declare that the Spirit of wisdom and knowledge shall rest upon me and in me in Jesus' name.

I decree and declare that the Spirit of counsel and might shall rest upon me and in me in Jesus' name.

I decree and declare that the Spirit of knowledge shall rest upon me and in me in Jesus' name.

I decree and declare that the fear of the Lord shall rest upon me and in me in Jesus' name.

I decree and declare that I will continue to walk in faith because God is with me.

July 30th

ISAIAH 54:17 (KJV), *"No weapon that is formed against thee shall prosper; and every tongue that shall rise up against thee in judgment thou shalt condemn. This is the heritage of the servants of the LORD, and their righteousness is of me saith the LORD."*

Weapon in the Merriam Webster Dictionary is defined as something used (such as club, knife, or gun) to injure, defeat, or destroy.[83] The Greek word for weapon is "Hoplon," meaning a tool, weapon, arms, or normally used for warfare.[84] This is another good scripture here that we can use to make it personal by adding our name to it.

Isaiah 54:17 (KJV) "No weapon that is formed against (Your name) _____ shall prosper; and every tongue that rise up against (your name) _____ in judgement thou shalt condemn. This is the heritage of the servants of the Lord, and their righteousness is of me saith the LORD."

---

83. Weapon Merriam-Webster.com https://www.Merriam-Webster.com Accessed June 2021
84. "Hoplon" The Greek word for Weapon https://www.biblehub.com Accessed June 2021

Every prayer we pray needs to have the Word of God in it because it moves God to see about you. When you are speaking His Word back to Him, He is obligated to answer His Word. God is listening for the Word of God coming out of our mouths so He can move mightily on our behalf. His Word declares that no weapon formed against us shall prosper. He didn't say that it would not form, but it will not prosper and do what the enemy wanted to do to us because God is protecting us behind His hedge of protection.

PRAYER

Father God, in the name of Jesus, we come before You today to thank You for protecting us from every illness or sickness that has been sent by the enemy against our lives right now in Jesus' name. Lord, we ask that You cover us under Your precious blood in Jesus' name. Lord, we bind every monitoring spirit that is sent by the enemy to keep up with our movements in Jesus' name. We cover every monitoring spirit's eyes with the blood of Jesus, blinding them in Jesus' name. Lord, Your Word declares that You will fight for us and vindicate us when the enemy tries to hurt or harm us in any way in Jesus' name. Lord, we ask that You send Your warring angels to surround each one of us and keep us safe from every attack of the enemy in Jesus' name. Lord, thank You for keeping us from things seen and unseen right now in Jesus' name. Lord, we ask that You cover our family members and keep us safe from all harm in Jesus' name. Lord, we love You and thank You for all that You have done and will do in our lives from this day forward in Jesus' name. Amen.

July 31st

*I*SAIAH 10:1 (KJV), "WOE unto them that decree unrighteous decrees, and that write grievousness
which they have prescribed."

Woe in the Merriam Webster Dictionary is defined as a condition of deep suffering from misfortune, affliction, or grief.[85]
The Greek word for Woe is "Ouai," meaning woe, alas, or uttered in grief or denunciation.[86]

Matthew Henry's Commentary Volume One talks about
woe to the person who makes these wicked laws that have been
placed on the books to oppress people and perverting justice in
the execution of the laws that were made by oppressing those
that lay at their mercy. They rob the fatherless of the little that
is left to them because they have no friend to appear for them.
The prophet is dealing with the proud oppressors of his people
at home that abused their power. This is the formal accusation
that was drawn up against the oppressors.[87]

85. Woe Merriam-Webster.com https://www.Merrian-Webster.com Accessed June 2021
86. "Ouai" The Greek Word for Woe https://www.biblehub.com Accessed June 2021
87. Matthew Henry's Concise Commentary Volume 1 2 1960 Zondervan Accessed June 2021

This story sounds so familiar with what is happening today. We have wicked leaders that have been elected in offices that have been making laws for years to oppress people of different races just because of the color of their skin. It seems like the poor or middle-class people have been oppressed repeatedly by all those unjust laws that are on the book in every city in the United States. No matter how God blesses and raises you up in a certain position, there is always someone judging you by the color of your skin tone. The children of God are not supposed to be operating like the world does. We must show the love of God regardless of another person's skin tone because God loves us all the same. He must teach all of us how to love people correctly. Truly none of us know how to love anybody correctly, especially if we do not have the Holy Ghost within our spirits. There is no way in the world that you love people right without Him helping you too.

DECLARATIONS

I decree and declare that I will love people the way God has taught me too.

I decree and declare that I will not be judging people according to the color of their skin but by their character.

I decree and declare that my spirit is full of the Holy Spirit in Jesus' name.

I decree and declare that I will always walk in love in Jesus' name.

I decree and declare that I will be loved because God is love.

I will love my enemies and those that despitefully misuse me in Jesus' name.

August 1st

*P*SALM 33:6 (KJV), "B*Y the Word of the LORD were the heaven made; and all the host of them by the breath of His mouth.*"

Word in the Merriam Webster Dictionary is defined as the expressed or manifested min and will of God.[88] The Greek work for Word is "Logos" meaning word (as embodying an idea), a statement, speech, or divine utterance.[89]

This scripture shows that God is the Creator of all things. He is entitled to be praised and adored by His creation. God has used wisdom, power, goodness, and skill to do it all. He did it by just speaking it into existence. The power of the spoken word is amazing and powerful. So, this lets you know that God's Word is true and gets the job done when it is spoken in authority. In *Genesis 1:14 (NLT)*, *God said, "Let light appear in the sky to separate the day from the night. Let them be signs to mark the season, days, and years."*

88. Word Merriam-Webster.com https://www.Merriam-Webster.com Accessed June 2021
89. "Logos" Greek for the Word (WORD) https://www.biblehub.com Accessed June 2021

PRAYER

Father God, in the name of Jesus, we come before You today, thanking You for speaking this world and everything in it into existence. Lord, in Your Word, You said, "Let there be," and everything became as You called it forth and this is a great reminder that we carry the same power to speak things into existence and to call things as not as though they were in our lives in Jesus' name. Lord, I decree and declare according to Your Word that I can speak things into existence if it is according to Your Word for our lives in Jesus' name. So, Lord, I decree and declare that I will not have another day of lack in my house because You have given me the power to get and retain wealth in Jesus' name. Lord, I realize that You named all the stars and the moons in the universe. You told them how bright to shine and where they would be positioned in the sky. Lord, Your Word declares that You divided the night from day, and You established the seasons so that we could tell them apart in Jesus' name. So that means that You established seed time and harvest time the moment you spoke the seasons into existence. Lord, we thank You for being the great Creator in this world. Thank You for creating things that we need like the light and the night so our crops can produce bountiful harvests in Jesus' name. Lord, we even thank You for even creating man in Your own image and likeness and placing us in the earth to subdue it for Your kingdom in Jesus' name. Amen.

August 2nd

Ezekiel 48:35 (NLT), "The distance around the entire city will be 6 miles. And from that day the name of the city will be "The Lord is there." (Jehovah Shammah)

Jehovah Shammah means that the Lord is there.[90] This was the name given to the city in Ezekiel's vision. *Matthew 28:20 (NLT) says, "Teaching them to observe all things that I have commanded you; lo, I am with you always, even to the end of the age. Amen."*

This verse means that God is not going to leave us, but He will be with us until the end of this age and not only that, but He is also going to be with us when we get to heaven. There is no where we can go to get out of the presence of God because He is everywhere at the same time. God is omnipresent. There is nowhere that we can go to get away from His presence. If we are doing wrong, He is there. If we are doing right, He is there. We cannot escape His presence no matter how hard we try to do it. Nobody can hide from God. *Psalm 139:7-12 (NLT), " 7 I can never escape from your Spirit! I can never get away from your*

90. Jehovah Shammah https://www.jesusplusnothing.com Accessed August 2021

presence! [8.] *"If I go up to heaven, you are there; if I go down to the grave, you are there."* [9.] *'If I ride the wings of the morning if I dwell by the farthest oceans."* [10.] *Even there your hand will guide me, and your strength will support me.* [11.] *"I could ask the darkness to hide me and the light around me to become night.* [12.] *"But even in darkness I cannot hide from you. To you the night shines as bright as day. Darkness and light are the same to you."* David wrote Psalm 139. No matter where he went, the presence of God was there. So, in other words, nobody is getting away with anything. God sees you.

Those that are believers of God are glad to know that He is here for us when we cry or call out to Him. He immediately comes to our rescue and helps us when we ask Him for help. If you can't count on anybody else, you can count on God to be there for you in the good times and in the troubled times. He is there to help us through every storm that we may encounter in our lives.

DECLARATIONS

I decree and declare that God is with me and for me and He will never leave me.

I decree and declare that I can count on God any time or day or night to come to   my rescue.

Lord, I thank You for being at my house and somebody else's house 4 blocks away at the same time.

Jehovah Shammah, thank You for always being present in my life.

Jehovah Shammah, with you on my side, I am a winner.

Jehovah Shammah is the on-time God that is never late.

Jehovah Shammah, thank You for never letting me face the loss of a loved one alone.

August 3rd

PSALM 27:1 (KJV), "THE LORD is my light and my salvation; whom shall, I fear? The LORD is the strength of my life; of whom shall I be afraid?"

Light in the Merriam Webster Dictionary is defined as something that makes vision possible.[91] The Greek word for light is "Phos," which means a source of light or radiance.[92]

Matthew Henry's Concise Commentary states that the Lord is the believer's light. It is the strength of his life, not only by whom, but in whom he lives and moves. God strengthens us. The gracious presence of God is His power, His promise, and His readiness to hear our prayers. The witness of His Spirit in the hearts of His people.[93]

91. Light Merriam-Webster.com https://www.Merriam-Webster.com Accessed August 2021

92. "Phos" Greek word for Light https://www.biblehub.com Accessed August 2021

93. Matthew Henry's Concise Commentary https://www.biblehub.com Accessed August 2021

PRAYER

Father God, in the name of Jesus, I come before You today to thank You for being my light and my salvation. With You as my light, I have no reason to fear what the enemy can do to me because I know that You are with me. Lord, thank You for being the strength of my life. With Your strength, I can continue to hold on and move forward into what You have carved out for my life. Lord, with You as the head of my life, there isn't anything to be afraid of because Your rod and staff shall comfort me all the days of my life in Jesus' name. Amen.

August 4th

*P*SALM 24:7-10 (KJV), " *⁷ Lift up your heads, O ye gates; and be ye lift up, ye everlasting doors, and the King of glory shall come in.*" *⁸.* "*Who is the King of glory? The LORD strong and mighty, the LORD mighty in battle.*" *⁹.* "*Lift up your heads, O ye gates; even lift them up, ye everlasting doors; and the King of glory shall come in. ¹⁰. Who is the King of glory? The LORD of hosts, he is the King of glory. Selah.*"

Everlasting in the Merriam Webster Dictionary is defined as continuing for a long time or indefinitely.[94] The Greek word for Everlasting is "Aionios," meaning age-long, and therefore practically eternal.[95]

This scripture talks about the arc of the covenant being brought back to Jerusalem. The arc of the covenant is the symbol of the presence of Jehovah Shammah, and it belongs in the city of God. Jerusalem is considered as the city of God because God had placed David as the king of Jerusalem. This is the song

94. Everlasting Merriam-Webster.com https://www.Merriam-Webster.com Accessed August 2021
95. Aionios" the Greek word for Everlasting https://www.biblehub.com Accessed August 2021

that the people of Jerusalem were signing. It was a song to welcome God's presence into the city. This Psalm looks much further into the future and is a prophecy that welcomes Jesus Christ into heaven at His ascension. The King of Glory here in this scripture is referring to Jesus.

God wants each of us to long for His Presence even more in our homes, churches and everywhere our feet shall tread. We will always take His presence with us. We will seek His face and pursue a deeper personal relationship with Him. He will never turn His back on us, and He will meet us in the secret place.

DECLARATIONS

I decree and declare that I will always stay in the Presence of God.

Lord, I long to feel Your glory in and on my life in Jesus' name.

Jesus is the King of Glory, and we give Him the glory and honor that He deserves.

Lord, You deserve the glory and the honor. I lift my hands in total worship unto You.

I decree and declare that Jesus is our deliverer, and we will seek Him in a time of need in Jesus' name.

Lord, thank You for opening the everlasting doors of our souls by Your grace, that we may now receive thee.

August 5th

*P*SALM 103:2-8 (KJV), "² *Bless the LORD, O my soul, and forget not all his benefits;* ³. *who forgiveth all thine iniquities; who healeth all thy diseases;* ⁴. *who redeemeth thy life from destruction; who crowneth thee with lovingkindness and tender mercies* ⁵. *who satisfieth thy mouth with good things; so that thy youth is renewed like the eagle's.* ⁶. *The LORD executeth righteousness and judgment for all the oppressed.* ⁷.*He made know his way unto Moses, His acts unto the children of Israel.* ⁸ *The LORD is merciful and gracious, slow to anger, and plenteous in mercy."*

Benefits in the Merriam Webster Dictionary is defined as something that produces good and helpful results or effects or something that promotes well-being.[96] The Greek word for Benefits is "Opheleia," which means usefulness, profit, advantage, benefit, or gain.[97]

96. Benefits Merriam-Webster.com https://www.Merriam-Webster.com Accessed August 2021
97. "Ophelia" Greek word for Benefits https://www.biblehub.com Accessed August 2021

<u>PRAYER</u>

Father God, in the name of Jesus, we come before You to-day, thanking You for the benefits that are mine according to Your Word in Jesus' name. Lord, thank You for forgiving all of my sins, past, present, and future. Your Word declares that You would not impute sin against me. Lord, thank You for healing all of my diseases and taking those 39 lashes over 2000 years ago for every sickness or disease that we would ever go through. I am healed because of Your stripes in Jesus' name. Lord, thank You for Your shed blood because it was only through Your blood that I could be redeemed back to God. Lord, thank You for crowning me with Your lovingkindness and tender mercies in Jesus' name. Lord, thank You for satisfying my mouth with good things. It is the only things that pertain to You and Your Word that are profitable for me to know and do. Lord, thank You for executing righteousness and justice for those that have tried to oppress me in Jesus' name. Lord, You said in Your Word that You are our vindicator, and You would repay all of those that have wronged and mistreated us. Lord, thank You for being merciful, gracious, and slow to anger when I fell short of what You have told me to do for Your kingdom. Lord, I thank You for giving me chance after chance and never giving up on me. Lord, thank You for Your compassion and love in Jesus' name. Amen.

August 6th

❦

*P*SALM *128:1-2 (KJV),* "¹ *Blessed is every one that fear the LORD; that walketh in his ways.* ². "*For thou shalt eat the labor of thine hands: happy shalt thou be, and it shall be well with thee.*"

Blessed In the Merriam Webster Dictionary is defined as bringing pleasure, contentment, or good fortune.[98] The Greek word for Blessed is "Makarios,"which means blessed, happy, and to be envied.[99]

These scriptures explain that if we fear the Lord in reverence for who He is and continue to walk in His ways, we will be able to eat the labor of our hands. He is going to bless everything that we put our hands to do. We will not be suffering and poor, but we will be prosperous and happy with joy in our hearts. God will bless everything that we do, and the people of this world are going to be looking at us and envying what God is doing in our lives because we are being obedient to Him. How-

98. Blessed Merriam-Webster.com https://www.Merriam-Webster.com Accessed August 2021
99. "Markarios" the Greek word for Blessed https://www.biblehub.com accessed August 2021

ever, those that pretend to fear the Lord will not receive the blessings because God knows all of our hearts. He knows if we are sincere about anything that we do for Him. He knows when we are faking until we make it. So the best thing to do with God is to be honest with Him. He can help you in whatever area you need help in.

DECLARATIONS

I decree and declare that I am in reverence of the Lord in every area of my life.

I decree and declare that I will forever walk in His ways, instead of my owns.

I decree and declare that I will not lean to my own understanding but acknowledge Him in every way.

I will allow the Spirit of God to come inside of my heart and make a new creature out of me.

I decree and declare that I will not turn my back on Your God or Your Commandments.

I decree and declare that I will be a lender and not a borrower because I am a faithful follower of Christ.

August 7th

*J*OEL 2:28-30 (KJV), "*²⁸ And it shall come to pass afterward, that I will pour out my Spirit upon all flesh; and your sons and your daughters shall prophesy, your old men shall dream dreams, your young men shall see visions:²⁹· "And also upon the servants and upon the handmaids in those day will I pour out my spirit. ³⁰· "And I will shew wonders in the heavens and in the earth, blood, and fire, and pillars of smoke."*

Pour in the Merriam Webster Dictionary means to move with a continuous flow.[100] The Greek word for Pour is "Spendo," which is to pour out (as drink offering) and to make a libation.[101]

Joel describes the day that God will generously send His Spirit to empower and work through those who call on the name of the LORD. As a result, prophetic gifts and experiences will be common among all the people who serve God, no matter what age, sex, or position in society. God is releasing pro-

---

100. Pour Merriam-Webster.com https://www.Merriam-Webster.com Accessed August 2021

101. "Spendo" The Greek Word for Pour https://www.biblehub. com Accessed August 2021

phetic gifts for the purpose of honoring Him and benefiting others. As God's people exercise these gifts, the Spirit works through them to reveal God's Presence in powerful and compelling ways.[102]

PRAYER

Father God, in the name of Jesus, I come before You because You declared in Your Word that in the last days that You would pour out Your Spirit on all flesh. So, Lord, I believe You at Your Word and I activate every gift on the inside of me that is lying dormant to come alive by Your Spirit. Lord, I am one of Your children and I need that empowerment to do all the things that You have required for me to do in Jesus' name. So, Lord I receive all that You have for me, and I will use it for the building up of Your kingdom and drawing people into the Kingdom as well. Lord, Your Word declares that out of my belly will come rivers of living water, so let it erupt right now in Jesus' name. Let the gifts come up and I will not be afraid to use them for Your glory from this day forward in Jesus' name. Amen.

---

102. Fire Bible study Bible (KJV) Hendrick and Henderickson Bibles Accessed September 2021

August 8th

*J*OEL 3:18 (KJV), "AND it shall come to pass in that day, that the mountains shall drop down new wine, and the hills shall flow with milk and all the rivers of Judah shall flow with waters, and a fountain shall come forth of the house of the LORD, and shall water the valley of Shittim."

Fountain in the Merriam Webster Dictionary is defined as a spring of water issuing from the earth.[103] The Greek word for Fountain is "Pege," which means a spring of water, a fountain, well, issue, or flow.[104]

Matthew Henry's Concise Commentary states that there shall be abundant divine influences, and the gospel will spread speedily into the remotest corners of the earth. The fountain is plenty in the House of God. Christ is this fountain. His suffering, merit, and grace, cleanse, refresh and makes us fruitful. The gospel of grace flowing from Christ shall reach the Gen-

103. Fountain Merriam-Webster.com https://www.Merriam-Webster.com Accessed September 2021
104. "Pege" the Greek word for Fountain. https://www.biblehub.com Accessed September 2021

tiles, the world, and the most remote regions and make them abound in the fruits of righteousness. [105]

Jesus is the living water that we all need to obtain eternal life and an abundant life here on earth. Without Jesus, nothing that we do will last. Jesus is the new wine in our lives. The old wine is our old man before we knew Christ. You cannot put new wine into old wineskins. New wine must go into a new wine skin to be preserved. Jesus is life. Eternal life is only found in Jesus and not anything or anyone else in this world.

DECLARATIONS

I decree and declare that I will put new wine into new wine skins.

I decree and declare that divine influences are coming into my life.

I decree and declare that the Word of God will make it to all parts of the world.

God, I thank You for Your grace that empowers me so that I can be fruitful in You.

I decree and declare that I am the righteousness of God in Christ Jesus.

---

105. Matthew Henry's Concise Commentary https://www.biblehub.com Accessed September 2021

Lord, thank You for Your compassion and grace that You have given us.

August 9th

AMOS 9:13-14 (KJV), "BEHOLD the days come, saith the LORD, that the plowman shall overtake the reaper, and the treader of grapes him that soweth seed; and the mountains shall drop sweet wine, and all the hills shall melt."

Plowman in the Merriam Webster Dictionary defined as a man who guides a plow.[106] The Greek word for Plowman is "Arotriao," which means plowing, to plow, or one who plows.[107]

The Fire Bible Study Bible shows how Amos speaks of a transformed and glorious earth where God's people can continuously plant and harvest at the same time. The land will be full of supernaturally productive people who will lack nothing and God's blessings will never end.[108]

106. Plowman Merrian-Webster.com https://www.Merriam-Webster.com Accessed September 2021
107. "Arotriao" the Greek word for Plowman https://www.biblehub.com Accessed September 2021
108. Fire Bible (KJV) Study Bible Hendrickson Publishing 2020 accessed September 2021

Wouldn't this be an awesome time when we can sow seed and it comes right back and blesses us without having to wait for a long time?

PRAYER

Precious Father, we come to You today because Your Word declares that there will come a day where we can continuously plant and reap at the same time. Our land will be supernaturally productive and we will not lack anything. We will have everything that we will ever need at our disposal. Lord, that will be a momentous day where Your blessing will never end in our lives in Jesus' name. Amen.

August 10th

ATTHEW 9:37-38 (KJV), "*37 Then saith he unto is disciples, The harvest truly is plenteous, but the laborers are few. 38. "Pray ye therefore the Lord of the harvest, that he will send forth laborers into the harvest."*

Laborers in the Merriam Webster Dictionary are defined as a person who does unskilled physical work for wages.[109] The Greek word for laborers is "Kopos," meaning labor, toil, or involving labor.[110]

The Fire Bible Study Bible states that Jesus challenges His followers to always remember that those who are spiritually lost, who do not know and follow God, have a priceless eternal soul and will spend eternity in heaven or hell. We must reach them with the love and the message of Christ while there is still time. Many of them are spiritually ready to receive the

---

109. Laborers Merriam-Webster.com https://www.Merriam-Webster.com Accessed September 2021
110. "Kopos" The Greek Word for Laborers https://www.biblehub.com Accessed September 2021

message. They can only be saved if someone presents the good news of forgiveness and a new life through Jesus Christ.

Our part in the work is necessary because before God acts, He usually inspires His people to pray. Only after they have prayed does God respond and finishes what He desires to happen.[111]

We are the laborers that this scripture is describing. God wants to send His people out to compel people to come to Christ while there is still time to come. God wants people saved from death, hell, and destruction. God is calling all of His children to stand up and do what He is telling us to do in the world before He comes back that second time to reclaim His people.

DECLARATIONS.

-

I decree and declare that I will move forward and be a laborer in the field for God.

I will tell them my testimony about how God has delivered and set me free, so they will know that God wants to deliver them too.

I will witness to the people that God tells me to witness too, so they can obtain salvation.

I will no longer be fearful but will go forth in boldness to be who God has called me to be.

111. Fire Study Bible (KJV) Hendrickson Publishing 2020 Accessed September 2021

God, I will make haste and get to work for the Kingdom of God.

Lord, You can use me to do Your will in the earth.

August 11th

*L*UKE 4:18 (KJV), "THE *Spirit of the Lord is upon me, because he hath anointed me to preach the gospel to the poor; he hath sent me to heal the broken-hearted, to preach deliverance to the captives, and recovering of sight to the blind, to set at liberty them that are bruised."*

Anointed in the Merriam Webster Dictionary means applying oil as part of a religious ceremony.[112] The Greek word for Anointed is "Chrisma," which is an anointing or unction.[113]

Anointing symbolizes pouring oil all over an individual who was being appointed, commissioned, and empowered for spiritual service. This anointing oil was symbolic of the Holy Spirit. Jesus was not anointed with literal oil but with the Spirit Himself.[114]

112. Anointed Merriam-Webster.com https://www.Merriam-Webster.com Accessed September 2021
113. "Chrisma" The Greek word for Anointed https://www.biblehub.com Accessed September 2021
114. Fire bible study Bible (KJV) Hendrickson Publishing 2020 Accessed September 2021

Jesus stated that the purpose of this Spirit anointed ministry is to:

1. Preach the Gospel to the poor.
2. Heal the broken hearted.
3. Preach deliverance to the captives.
4. Recovering sight to the blind
5. To set the captives free.

This is what the ministry of Jesus Christ represents to His believers and for the ones that does not know Him as their personal Savior. Jesus's ministry is designed to heal every person's need.

<u>PRAYER</u>

Father God, in the name of Jesus, I come before You today to thank You for sending Your Son Jesus so that He could take care of all of our needs. Jesus was anointed by You to preach the gospel to the poor in spirit. You also sent Him to heal the broken-hearted, so I declare that every heart that is broken will be healed on today in Jesus' name. Lord, Your Word declares that Jesus was sent to preach deliverance to those who are oppressed by the enemy. You came to set the captives free from sin. Lord, thank You for sending Him to recover sight to the blind (those spiritually and physically blind) in Jesus' name. Lord, thank You for sending Him to set the captives free from sin in Jesus' name. You placed all the sins of this world on Jesus on the cross over 2,000 years ago. Lord, thank You for sending Him to preach the acceptable year of the Lord. Now is the time for us to give our lives to Christ and be an example for Him in this world. Lord, I thank You for moving mightily in our lives from this day forward because of our surrender to You in Jesus' name. Amen.

August 12th

*L*UKE *6:27-28 (KJV), "BUT I say unto you which hear, love your enemies, do good to them which hate you." 28. "Bless them that curse you and pray for them that despitefully use you."*

Enemies in the Merriam Webster Dictionary is defined as one that is antagonistic to another, one seeking to injure, or overthrow.[115] The Greek word for Enemies is "Echthros," which means hostile, hated, or an enemy.[116]

The Fire Bible Study Bible states that Jesus tells us how we are to conduct ourselves toward others, particularly those who oppose or disagree with us. As believers, we are to accept responsibility of the requirements He outlines here. Loving our enemies does not mean emotional love, such as showing affection for them. This love speaks of the genuine concern for their good, especially for their eternal spiritual salvation. Since we know the terrible consequences awaiting those who are hostile

115. Enemies Merriam-Webster.com Https://www.Merriam-Webster.com Accessed September 2021
116. "Echthros" the Greek Word for Enemies https://www.biblehub.com Accessed September 2021

to God and His people, we must pray for them and attempt to introduce them to Christ. We can only do this through kind and gracious actions: repaying love for hate and good for evil. We will take a stand against evil and ungodliness in this world today.[117]

DECLARATIONS

I will bless and be good to those that curse me.

I will exchange love with hate and good with evil.

I will take a stand against evil in this world in Jesus' name.

I will pray for those that say all manner of evil against me.

I will pray for them and attempt to introduce them to a risen Christ.

I will use kind and generous actions toward my enemies so they can be drawn to Christ.

117. Fire study Bible (KJV) Hendrickson Publishing 2020 Accessed September 2021

August 13th

*L*UKE 6:38 (KJV), *"GIVE and it will be given unto you; good measure, pressed down, and shaken together, and running over, shall men give unto your bosom."*

Good measure in the Merriam Webster Dictionary means additionally, more, or in addition to.[118] The Greek word for Good Measure is "Metron," which means a measure or a measuring rod.[119]

This scripture states that we are to give to those who are in need and then in turn, God will bless us with more to give. God will multiply what is given back to us: pressed down, shaken together, or running over. God will cause men to give unto our bosom. The Word of God states that God will give seed to a sower (giver) and bread to the eater. So, whatever you give, God will make sure you get that back and more added to it. You can never out give God no matter how hard you try. God

118. Good measure Merriam-Webster.com https://www.Merriam-Webster.com Accessed September 2021
119. "Metron" the Greek word for Good Measure https://www.biblehib.com Accessed September 2021

does not always give back money when we give money, but He blesses us in other ways like physically, mentally, financially, and many other ways. The Word states that He will rebuke the devourer for His name's sake. He will close the mouth of anything that is eating up your seed. God is our source and supplier. He will supply every need that we will ever have in life.

PRAYER

Precious Father, I thank You for supplying my every need, such as Your riches in glory by Christ Jesus. Lord, we thank You for making a way out of no way in our lives. Lord, we thank You for rebuking the devourer to our harvest in Jesus' name. Lord, thank You for multiplying what You give back to me before it comes back to me in Jesus' name. Lord, I give to the poor every chance that I get. I sow into other people's lives and will be a blessing to them so they can do the work that You have called them to do in this earth. Lord, I thank You for moving mightily in everything that concerns me in Jesus' name. Lord, I see Your hand upon my life and resources in Jesus' name. Lord, I thank You for every increase that You have given to me and my home in Jesus' name. Amen.

August 14th

LUKE 9:23 (KJV), "AND he said to them all, if any man will come after me, let him deny himself, and take up his cross daily, and follow me."

Deny in the Merriam Webster Dictionary is defined as to restrain (oneself) from the gratification of desires.[120] The Greek word for Deny is "Aparneomai," meaning to deny, disown, repudiate (either another person or myself), or disregard.[121]

The Fire Bible Study Bible states that accepting Jesus as Savior and Lord the forgiver of sins and the Leader of your life requires believing the truth of His message. It also requires a commitment to follow Him, no matter the cost. The sacrifice that Jesus made on the cross provided us with an opportunity for an eternal relationship with God. We must be willing to identify with Christ and His sufferings, allowing our own reputations to become wrapped up in our devotion to Him.[122]

120. Deny Merriam-Webster.com https://www.Merriam-Webster.com Accessed September 2021
121. "Aparneomai" The Greek word for Deny https://www.biblehub.com Accessed September 2021
122. Fire study Bible Henderickson Publishing 2020 Accessed September 2021

DECLARATIONS

Jesus, I accept You as my Lord and Savior and as the Leader of my life.

Lord, thank You for forgiving all of my sins, past, present, and future in Jesus' name.

God, You sent Jesus to die for our sins, and He rose on the 3rd day with all power in the palm of His hands.

Lord, I will follow You no matter what the cost.

No matter who walks away from my life, I will never walk away from You.

Lord, I surrender all to You because You are my Precious Savior.

August 15th

*R*OMANS 8:31, "WHAT SHALL *we then say to these things? If God be for us, who can be against us?"*

Say in the Merriam Webster Dictionary is defined as to express in words or state.[123] The Greek word for Say is "Phemi," meaning to declare or say.[124]

Barnes Notes on the Bible states that God is for us, lives on the inside of us, and is our friend because we were adopted into the beloved as His children. He gave us His Spirit to live on the inside of us and saved us from a life of sin. Who can injure or destroy us? Sinners may be against us and the great enemy of our souls, but their power to destroy us is taken away. God is mightier than all of our foes and He can defend and save us.[125] *Psalm 118:6 (ESV), "The Lord is on my side; I will not fear what man can do unto me."*

123. Say Merriam-Webster.com https://www.Merriam-Webster.com Accessed September 2021
124. "Phemi" The Greek word for Say https://www.biblehib.com Accessed September 2021
125. Barnes Notes on the Bible Romans 8 :31 https://www.biblehub.com Accessed October 2021

PRAYER

Father God, in the name of Jesus, I come before You today to thank You for watching out for me. When the enemy revolts against me, and try to harm or hurt me, You come to my rescue and defend me. Lord, thank You for Your protection and the hedge of protection that You have placed around my family. Lord, thank You for saving me from a life of sin. Thank You for sending Your Son Jesus to die for my sin. Through Jesus' redeeming blood, I can now become Your beloved son/daughter. Lord, thank You for engrafting me into Your body in Jesus' name. I know according to Your Word that since You are for me, no one can be against me. Lord, thank You for loving, keeping, and defending me when I need defending from the enemy in Jesus' name. Amen.

August 16th

*R*OMANS 11:29 (KJV), "FOR *the gifts and calling of God are without repentance.*"

Repentance in the Merriam Webster Dictionary is defined as turning from sin and dedicate oneself to the amendment of one's life or change one's mind.[126] The Greek word for Repentance is "Metanoeo," meaning to change one's mind or purpose, repent, or change the inner man (particularly with reference to acceptance of the will of God).[127]

God has given everyone a gift and the gifts and callings that He has given us are without repentance. We do not have to be saved to operate in them. If you are not saved and operating in them, you are operating in them illegally. You need to accept Jesus as your Lord and Savior to operate through His Spirit. Anything else is strange fire and it is not of God. It comes from the enemy Satan. That is why repentance is so important because without it, you will not be able to come to Christ. It will take

126. Repentance Merriam-Webster.com https://www.Merriam-Webster.com Accessed October 2021
127. "Metanoeo" The Greek Word for Repentance https:///www.biblehub.com Accessed Octobeer 2021

repentance before you can be saved and adopted in the Body of Christ. The enemy is fooling thousands of people every day about where they will spend eternity. If you leave this world without God, it will not be good for you. In Hell, you will lift your eyes. If you leave this world in Christ, to be absent from the body is to be present with the Lord. We must do repentance often to stay in right standing with God.

DECLARATIONS

I decree and declare that I will repent to God and change my ways in Jesus' name.

I decree and declare that I will not try to use my gift or calling without God backing me.

I decree and declare that I will surrender my life to Christ to operate legally in my gifts and callings.

I decree and declare that I want to spend eternity with the Lord in Jesus' name.

I decree and declare I will not be using my gifts illegally, but I will have a legit relationship with Christ.

August 17th

❧

*R*OMANS 12:21 (KJV), "BE *not overcome with evil but overcome evil with good."*

Overcome in the Merriam Webster Dictionary means to get the better of.[128]

The Greek word for Overcome is "Nikao," which means to conquer, to prevail, or subdue.[129] The Barnes Notes on the Bible says, "Be not vanquished or subdued by injury received from others. Do not suffer your temper to be excited. Don't allow your Christian principles, mild, amiable, kind, and benevolent temper to be ruffled by any opposition or an injury which you may experience or abandon. Maintain your Christian principles amidst all opposition and thus show the power of the gospel. We will not be overcome with evil to have our temper get out of hand, enraged, or revengeful. We will not engage in contention with those that injure us. If Christians show benevolence,

128.. Overcome Merriam Webster.com https://www.Merriam-Webster.com Accessed October 2021
129. "Nikao" The Greek word for Overcome https://www.biblehub.com Accessed October 2021

they will send forth proofs of love to the ends of the earth, then the evils of the world will be overcome."[130]

PRAYER

Father God, in the name of Jesus, I come before You today to thank You for Your Word that I hide in my heart daily so that I will not sin against You. I will not repay evil for evil when it has been done against me. I will pray for the person and show them the love of God regardless of how they are treating me. Lord, thank You for blocking every attack that the enemy has sent against me. Thank You for Your precious blood in Jesus' name. Lord, we pray for the ones that are doing evil. Lord, save and fill them with Your Holy Spirit right now in Jesus' name. Lord, give Your people the strength that when someone is coming up against them, they will have the power to stand strong in You. Lord, help us to walk in forgiveness toward the people that the enemy has used to try to hurt us. Lord, Your word declares that no weapon that is formed against us shall prosper. Thank You for reassuring us that we do not have anything to worry about if You are in our corner in Jesus' name. Amen.

---

130. Barnes Notes on the Bible Commentary https://www.biblehub.com Accessed October 2021

August 18th

ROMANS 13:11 (KJV), "AND that, knowing the time, that now it is high time to awake out of sleep: for now, is our salvation nearer than when we believed."

Salvation in the Merriam Webster Dictionary is defined as a deliverance from the power and effects of sin.[131] The Greek word for Salvation is "Soteria," meaning deliverance, safety, or salvation.[132]

Matthew Henry's Concise Commentary states that we need to wake up out of carnality, carnal security, sloth, negligence, and spiritual death, considering that this time is a busy or perilous. Salvation is nigh at hand. Let us mind our ways and mend our pace. We are nearer to our journey's end. It is time to dress ourselves. Observe what we must put off and cast off sinful works of darkness and put on the armour of light. Put on

131. Salvation Merriam-Webster.com https://www.Merriam-Webster.com Accessed October 2021
132. "Soteria" The Greek word for Salvation https://www.biblehub.com Accessed October 2021

Christ. Put on righteousness. Put on the Spirit of Christ. Put on the grace of Christ.[133]

DECLARATIONS

I decree and declare that I will give my life to Christ and become serious in my walk with Him.

I decree and declare that I will not be the walking dead and live without Christ.

I decree and declare I will wake up out of spiritual deadness in my life.

I decree and declare that the salvation of God is at hand, and I must seek Him while He may be found.

I decree and declare I will not be left when the bridegroom comes like the five   foolish virgins.

I decree and declare that I will no longer be walking or operating in carnality   anymore, but I will be led by the Holy Spirit.

---

133. Matthew Henry's concise Commentary https:/www.biblehub.com Accessed October 2021

August 19th

*R*OMANS 14:17 (KJV), "FOR *the kingdom of God is not meat and drink; but righteousness, and peace, and joy in the Holy Ghost."*

Righteousness in the Merriam Webster Dictionary is defined as acting in accord with divine or moral law; free from guilt or sin.[134] The Greek word for Righteousness is "Dikaiosune," meaning righteousness, justice, or righteousness (God is the source or author).[135]

Matthew Henry's Concise Commentary states that righteousness, peace, and joy are words that mean a great deal. As to God, our great concern is to appear before Him justified by Christ's death and sanctified by the Spirit of His grace; for the righteousness of the Lord loveth righteousness.[136] God is expecting His people to live righteous lifestyles because we represent Him, and He is a God of righteousness. He wants each of

134. Righteousness Merriam-Webster.com https://www.Merriam-Webster.com Accessed October 2021
135. "Dikaiosune" Greek word for Righteousness https://www.biblehub.com Accessed October 2021
136. Matthew Henry's Concise Commentary https://www.biblwehub.com Accessed October 2021

us to have peace and joy in the Holy Ghost. That spiritual joy is wrought by the blessed Spirit in the hearts of the believers that respects God as their reconciled Father and expects heaven as their home. When we walk in God's righteousness, we are not a slave to sin. Sin has no dominion over us.

PRAYER

Father God, in the name of Jesus, I come before You today. Thank You for Your peace, righteousness, and joy through the Holy Spirit that lives on the inside of me. Lord, I am the righteousness of God in Christ Jesus and not walking in religion, tradition, or in my own righteousness. Lord, thank You for sending Your Son Jesus to redeem us back to You through salvation in Jesus' name. Lord, thank You for being my Abba Father, the one who I can lean on when I need to. By Jesus's perfect sacrifice, I do not have to be a slave to sin any longer. Thank You for delivering and setting me free in Jesus' name. Amen.

August 20th

1 Corinthians 8:6 (KJV), "*But to us there is but one God, the Father, of whom are all things, and we in him; and one Lord Jesus Christ, by whom are all things, and we by him.*"

Father in the Merriam Webster Dictionary is defined as GOD, the first person in the Trinity.[137] The Greek word for Father is "Pater," meaning a father, ancestor, elder, or senior.[138]

Matthew Henry's Concise Commentary states that One God made all, and has power over all. The One God, even the Father, signifies the Godhead as the sole object of all religious worship, and the Lord Jesus Christ denotes the person of Emmanuel, God manifested in the flesh. One with the Father, and with us is the appointed Mediator, and Lord of all, through whom we come to the Father. Through whom the Father sends all blessings to us, by the influence and the working of the Holy Spirit. We refuse to worship any other god but the only true God.[139]

137. Father Merriam-Webster.com https://www.Merriam-Webster.com Accessed October 2021
138. 'Pater" The Greek word for Father https://www.biblehub.com Accessed October 2021
139. Matthew Henry's Concise Commentary https://www.biblehub.com Accessed

DECLARATIONS

I decree and declare that I will only serve the Godhead, the Father, the Son, and the Holy Spirit.

I decree and declare that Jesus is Emmanuel meaning God with us.

I decree and declare that Jesus is the Mediator between God and man.

I decree and declare that God is Lord over all.

I decree and declare that God has all power in His hands.

I decree and declare that there is not another person that is more powerful than God.

August 21st

1 CORINTHIANS 9:14 (KJV), "EVEN so hath the Lord ordained that they which preach the gospel should live the gospel."

Ordained in the Merriam Webster Dictionary is defined as to invest officially (as by the laying on of hands) with ministerial or priestly authority.[140] The Greek word for Ordained is "Diatasso," meaning to give orders or to charge.[141]

This scripture explains that it is the churches' (body of believers) responsibility to take care of their ministers, especially if they are feeding them the Word of God. Those who seek to do our souls good should have food provided for them and should not be laboring with their own hands to get it. The ministers may wave their rights like Paul did, but those who transgress a precept of Christ, deny or without due support to our pastors.

140. Ordained Merriam-Webster.com https://www.Merriam-Webster.com Accessed October 2021
141. "Diatasso" The Greek Word for Ordained https://www.biblehub.com Accessed October 2021

PRAYER

Father God, help me to be able to take care of the ministers of the gospel without any strain in Jesus' name. Lord, give us witty ideas and dreams to make a substantial income to take care of the needs of our leaders in Jesus' name. Some do not ask for anything extra from their members because they know their financial situations in Jesus' name. Lord, give us all wisdom on how to be blessed beyond measure so we can bless our leaders beyond measure so, they will not have to work regular jobs unless they just want to. Lord, You said in Your Word that You would supply our needs such as Your riches in glory by Christ Jesus. Lord, You also said that we could speak a thing and it shall be established in Jesus' name. Lord, we speak increase in everyone's life so we can be a blessing to our leaders in Jesus' name. Amen.

August 22nd

1 CORINTHIANS 10:16 (KJV), "THE cup of blessing which we bless, is it not the communion of the blood of Christ? The bread which we break, is it not the communion of the body of Christ?"

Communion in the Merriam Webster Dictionary is defined as a Christian sacrament in which consecrated bread and wine are consumed as memorials of Christ's death. It also symbolizes the realization of the spiritual union between Christ and the communicant or as the body and the blood of Christ.[142] The Greek word for Communion is "Koinonia," meaning fellowship, partnership, spiritual fellowship, or a fellowship in the spirit.[143]

Matthew Henry's Concise Commentary talks about the Lord's Supper and taking part in it is a profession of faith in Christ crucified and the adorning gratitude to Him for salvation.[144] Taking communion regularly is also good for being pro-

142. Communion Merriam-Webster.com https://www.Merriam-webster.com Accessed October 2021
143. "Koinonia" The Greek word for Communion https://www.biblehub.com Accessed October 2021
144. Matthew Henery's Concise Commentary https://www.biblehub.com Accessed October 2021

tected from backlash, retaliation, and demonic attacks from the enemy, Satan. We are covered by Jesus's precious blood. We can take communion to receive healing in our bodies because Jesus took 39 lashes for every sickness or disease that we would ever experience. All these diseases, including the COVID-19 virus and the Delta Variant have already been placed on Jesus over 2,000 years ago. We do not have to be sick, or come into agreement with what the doctor said about us. Communion belongs to the believers of Christ.

DECLARATIONS

I decree and declare that I will take communion daily because that is a benefit of a child of God.

I decree and declare as I take this communion, by His stripes, I am healed in Jesus' name.

I decree and declare that I am covered under the blood of Jesus.

I decree and declare that I am protected from all manner of sicknesses and   diseases because of communion.

I decree and declare that through Jesus' obedience, I am now healed in my body and mind.

I decree and declare that communion only belongs to those in the Body of Christ.

August 23rd

*J*UDGES 6:12 (KJV), "AND the angel of the LORD appeared unto him, and said unto him, The Lord is with thee, thou mighty man of valor."

Valor in the Merriam Webster Dictionary is defined as strength of the mind or spirit that enables a person to encounter danger with firmness and personal bravery.[145] The Greek word for Valor is "Andreia," meaning the qualities of a hero or heroine, exceptional or heroic courage when facing danger, especially in battle.[146]

In this scripture, the angel of the Lord came to Gideon to let him know that God had called Gideon a mighty man of valor because he was in a battle with the Midianites. He would be able to win the battle with the help of the Lord. Gideon was weak in faith, and he believed that he could not complete the task set before him. Gideon wanted to have his faith confirmed and the angel was there to confirm his faith. Gideon asked God

145. Valor Merriam-Webster.com https://www.Merriam-Webster.com Accessed October 2021
146. "Andreia" Greek word for Valor https://www.biblehub.com Accessed October 2021

to show him a sign that he was with him, and he was shown a sign by the angel. The angel turned the meat into an offering consumed by fire. Gideon had found grace in God's sight. Then Gideon believed that God was with him.[147]

God will show us a sign in our hearts when we pray to Him about a matter by the working power of His Spirit. We will find grace in God's sight as well and He will give us peace.

PRAYER

Precious Father, I thank You for calling me a mighty woman or man of valor because of the courage that I have going through these attacks of the enemy. I will not be afraid of what man can do unto me. I know that Your Word declares that no weapon formed against me shall be able to prosper. The weapon would form, but it would not prosper because You have me hedged in Your arms of protection. Lord, thank You for protecting me from the fiery darts of the enemy against my life in Jesus' name. I will wear the shield of faith so nothing that the enemy does or throws at me will prosper. We cast down every demon, witchcraft, backlash, and retaliation from the enemy. We plead the blood of Jesus over everything and everyone that concerns us in Jesus' name. Amen.

---

147. Matthew Henry's Concise Commentary https://www.biblehub.com Accessed October 2021

August 24th

1 CHRONICLES 16:10 (KJV), "GLORY ye in the holy name; let the heart of them rejoice that seek the LORD."

Rejoice in the Merriam Webster Dictionary is defined as to give joy to or great delight.[148] The Greek word for Rejoice is "Sugchairo," which means to rejoice with or congratulate.[149]

Matthew Henry's Concise Commentary says, "Let God be glorified in our praises. Let others be edified and taught that strangers to Him may be led to adore Him. Let us ourselves triumph and trust in God. Those that give glory to His name are allowed to glory in it. Let His everlasting covenant be our joy and thankfulness to Him."[150]

DECLARATIONS

I decree and declare His glory among the nations.

148. Rejoice Merriam-Webster.com https://www.Merriam-Webster.com Accessed October 2021
149. "Sugchairo" The Greek word for Rejoice httos://www.biblehub.com Accessed October 2021
150. Matthew Henry's Concise Commentary https://www.biblehub.com Accessed October 202

I sing Glory ye His Holy name.

I take delight and joy in praising His name.

I will sing praises to His name as I worship Him in Spirit and in truth.

I am rejoicing that God is so good.

Let the praises ring on high, Oh Lord.

August 25th

GENESIS 1:27 (NKJV), *"So God created man in His own image; in the image of God, He created him; male and female He created them."*

Created in the Merriam Webster Dictionary is defined to bring into existence.[151] The Greek word for "Created" is Ktizo," which means to build, to create, form, shape, or always of God.[152]

The following passage is taken from *Woman Thou Art Loosed Holy Bible* by T.D. Jakes. God looked out across eternity. He saw you. He saw everything He had created and everything He would create around you. He saw the specific need on this earth that He would make you meet. He saw the full set of traits and abilities that you would need to complete His purpose for your life. He knew what kind of environment would be necessary for you to properly develop the gifts He would give you.

151.Created Merriam-Webster.com https://www.Merriam-Webster.com Accessed October 202
152. "Ktizo" Greek word for Created https://www.biblehub.com Accessed October 2021

God looked and then He created. He created you. God looked at you and said, "This is good."

Do you have the same opinion of yourself? Do you agree with God's opinion of you? You must appreciate the way God created you because other people will treat you the way you treat yourself. They will respect you only to the degree that you respect yourself.[153]

Prayer

Father God, in the name of Jesus, we come before you today to acknowledge that we were created in Your image and likeness. Lord, thank You for seeing me as Your daughter and something that You have created as good according to Your Word in Jesus' name. Lord, thank You for maturing me to move me closer to my purpose in this earth in Jesus' name. Lord, thank You for connecting me to the right people to help birth the gifts You have placed deep within me in Jesus' name. Amen.

153. Woman thou art Loosed Holy Bible by T.D. Jakes 1998 Accessed October 2021

August 26th

*N*UMBERS 6:24-26 (NKJV), "²⁴ *The LORD blesses you and keep you; ²⁵. "The LORD makes His face shine upon you. ²⁶. "The LORD lifts up His countenance upon you and give you peace."*

Blesses in the Merriam Webster Dictionary is defined as very welcome, pleasant, or appreciated.[154] The Greek word for Blesses is "Makarios," which means blessed, happy, or to be envied.[155]

These verses are a prayer that the priests prayed to bless the people in the name of the Lord. They prayed the following:

- To be under the almighty protection of God our Savior;
- to enjoy His Favor as the smile of a loving Father or as the cheering beams of the sun;

He mercifully forgives our sins, supplies our wants, consoles the heart, and prepares us by His grace for eternal glory.

---

154. Blesses Merriam-Webster.com https://www.Merriam-Webster.com Accessed October 2021
155. "Markarios" Greek Word for Blesses https://www.biblehub.com Accessed October 2021

These things form the substance of this blessing and the total of all blessings.[156]

DECLARATIONS

I decree and declare that the Lord blesses and keep you.

Lord, thank You for blessing and keeping us.

Lord, thank You for Your face shining upon me.

Lord, thank You for giving me peace.

Lord, thank You for being gracious to us.

Lord, I thank You for Your favor and protection over my life.

---

156. Matthew Henry's Concise Commentary https://www.biblehub.com Accessed October 2021

August 27th

*D*EUTERONOMY 10:12-13 (NKJV), "¹²AND now, Israel what does the LORD your God require of you, but to fear the LORD your God, to walk in all His ways and to love Him, to serve the LORD your God with all of your heart and with all your soul, ^{13.} "And to keep the commandments of the LORD and His statues which I command to you today for your good?"

Commandments in the Merriam Webster Dictionary is defined as the act or the power of commanding or something that is commanded.[157] The Greek word for commandments is "Entole," which means an injunction, order, command, ordinance, or command.[158]

Matthew Henry's Concise Commentary says that we are taught our duty to God in our principles and practices. We must fear the Lord our God. We must love and delight in communion with Him. We must walk in how He has appointed us to walk.

---

157. Commandments Merriam-Webster.com https://www.Merriam-webster.com Accessed October 2021
158. "Entole" the Greek word for Commandment https://www.biblehub.com Accessed October 2021

We must serve Him with all our hearts and souls. What we do in His service, we must do cheerfully and with good will. We must keep His commandments. There is true honor and pleasure in obedience.[159]

PRAYER

Father God, in the name of Jesus, I come before You today to thank You for Your commandments that You have given us to go by in Jesus' name. Lord, I will forever praise Your name and honor Your Word. Lord, I will walk in reverential fear toward the precepts of Your Word in Jesus' name. Lord, I love You and delight in communion with You. I will walk in the ways that You have appointed me to walk in for my life in Jesus' name. Lord, I will serve You with my whole heart and soul. Lord, I will do Your good will cheerfully whenever You tell me to do it in Jesus' name. Amen.

---

159. Matthew Henry's Concise Commentary https://www,biblehub.com Accessed October 2021

August 28th

ᴘsᴀʟᴍ 138:8 (KJV), "ᴛʜᴇ LORD will perfect that which concerneth me: thy mercy, O LORD, endureth forever; forsake not the works of thine own hands."

Perfect in the Merriam Webster Dictionary is defined as lacking in no essential detail or complete.[160] The Greek word for Perfect is "Teleios," which means having reached its end, complete, perfect, full grown, especially the completeness of Christian character.[161]

Matthew Henry's Concise Commentary explains how this scripture lets us know that whatever God has begun in each of us who serve Him, He will perform it. He will perfect that which concerns us. That is what is most needful for us. Every good man is most concerned about his duty and happiness in God that the former may be faithfully done, and the latter effectually secured. If indeed these things are the things that our

160. Perfect Merriam-Webster.com https://www,Merriam-Webster.com Accessed October 2021
161. "Teleios" The Greek word for Perfect https://www.biblehub.com Accessed October 2021

hearts are most upon, there is an excellent work begun in us. He that begun it, will perfect it. Our hopes we shall preserve must be founded, not in our own strength, for that will fail us, but upon the mercy of God, for that will not fail us.[162]

DECLARATIONS

God will perfect everything that concerns us in Jesus' name.

God will perform everything that He has promised in my life.

God will faithfully complete every task that He has set out to do in my life.

We will not look to our own understanding, trying to get ahead of God.

We will acknowledge God in everything that we have done for Him in Jesus' name.

God, thank You that Your mercy endureth forever and ever.

---

162. Matthew Henry's Concise Commentary, https://www.biblehub.com Accessed October 2021

August 29th

*T*HE FIRE BIBLE KING James version talks about the unique attributes of God. We will talk about some of them today, so you can get to know God a little better.

1. God is Omnipresent. He is present everywhere at the same time. In *Psalm 139:17 (NLT), David is talking to the Lord. He said to God, "I can never escape from your Spirit! I can never get away from your presence! So, no matter where we go, God is there."*

2. God is Omniscient. He knows everything. Nothing gets by Him at any time. *Psalm 139:1 (NLT), "O LORD, you have examined my heart and know everything about me."*

3. God is Omnipotent. He is all powerful and has the authority over all things and creatures. *Psalm 147:13(NLT), "For He has strengthened the bars of your gates and blessed your children within you."* God has the power to do anything. Nothing is impossible for God.[163]

---

163. Fire Bible study Bible Zondervan @2012 Accessed October 2021

Once we get it into our minds and hearts that God is all-knowing, all-seeing, and all-powerful in our lives, the better off we will be. We should not turn from Him but turn to Him as our source here on earth because He is our only hope.

August 30th

*A*CCORDING TO FIRE BIBLE Study Book, the following are some characteristics of a true, faithful, and dependable God.

1. God is good. All that God created was good because it was an extension of His nature. *Mark 10:18 (NLT), "Why do you call me good? Jesus asked."* Only God is genuinely good.

2. God is love. His love is completely selfless. His love embraces the entire world of sinful people. The greatest expression of that love is when He sent His Son Jesus to die for our sins, to satisfy the complete penalty of our rebellion to God. *1 John 4:8 (NLT), "But anyone who does not love does not know God, for God is love."*

3. God is merciful and gracious. Grace can be described as God giving us the benefits of salvation that we do not deserve. Mercy is expressed as God saving us from the punishment of our sins we deserve. God offers forgiveness as a gift that we will receive by faith. *Joel 2:13 (NLT), "Don't tear your clothing in your grief but tear your hearts instead. Return to the LORD your God, for He is merciful*

and compassionate, slow to get angry and filled with unfailing love. He is eager to relent and not punish."

4. God is truth. Jesus called Himself the truth. The Holy Spirit is known as the Spirit of Truth because God is completely trustworthy and true in all He says and does. His Word is also described as truth. It really reveals things as they are really are, and it shows us the right way to do things. *Psalm 31:5 (NLT), "I entrust my spirit into your hand. Rescue me, LORD, for you are a faithful God."*

There are many more characteristics of God. However, the points above will get you thinking and meditating on who God is so you can get to know Him in various aspects as you walk to your destiny in Him. God has everything that we would ever need wrapped up in Him.[164]

---

164. Characteristics of a true faithful and dependable God Fire Bible Study Bible Zondervan Accessed October 2021

August 31st

*P*SALM 144:1-2 (KJV), "¹ *Blessed be the LORD my strength, which teacheth my hands to war, and my fingers to fight.* ². *My goodness, and my fortress; my high tower, and my deliverer; my shield, and he is whom I trust; who subdueth my people under me.*"

Teacheth in the Merriam Webster Dictionary is defined as to cause to know something.[165] The Greek word for Teacheth is "Didasko," which means a teacher of good and that which is noble, or honorable.[166]

In these scriptures, David prayed and He asked God to be His teacher on how to fight and war effectively against his enemies. God will give us victory over our own spirit. David praised God for the victory. God is our strength. God is full of power and He becomes the power of those that put their trust in Him.

165. Teacheth Merriam-Webster.com https://www.Merriam-Webster.com Accessed October 2021
166. "Didasko" Greek Word for Teacheth https://www.biblehub.com Accessed October 2021

PRAYER

Father God, in the name of Jesus, I come before You today to thank You for being my strength every day. Lord, teach my hands to war and my finger to fight, so I can effectively win against the enemy's attacks in Jesus' name. Lord, You are my goodness and my fortress, and I can run into the arc of safety when I need it. Lord, You are my strong tower and my deliverer in Jesus' name. Lord, thank You for being my shield and someone I can trust not to tell my secrets in Jesus' name. Lord, I thank You for Your listening ear that all I have to do is cry out to You and You will see about us in Jesus' name. I put on the shield of faith to stand against every fiery dart of the enemy in Jesus' name because I am victorious in You God.

September 1st

PROVERBS 13:20 (KJV), "He that walketh with wise men shall be wise: but a companion of fools shall be destroyed."

Wise in the Merriam Webster Dictionary is defined as exercising and showing sound judgment or prudent.[167] The Greek word for wise is "Sophia," which means skill (human or divine), wisdom, insight, or intelligence.[168]

This scripture talks about wisdom. If we need wisdom, we are to ask of God, who gives it generously to all that will ask Him. Wise men get their wisdom from God and not the world. They will make the best decisions and will be able to stay on track because they are using something more than their wisdom. If we pray or ask God for the solution to our problems, He will give us the best solution that we need to benefit us in our lives. A companion of fools has nobody into the group with any wisdom. They will fall in the ditch time after time because

---

167. Wise Merriam-Webster.com https://www.Merriam-Webster.com Accessed October 2021
168. "Sophia" Greek word for Wise https://www.biblehub.com Accessed October 2021

they will be leaning on their own understanding and not God's wisdom.

DECLARATIONS

I decree and declare that I will ask God for His wisdom if I lack it.

I will not lean to my own understanding about anything that God is getting ready to do in my life.

I will use God's wisdom on make the right decisions in my life.

I will not let a companion of fools influence me to do anything foolish in Jesus' name.

I will walk in the Wisdom that God has given me to walk in and I will stay rooted in the truth of God.

I will pray and ask God about a matter before I set out to do it in Jesus' name.

September 2nd

PROVERBS 16:7 (KJV), "WHEN a man's ways please the LORD, he maketh even his enemies to be at peace with him."

Peace in the Merriam Webster Dictionary is defined as freedom from disquieting or oppressive thoughts or emotions.[169] The Greek word for Peace is "Eirene," which means peace, quietness, rest, or peace of mind.[170]

God has all the hearts of man in His hands, and He can make your enemies be at peace with you. If a man makes God's glory their end, and His will their rule, He will direct their steps by His Spirit and grace. Are your ways pleasing God? If not, what is going on in your life that is stopping you from pleasing God? Is it your desire to please God with your life?

169. Peace Merriam-Webster.com https://www.Merriam-Webster.com Accessed October 2021
170. "Eirene" Greek word for Peace https://www.biblehub.com Accessed October 2021

PRAYER

Father God, in the name of Jesus, we come before You today to allow You to change the necessary things in me so that my life will please you. Lord, You have my permission to get anything that is hindering my walk with You out of me. Lord, show me what I can do to help with my recovery in Jesus' name. Lord, cleanse me of all past hurts, rejections, abuse, unforgiveness, and bitterness so that I can walk pleasing in Your sight in Jesus' name.

September 3rd

❧

*P*SALM 23:4 (*NLT*), "*EVEN when I walk through the darkest valley, I will not be afraid, for you are close beside me. Your rod and your staff protect and comfort.*"

Valley in the Merriam Webster Dictionary is defined as a low point or condition and depression.[171] The Greek word for Valley is "Koilada."[172]

This scripture talks about going through the darkest time in your life when you don't have to be afraid. The loss of a loved one can really be a dark time. Also, when a marriage or relationship ends that can be a very dark time. We don't have to go through the dark times alone because He is there for us. He will protect and comfort us when we are going through these types of storms in our lives. God will give each of us His supernatural strength to be able to go through the hardest times in our lives.

---

171. Valley Merriam-Webster.com https://www.Merriam-Webster.com Accessed October 2021
172. "Ikoiladu" Greek word for Valley https://www.wordhippo.com Accessed October 2021

Whatever may come my way, I can rest assured that God is with me and looking out for my well-being.

DECLARATIONS

Even though I may be walking through the darkest time in my life, I know that I am not alone.

Lord, hold me up on my weak side and help me to overcome this storm.

Lord, thank You for being a shelter in the time of a storm.

Lord, thank You for protecting me when I can't protect myself.

Lord, thank You forgiving my family and me Your supernatural strength.

Lord, Your Word declares that You are my comforter when I need comforting in Jesus' name.

September 4th

PSALM 85:2 (NLT), "You forgave the guilt of your people—yes, you covered all their sins. Interlude."

Forgave in the Merriam Webster Dictionary is defined as to cease to feel resentment against or pardon.[173] The Greek word for Forgave is "Aphesis," which means dismissal, release, pardon, sending away, or complete forgiveness.[174]

The Pulpit Commentary states that God's remission of punishment, and restoration of His people to favor, was a full indication that He had forgiven their iniquity and covered their sins.[175] God will forgive our iniquity and sin when we ask Him to forgive us with a sincere heart. God sent Jesus to go on our bond for our sins and iniquity. That was the only way that we could be redeemed back to God by Jesus's precious shed blood. After we accept Jesus as our Lord and Savior, we are accepted into the Sonship with Christ.

173. Forgave Merriam-Webster.com https://www.Merriam-Webster.com Accessed October 2021
174. "Aphesis" Greek word for Forgave https://www.biblehub.com October 2021
175. The Pulpit Commentary https://www.biblehub.com Accessed October 2021

PRAYER

Father God, in the name of Jesus, I come before You today to thank You for forgiving me when I repented to You. Lord, thank You for forgiving my sins and iniquity. Lord, through Your shed blood, I could be redeemed back to right standing with God. Lord, thank You for Your grace and mercy. Thank You for not giving me what my sins deserved in Jesus' name. Lord, we ask You to help us walk in forgiveness with other people like how You forgave us. Lord, we will walk in complete forgiveness of other people who have hurt or mistreated us because we know You have forgiven us. Lord, we thank You for Your complete and total love of each of us in Jesus' name. Amen.

September 5th

PSALM 19:14 (NLT), "MAY the words of my mouth and the meditation of my heart be pleasing to you, O LORD, my rock and my redeemer."

Meditation in the Merriam Webster Dictionary is defined as to spend time in quiet thought for religious purposes and relaxation.[176] The Greek Word for Meditation is "Dialogismos," which means thought, thinking, reflection, or speculation.[177]

This scripture talks about meditating on the Word of God and not thinking anything contrary to it. God listens to our thoughts daily, so "God, may all our thoughts please You." The Word of God said that we are supposed to cast down every imagination of anything that tries to acknowledge itself that does not come from God's Word. We are to think about the Word of God no matter what we may be seeing with our natural eyes. Think on the good things that come from above in

---

176. Meditation Merriam-Webster.com https://www.Merriam-Webster.com Accessed October 2021
177. "Dalogismos" Greek Word for Meditation https://www.biblehub.com Accessed October 2021

heaven. We can't go wrong with thinking of things in heaven. God is my rock and redeemer, and I can find it all in His Word.

DECLARATIONS

I will meditate on your Word day and night, so I will not sin against thee.

Let the things that I think be pleasing unto You, God.

I decree and declare that I am a vessel of purity and honor in Jesus' name.

I will walk uprightly and stay in right standing with You, God.

I will not give into impure thoughts that will grieve the Holy Spirit in me.

May the Words of my mouth be always seasoned with salt.

September 6th

❧

PSALM 145:18 (NLT), "THE Lord is close to all who call on him, yes, to all who call on him in truth."

Call in the Merriam Webster Dictionary is defined as to speak in a loud voice.[178] The Greek word for Call is "Klesis," which means a calling, invitation, or always a divine call.[179]

This scripture let us know that God draws near to those that draw near to Him. He makes sure His presence is always felt by them. So, if you feel like you are not close enough to God, He is waiting on you to get closer to Him. When You draw closer to Him, He will draw closer to you. He wants to have an intimate relationship with you and consider you a friend, but it must be done by going deeper into His presence regularly. His heart is pure toward you. Call upon Him in truth by studying, eating His Word, and saying what His Word says back to Him.

178. Call Merriam-Webster.com https://www.Merriam-Webster.com Accessed October 2021
179. "Klesis" Greek word for Call https://www.biblehub.com Accessed October 2021

PRAYER

Father God, in the name of Jesus, I come to You today to ask that as I draw closer to You, You will in turn, draw closer to me. Lord, I need an intimate relationship with You in Jesus' name. Lord, order my steps in the right way that I need to go in my life. Lord, I decree and declare that I will not let distractions stop me from getting closer to You in Jesus' name. I bind all distractions that the enemy sent to stop me from moving forward in an intimate relationship with Jesus. Lord, I know that You are much closer than I ever realized in my life. Lord, thank You for fighting for me behind the scenes when an issue arises in my family, marriage, business, or children in Jesus' name. Lord, I trust You to work everything out for my good in Jesus' name. Amen.

September 7th

Proverbs 17:28 (NLT), "Even fools are thought wise when they keep silent, with their mouths shut they seem intelligent."

Silent in the Merriam Webster Dictionary is defined as making no utterance, not speaking, or making noise.[180] The Greek word for Silent is "Sigao," which means to keep silent or to keep secret.[181]

This scripture talks about being wise and keeping your mouth shut. Do not tell people all of your business, especially the plans that God has given you. Keep them to yourselves so no one will try to prey against you or beat you doing it. Your business is not everybody's business. So, people will get close to you for you to let your guard down to find out confidential information so they can spread it to other people. Just make sure your friend is not throwing you under the bus when you are not around. Keep silent and keep those secrets because

---

180. Silent Merriam-Webster.com https://www.Merriam-Webster.com Accessed October 2021
181. "Sigao" Greek word for Silent https://www.biblehub.com Accessed October 2021

when you can keep secrets, God won't mind telling you more things.

DECLARATIONS

I decree and declare that I will hold my tongue and be quiet.

I decree and declare that I will not tell my dreams to a dream crusher.

I decree and declare that I will be more discerning to see who is really for or against me.

I decree and declare that I will ask God if I can tell anybody else our secrets.

I decree and declare that I will not be telling my personal business on social media for any reason.

September 8th

*J*OHN 15:4 (NLT), "*REMAIN in me, and I will remain in you. For a branch cannot produce fruit if it is severed from the vine, and you cannot be fruitful unless you remain in me.*"

Fruitful in the Merriam Webster Dictionary is defined as yielding or producing fruit, or abundantly productive.[182] The Greek word for Fruitful is "Karpos," which means fruit, action, result, or profit.[183]

This scripture talks about the life of the believer. They have to stay rooted and grounded in God. If not, they will operate out of their flesh. When they are rooted in Jesus, their faith will be built on a firm foundation. We are not able to do anything on our own. We need God for everything. We must remain in God and He will remain in us. He will not leave us, so we do not need to leave Him either. We can't even use the gifts He has given to us to be proficient with the Holy Spirit. If we are using them

182. Fruitful Merriam-Webster.com https://www.Merriam-Webster.com Accessed October 2021
183. "Karpos" Greek word for Fruitful https://www.biblehub.com Accessed October 2021

without the Holy Spirit, we are using them illegally. When we use them illegally, we are more than likely using them for the enemy and not God. So, if you want to bear much fruit, stay in God and He will use you for His glory here on earth.

PRAYER

Father God, in the name of Jesus, I come to You today to draw closer to You so that I can stay within the vine. So, I will be able to continue to bear much fruit because I am a follower of Christ. Lord, apart from You, I cannot do anything that would be successful. Lord, I know at some point in my life that You will prune me so that I can bear much more fruit in You. Lord, I know that there are many branches that are connected to the vine. We all have our own functions in the body, but we will continue to produce only what being connected to the vine can produce in Jesus' name. Lord, we will bring forth good and healthy fruit. Lord, do a magnificent work in me so that I can continue to produce righteous fruit in Jesus' name. Amen.

September 9th

ROVERBS 18:4 (NLT), "WISE words are like deep waters; wisdom flows from the wise like a bubbling brook."

Bubbling in the Merriam Webster Dictionary is defined as a flow with a gurgling sound.[184] The Greek word for Bubbling is "Zelos," which means to have a warmth of feeling for or against, to be zealous or jealous.[185]

Matthew Henry's Concise Commentary states that the well-spring of wisdom in the heart of the believer, continually supplies words of wisdom.[186] The Word of God states that if we need wisdom, we are to ask of God, who gives it to us generously. We need to operate in Godly wisdom at all times and not worldly wisdom. Godly wisdom comes from the heart of God on a subject or matter. Using the wisdom of God will get you further than using the wisdom from the world. Worldly

184. Bubbling Merriam-Webster.com htttps://www.Merriam-Webster.com Accessed October 2021
185. "Zelos" Greek word for Bubbling https://www.biblehub.com Accessed October 2021
186. Matthew Henry's Concise Commentary https://www.biblehub.com Accessed October 2021

wisdom is founded on intellect, and it is not based on what the Bible says. So, if you need more wisdom, just ask for it and you will get it. Wise words run deep and sets up roots in the soil, but foolish words don't even have any legs to stand on.

DECLARATIONS

I decree and declare that I will ask God for more wisdom and not lean to my own understanding.

I will use the wisdom of the Word to lead and guide me.

Walking in wisdom is better than being a foolish person.

I have wisdom in my heart because the Word of God is in my heart.

I will not be wise in my own eyes and will not lean on my own understanding about anything.

I will use the wisdom of God in every area of my life so I can be fruitful and multiply.

September 10th

PSALM 100:2 (NLT), "WORSHIP the LORD with gladness. Come before him, singing with joy."

Gladness in the Merriam Webster Dictionary is defined as a feeling or state of well-being and contentment.[187] The Greek word for Gladness is "Euphrosune," which means joy, rejoicing, or gladness.[188]

We are to worship the Lord with gladness about all the things that He has done for each of us. We are to serve the Lord with gladness. Lord, we will serve you whether we are rich or broke. Nothing will stop me from worshipping You and staying in Your presence daily. Lord, no matter who walks away from me, I will not leave You because You will not leave me. Regardless of the troubles and trials that may come our way, we will still hold fast to Your Love, God. We sing songs of praise and adoration because of who He is in our lives.

---

187. Gladness Merriam-Webster.com https://www.Merriam-Webster.com Accessed October 2021
188. "Euphrosune" Greek word for Gladness https://www.biblehub.com Accessed October 2021

PRAYER

Father God, in the name of Jesus, we come before You today to worship You and sing praises unto Your name. Lord, we will worship You with gladness in our hearts, and we will come before You with thanksgiving and praises for all that You have done for all of us. Lord, thank You for the doors that You open that no man can close and thank You for the doors that You closed that no man could open. Lord, we thank You for taking care of all of our needs in our lives right now in Jesus' name. Lord, we thank You for life, health, and strength that You have given us every day. Lord, we praise You and adore You because You are a compassionate God in Jesus' name. Amen.

September 11th

PSALM 116:8 (NLT), "HE has saved me from death, my eyes from tears, my feet from stumbling."

Saved in the Merriam Webster Dictionary is defined as delivered from sin and from spiritual death, and rescued from eternal punishment.[189] The Greek word for Saved is "Sozo," which means to save, heal, preserve, or rescued.[190]

Matthew Henry's Concise Commentary states that we should deem ourselves bound to walk in His presence. It is a great mercy to be kept from being swallowed up with over-much sorrow. It is a great mercy for God to hold us by the right hand, so that we are not overcome and overthrown by a temptation. But when we enter that heavenly rest, deliverance from sin and sorrow will be complete. We shall behold the glory of the Lord and walk in His presence with delight we can now conceive.[191]

---

189. Saved Merriam-Webster.com Https://www.Merriam-Webster.com Accessed October 2021
190. "Sozo" Greek word foe Saved https://www.biblehub.com Accessed October 2021
191. Matthew Henry's Concise Commentary https://www.biblehub.com Accessed October 2021

DECLARATIONS

-

I will always keep my eyes on the Lord.

Jesus is sitting at the right hand of the Father, interceding for us.

I am the righteousness of God, and I will not be shaken.

I decree and declare that I do not care who the devil uses. God is protecting me.

We will not be shaken when troubles, trials, and tribulations come our way.

September 12th

ALATIANS 6:10 (NLT), "THEREFORE, whenever we have the opportunity, we should do good to everyone—especially to those in the family of faith."

Opportunity in the Merriam Webster Dictionary is defined as an amount of time or a situation in which something can be done.[192] The Greek word for Opportunity is "Efkairia," which means chance, occasion, bargain, sale, or scope.[193]

Matthew Poole's Commentary states, "God gives us time and ability to be good to all men. Let it be our business not to harm anyone, but supply necessities of all men, either with our spiritual advice or counsels with all the assistance we can give them that may any way be of spiritual profit or advantage to them, preferring Christians before others; those that belong to the church."[194]

192. Opportunity Merriam-Webster.com https://www.Merriam-Webster.com Accessed October 2021
193. "Efkaina" Greek word for Opportunity https://www.wordhippo.com Accessed October 2021
194. Matthew Poole's Commentary https://www.biblehub.com Accessed October 2021

PRAYER

Father God, in the name of Jesus, I come before as humble as I know. Your Word declares that whenever we could bless those that are in the household of faith, we are to bless them in Jesus' name. Lord, Your Word declares that we are supposed to help them with spiritual advice and counsel and whatever else they need in Jesus' name. Lord, we ask that You lead and guide all of us in the way that we should treat everybody that we come into contact with in Jesus' name. Lord, help us all to do good to all those that are in the Body of Christ and help us to always treat each other right in Jesus' name. Lord, we ask that You make us into the people of God that You want us to be in Jesus' name. Lord, we want to represent You the right way at all times in Jesus' name. Amen.

September 13th

Psalm 147:1 (NLT), "Praise the LORD! How good to sing praises to our God! How delightful and how fitting!"

Praises in the Merriam Webster Dictionary is defined as to glorify (a god or saint) especially by the attribution of perfections or worship.[195] The Greek word for Praises is praise, which means commendation or approval.[196]

Matthew Henry's Concise Commentary states that praising God is work with its own wages. It is comely; it becomes us as reasonable creatures, much more as people in covenant with God.[197] We are to sing praises to God because His Word declares that when praises go up, blessings come down. God will reign down His blessings, His presence, and His strength to all those that need it. We are to sing praises to Him because of who He is and what He has done for us. If we had 10,000

---

195. Praises Merriam-Webster.com https://www.Merriam-Webster.com Accessed October 2021

196. "Epainos" Greek word for Praises https://www.biblehub.com Accessed October 2021

197. Matthew Henry's Concise Commentary https://www.biblehub.com Accessed October 202

tongues, we could not praise Him enough for the things that He has protected us from. Some of them we were able to see and some of them we could not see. God is worthy of all the praise, the honor and glory. It all belongs to Him.

DECLARATIONS

Lord, if I had 10,000 tongues, I could not praise You enough for all You have done for me.

Lord, I will praise Your name forever and ever in Jesus' name.

What is the highest praise? Hallelujah

Lord, I thank You for waking me up this morning. I am closed in my right mind with the activity of my limbs.

Lord, thank You for taking care of all of my needs, such as Your riches in glory by Christ Jesus.

September 14th

MATTHEW 9:37-38 (NLT), "[37] He said to his disciples, "The harvest is great, but the workers are few. [38.] "So, pray to the Lord who is in charge of the harvest; ask him to send more workers into his fields."

Harvest in the Merriam Webster Dictionary is defined as the season when crops are gathered from the fields or the activity of gathering crops.[198] The Greek Word for Harvest is "Thermismos," which means reaping, harvest, or crop.[199]

These scriptures talk about the harvest of souls into the kingdom of God. God is raising up and training laborers to send into the world to draw people into the kingdom by telling our testimonies and witnessing to a lost and dying world. The world will die and everybody in it without God's intervention. He will send His people into the hedges and by ways to compel people to come to Christ before it is too late. He will send them

---

198. Harvest Merriam-Webster.com https://www.Merriam-Webster.com Accessed October 2021
199. "Therismos" Greek word for Harvest https://www.biblehub.com Accessed October 2021

as soon as they are ready to be released after they have been equipped to do the tasks that God has set before them.

PRAYER

Father God, in the name of Jesus, we come before You today to ask You to equip and send more laborers into the fields to preach, teach, witness and compel people to come to Christ while there is still time. Lord, give us a spirit of boldness so we will not be afraid to tell the people what You have told us to tell them in Jesus' name. Lord, we surrender our will for Your will so we can do the work of an evangelist. Lord, You have given all Your blood washed believers the commission to make disciples to all the nations in Jesus' name. Lord, help us to move forward without the fear of rejection in Jesus' name. Lord, strengthen each one of us from the top of our heads to the soles of our feet in Jesus' name. Amen.

September 15th

Samuel 26:3 (NLT), "Saul camped along the road beside the hill of Hakilah, near Jeshimon, where David was hiding. When David learned that Saul had come after him into the wilderness."

Learned in the Merriam Webster Dictionary is defined as characterized by or associated with learning.[200] The Greek word for Learned is "Manthano," which means to learn, a person who is the object of knowledge, or someone learns from experience.[201]

Saul was jealous of David, so he chased after David, trying to kill him. David walked up on Saul and his men while they were asleep and he didn't do anything to them because Saul was God's anointed, so he left him alone. He did cut part of his garment as a souvenir. David was anointed to be king, but it was not yet his time, so he waited on the timing of God. He respected that God had placed Saul in the palace to be king at

---

200. Learned Merriam-Webster.com https://www.Merriam-Webster.com Accessed October 2021
201. "Manthano" Greek word for Learned https://www.biblehub.com Accessed October 2021

that time. The respect that David showed to Saul is something that we must all do to those that God has put to rule over us. Respect their choice. God will release and elevate you in His timing for your life. Continue to stay hidden until God releases you into further promotion.

DECLARATIONS

I will remain hidden in God until He releases me into promotion in Jesus' name.

I will not touch the anointed of God or do His prophets no harm according to God's Word.

I will wait until the perfect timing of God to be promoted by Him.

I will give respect to the anointed of God.

I will not go against the wishes of God for my own gain.

September 16th

ISAIAH 26:3 (NLT), "YOU will keep in perfect peace all who trust in you, all whose thoughts are fixed on you!

Perfect in the Merriam Webster Dictionary is defined as having no mistakes, or flaws, or accurate.[202] The Greek word for Perfect is "Teleios," which means complete in all parts, full grown, full age, or especially of the completeness of Christian character.[203]

God will keep us in perfect peace because our minds and our thoughts will be placed in You and not in us. We will have the peace that passeth all understanding that will guard our hearts and minds through Christ Jesus. I will walk in perfect peace with my mind stayed on thee. Lord, my thoughts will only be focused on You and not on my problems or my issues. Lord, I release everything to You for You to take care of everything that concerns me.

202. Perfect Merriam-Webster.com https://www.Merriam-Webster.com Accessed October 2021
203. "Teleios" Greek for Perfect https://www.biblehub.com Accessed October 2021

PRAYERS

Father God, in the name of Jesus, we come before You today to ask that You will keep me in perfect peace with my mind stayed on You. Lord, help me to keep my mind stayed on You right now in Jesus' name. Lord, we ask that You give us Your perfect peace so we can continue to move forward and do what You are telling us to do. Lord, we lay all of our cares to You because You care for us. Lord, we are asking that You move mightily on our behalf right now in Jesus' name. I decree and declare that peace will be my portion right now in Jesus' name. I know that peace is a gift, and I will cherish it and not let anything, or no one destroy my peace. I cast down every negative thought and surrender it to You right now in Jesus' name. I will keep my mind on Christ. I put on the helmet of salvation, and I have a sound mind and the mind of Christ in Jesus' name. Amen.

September 17th

1 JOHN 4:16 (NLT), "WE know how much God loves us, and we have put our trust in his love. God is love, and all who live in love live in God, and God lives in them."

Love in the Merriam Webster Dictionary is defined as the fatherly concern of God for humankind.[204] The Greek word for love is "Agape," which means love, goodwill, esteem, and benevolence.[205]

Matthew Henry's Concise Commentary states true love for God assures believers of God's love for them. Love teaches us to suffer for Him and with Him. Therefore we may trust that we shall also be glorified with Him. Obedience and good works are done from the principle of love.[206]

God loves every one of us so much that He sent His only Son to die for us. God wants us to trust in His love and He wants the best for each of us. We must surrender ourselves to Him. God

---

204. Love Merriam-Webster.com https://www.Merriam-Webster.com October 2021
205. "Agape" Greek word for Love https://www.biblehub.com Accessed October 2021
206.. Matthew Henry's Concise Commentary https://www.biblehub.com Accessed October 2021

has a future and a hope for each of us. We can't say we love God and hate our brother or sisters. God's perfect love cast out fear. God loves to set the captives free and those that He set free are free indeed. We can't say that we love God and be nasty to people. God's love will renew every one of our hearts if we allow Him to do so.

DECLARATIONS

I decree and declare that the love of God is stronger than ever before in Jesus' name.

Lord, I will put my complete trust in You and Your Word in Jesus' name.

I decree and declare that God is love and He is peace.

I decree and declare that perfect love casts out fear in Jesus' name.

Lord, Your perfect love will cast all the captives free in Jesus' name.

I decree and declare that God's love is everlasting and never runs dry in Jesus' name.

September 18th

Philippian's 4:8 (NLT), "And now, dear brothers and sisters, one final thing. Fix thoughts on what is true, and honorable, and right, and pure, and lovely, and admirable. Think about things that are excellent and worthy of praise."

Excellent in the Merriam Webster Dictionary is defined as very good of its kind and eminently good.[207] The Greek Word for Excellent is "Arete," which means goodness, a gracious act, virtue, or uprightness.[208]

We are encouraged to think only on the good things because there is power in our thoughts. Your thoughts can lead to a change in your direction and actions. Your thoughts can determine where you go in life. So, redirect your thoughts from negative things and replace them with positive things. You must even speak positive things over yourself and not negative things because what is in you will eventually come out of your

---

207. Excellent Merriam-Webster.com https://www.Merriam-Webster.com Accessed October 2021
208. "Arete" Greek word for Excellent https://www.biblehub.com Accessed October 2021

mouth or thoughts. We have to be careful not to think about things to hinder or hurt us.

PRAYER

Father God, in the name of Jesus, we come before You today to ask that You help us to think only on things that are pure and nothing that is evil. I put on the mind of Christ today so I can only think like Jesus thinks in Jesus' name. I have a sound mind and I will not keep thinking about negative things, but only on the pleasant ones. I will always rise in faith and believe God at His word and only think about things to increase my faith in Jesus' name. Lord, help me to get rid of thoughts that is sent to distract me from my destiny in Jesus' name. I will continue to meditate on the Word of God daily and hide Your Word in my heart so I will not sin against thee.

September 19th

❧

ROVERBS 1:7 (NLT), "*FEAR of the LORD is the foundation of true knowledge, but fools despise wisdom and discipline.*"

Fear in the Merriam Webster Dictionary is defined as an unpleasant emotion caused by being aware of danger, or a feeling of being afraid.[209] The Greek word for Fear is "Phobos," which means panic, flight, fear, the object or cause of fear, reverence, or respect.[210]

Matthew Henry's Concise Commentary states that fools have no true wisdom, follow their own devices, without regard to reason, or reverence for God.[211] Many people think they know everything and they do not know anything. They refuse to let you tell them anything, and they do not listen to sound doctrine or take your advice.

---

209. Fear Merriam-Webster. https://www.Merriam-Webster.com Accessed October 2021
210. "Phobos" Greek word for Fear https://www.biblehub.com Accessed October 2021
211. Matthew Henry's Concise Commentary https://www.biblehub.com Accessed October 2021

DECLARATIONS

I decree and declare that I am walking in the fear of the Lord.

Fools refuse to take the wisdom that is given to them.

Nobody knows everything. We all could learn something new.

We are to reverence God for who He is: our Creator, Lord, and Savior.

Those that despise wisdom and discipline are prone to keep repeating mistakes.

Be humble and let God lead you instead of leaning on your own understanding.

September 20th

2 CORINTHIANS 4:16 (NLT), "THAT is why we never give up, though our bodies are dying, our spirits are being renewed day by day."

Renewed in the Merriam Webster Dictionary is defined as to make new spiritually or regenerate.[212] The Greek Word for Renewed is "Anakainoo," which means renew or make new again.[213]

The Holy Spirit will continue to transform us into Christ-like people and make us new all over again from the inside out. He will change our hearts and minds. God will help build up our faith, patience, and endurance as He begins to take us through the process of maturity. Our bodies are the outer shell and as the years go by, our bodies are deteriorate and get older. We once were young, but our natural bodies are wasting away. We will continue to renew our spirit with the Word of God. We must read and study the Word of God to get it into our hearts

212. Renewed Merriam-Webster.com https://www.Merriam-Webster.com Accessed October 2021
213. "Anakainoo" Greek word for Renewed https://www.biblehub.com Accessed October 2021

and minds. We are steadily growing from level to level as we get closer to God in an intimate relationship with Him.

PRAYER

Father God, in the name of Jesus, we thank You for renewing our spirits daily. Your Word declares that our bodies are wasting away daily. Lord, we know that with every year we are getting older in Jesus' name. I decree and declare that my body will remain youthful, and I will never look my exact age. Lord, take back the years that the locust, cankerworm, palmerworm, and caterpillar have taken from me. God, You will give it all back to us. Lord, rejuvenate me from the top of my head to the soles of my feet right now in Jesus' name. I will not look like what I have been through, regardless of the trouble and trials that I have endured. Lord, I will not even smell like smoke from the fires that I have experienced. You were with me in the fire and in the troubles and trials and I have lived to tell the story in Jesus' name. Amen.

September 21st

ZEPHANIAH 3:17 (NLT), "*FOR the LORD your God is living among you. He is a mighty savior. He will take delight in you with gladness. With his love, he will calm all your fears. He will rejoice over you with joyful songs.*"

Savior in the Merriam Webster Dictionary is defined as one that saves from danger or destruction, or one who brings salvation.[214] The Greek word for Savior is "Soter," which means a savior, deliverer, or preserver.[215] Matthew Henry's Concise Commentary talks about Jesus saving His people from their sins. The Lord will save the weakest believer and cause true Christians to be honored where they have been treated with contempt.[216]

God will show up and show out for His people. It does not matter what you are going through. God can take care of your problems and situations. All we have to do is rest in His love

214. Savior Merrriam-Webster.com https://www.Merriam-Webster.com Accessed October 2021
215. "Soter" Greek word for Savior https://www.biblehub.com October 2021
216. Matthew Henry's Concise Commentary https://www.biblehub.com Accessed October 2021

and He will take care of the rest. God wants us to rest in Him and trust Him to work everything out for our good. If you need your fears calmed, Jesus is the only One that will be able to do it effectively. Many of us have mistakenly reached out to people when we should have asked God for help. Jesus is the only present help in the time of trouble. Nobody can do for you what God can do.

DECLARATIONS

I will trust God no matter what I am going through in Jesus' name.

Jesus is the only One that I can truly depend on to work everything out for my good.

When I get through running to people and they let me down, I will run to the Rock that is higher than I.

I know that God will come through for me in a mighty way.

Jesus has the answer to all of my problems.

I decree and declare that God will show up and show out on my behalf.

September 22nd

❧

MATTHEW 6:6-7 (AMP), "*⁶ But when you pray, go into your most private room, close the door, and pray to your Father who is in secret, and your Father who sees (what is done) in secret will reward you. ⁷· "And when you pray, do not use meaningless repetition as the Gentiles do, for they think they will be heard because of their many words."*

Secret in the Merriam Webster Dictionary is defined as kept hidden from others or known only to a few people.[217] The Greek word for Secret is "Kruptos," which means hidden or secret.[218]

These scriptures tell us to pray. Prayer is the key to everything that you may want to do in life and ministry. Prayer is one-on-one with God. When we pray things unto God, He will reward us openly for what we have prayed. Those who see the manifestation of your prayer will know that God is the One that did it. God wants an intimate relationship with all of His

217. Secret Merriam-Webster.com https://www.Merriam-Webster.com Accessed January 2022
218. "Kruptos" Greek word for Secret https://www.biblehub.com Accessed January 2022

children. He loves it when we talk to Him and ask His opinion about everything we are doing or want to do in our lives and ministries. God wants to see every one of us successful and walking into our destinies. We must pray before we act on a thing to make sure we are in the right timing of God for our lives. Don't be in public praying like the Sadducees and Pharisees. They were praying in the streets, but there was no power behind what they were praying because they were not in a relationship with God. They were walking around with religious spirits, denying the power thereof. When the righteous pray, they produce wonderful results and answers to their prayers because they have a relationship with Christ.

PRAYER

Father God, in the name of Jesus, we come before you today to ask that You would lead and guide me in all truth. Lord, teach me how to pray, not as the Pharisees, but powerful prayers that will bring heaven down to earth in Jesus' name. Lord, teach me how to bind and loose in the spiritual realm so it can manifest in the natural realm in Jesus' name. Lord, if anything is blocking me from having a closer relationship with You, remove it. If there is something that I need to do, reveal it so I can take care of it and go forward in You in Jesus' name. Lord, teach me to trust You after I have prayed the prayer of faith over my life and body in Jesus' name. Amen.

September 23rd

Ecclesiastes 12:13 (AMP), "When all has been heard, the end of the matter is; fear God (worship Him with awe-filled reverence, knowing that He is almighty God) and keep His commandments, for this applies to every person."

Commandments in the Merriam Webster Dictionary is defined as something that is commanded, especially one of the Biblical Ten Commandments.[219] The Greek word for Commandments is "Entole," which means injunction, order, command, or law.[220]

The Amplified Bible Study Bible states that Jesus summed up the commandments by saying, "Love the Lord your God and love your neighbor as yourself." We are whole and complete only when we fear God and obey His commandments. What profit is there in living? If we follow what this book has said, we will have a relationship with God and find life in Him.[221]

219. Commandments Merriam-Webster.com https://www.Merriam-Webster.com Accessed January 2022
220. "Entole" Greek word for Commandments https://www.biblehub.com Accessed January 2022
221. The Amplified Study Bible Zondervan 2017 Accessed January 2022

It is very profitable when we obey the commandments of God because all will be well with us when we do follow God's instructions. We are to walk in love even when people mistreat us and say all manner of evil against us. We are to pray for God to bless them and keep them in Jesus' name.

DECLARATIONS

I decree and declare that I will love God with all of my heart, mind, and soul in Jesus' name.

I decree and declare that I will love my neighbor regardless of how they treat me.

I will fear God and obey His Word every day of my life.

If I cannot love my brother like God said to love them, I will ask God for more grace to do so.

Lord, teach me how to love people the way that You love them in Jesus' name.

Lord, teach Your people to walk in love just like You did when You were on this earth.

September 24th

JAMES 1:22 (AMP), *"BUT prove yourselves doers of the word (actively and continually obeying God precepts), and not merely listeners (who hear the Word but fail to internalize its meaning), deluding yourselves (by unsound reasoning contrary to the truth)."*

Doers in the Merriam Websters Dictionary is defined as one that takes an active part or moving, applying it to your life.[222] The Greek word for Doers is "Poietes," which means a doer, a maker, carrying it out, or performer.[223]

We have to be doers of the Word so our lives will begin to line up with the Word of God. When we read and study the Word of God and begin to apply it, then God does a transformation in our lives and changes us from the old man into the new man. The new man has the Holy Spirit living on the inside of us and allows the Holy Spirit to lead and guide us in all truth. The new man loves the Word of God because it comes from

222. Doers Merriam-Webster.com https://www.Merriam-Webster.com Accessed January 2022
223. "Poietes" Greek word for Doers https://www.biblehub.com Accessed January 2022

God. We will not sit up in church every Sunday and hear the Word of God without it causing a transformation in our lives. We will allow God to change whatever He needs to in us so we can make the 180-degree transformation from the old man into the new man. We will continue to grow into full spiritual maturity and not stay as babes who are on milk. We will mature into being able to accept meat as a staple in our diets.

PRAYER

Father God, in the name of Jesus, we come before You today to ask You to help us retain Your Word so that when we read and study it and when the opportunity comes, the Holy Spirit can bring it to our remembrance. Lord, we ask that You touch our minds and memory, so we can remember what we are studying in Jesus' name. Lord, we desire to be doers of the Word of God instead of just letting the Word go into one ear and out the other one in Jesus's name. Lord, gives us clarity on the right Bible that we need to purchase to understand Your Word better in Jesus' name. Lord, give us a fresh filling of Your Holy Ghost Power so we can keep Your Word in our hearts in Jesus' name. Lord, we lay every sin aside that may be blocking us from having a clear understanding of Your Word in Jesus' name. Lord, we desire to be closer to You this year than ever before in Jesus' name. Amen.

September 25th

UKE 6:35 (AMP), "BUT love (that is, unselfishly seek the best or higher good for) your enemies, and do good, and lend, expecting nothing in return; for your reward will be great (rich, abundant), and you will be sons of the Most High; because He Himself is kind and gracious and good to the ungrateful and the wicked."

Ungrateful in the Merriam Webster Dictionary is defined as showing no gratitude or making a poor return.[224] The Greek word for Ungrateful is "acharistos," which means ungracious, unpleasing, unthankful, or ungraceful.[225]

This verse talks about loving people unconditionally. Real love is not selfish. A selfish person only thinks about themselves and how they feel. They have no regard for anyone else, nor is their love real. Their love is superficial, and it will not last long. The only way a person can be taught to love is by having a loving relationship with God. If that person does not

224. Ungrateful Merriam-Webster.com https://www.Merriam-Webster.com Accessed January 2022
225. "Acharistos" Greek word for Ungrateful https://www.biblehub.com Accessed January 2022

know God, then their relationships will not last long because it is always "I" with them and they never consider someone else's feelings over their own. You will know this type of person because they will always have to be the center of attention. If, for one moment, the attention is not on them, then they will regress back up into their shell and cut off communication with other people. Luke 6:35 provides an example of someone who knows how to love without conditions. Their love will not falter when things do not go their way because they have been given the grace of God to love people genuinely and not falsely. When you love someone genuinely regardless of how you are treated, that shows you have the love of God in your heart and now you can be called a child of the Most High God.

DECLARATIONS

I decree and declare that I will love my enemies and those who despitefully misuse me.

Lord, help me to always be a lender and not a borrower. Your Word declares that I will lend to many nations.

God, help me to be kind even to the ungrateful and wicked who don't appreciate anything that you do for them.

Lord, help us to bless those who have hurt us and show your agape love toward t hem.

Lord, I will love people genuinely so that I can seek the higher good in Jesus' name.

Lord, help me to die to myself, stop putting me first, and put other people's feelings above my own in Jesus' name.

September 26th

MARK 11:24 (AMP), "FOR this reason I am telling you, whatever things you ask for in prayer (in accordance with God's will), believe (with confident trust) that you have received them, and they will be given to you."

Believe in the Merriam Webster Dictionary is defined as accepting or regarding something as true, or accepting the truth of what is said.[226] The Greek word for Believe is "Pisteuo," which means believe, belief, believers, to be persuaded, place confidence and trust in.[227]

This scripture states that we have to believe what we are praying and pray according to God's will for our lives. What we have been praying for will soon manifest in our lives. We are to have strong faith that we will have what we are decreeing and declaring before we even get them in the natural realm. We have to trust that God will answer our prayers when we are

226. Believe Merriam-Webster.com https://www.Merriam-Webster.com Accessed January 2022
227. "Pisteuo" Greek word for Believe https://www.blueletterbible.com Accessed January 2022

praying and asking for things to happen in our lives in Jesus' name. We can totally put all of our trust in God because He always has our best interest at heart. So, we can trust Him to tell our innermost secrets too. He will help us get through some trying times in our lives when we lean and fully trust Him.

PRAYER

Father God, in the name of Jesus, I come before You today because Your Word declares that the prayers of the righteous availeth much and produces wonderful results in Jesus' name. Lord, I believe but help my unbelief so I can take You at Your Word when You tell me something to do in Jesus' name. Lord, help me to be a doer of the Word instead of just a hearer in Jesus' name. Lord, help me to put everything that You are teaching me into practice instead of just sitting on it in Jesus' name. Lord, forgive me all the time when I did not believe You when you told me that You were going to supply my every need such as Your riches in glory by Christ Jesus. Lord, help me to believe that my requests are heard by You when I pray them on the first day in Jesus' name. Lord, help me not to get weary in well doing in Jesus' name. Lord, I thank You for always being available when I need You in Jesus' name. Amen.

September 27th

PHILIPPIANS 3:14 (AMP), "*I press toward the goal to win the (heavenly) prize of the upward call of God in Christ Jesus.*"

Goal in the Merriam Webster Dictionary is defined as something that you are trying to do or achieve.[228] The Greek word for Goal is "Telos," which means to full potential or inherent purpose or objective of a person or thing.[229]

Paul says, "that he pressed toward the mark." Whenever there is a challenge facing you, you must learn how to press on despite the opposition. Paul uses the analogy of a race to show that we are constantly striving toward our goal. We cannot constantly run looking behind us because we cannot see the constant dangers that may lay ahead of us. No matter how the long the race that we have to run, we will not give up or look back any longer, but we will keep on striving because our goal is to access the finish line.[230]

228. Goal Merriam-Webster.com https://www.Merrriam-Webster.com Accessed January 2022
229. "Telos" Greek word for Goal https://www.wikipedia.org Accessed January 2022
230. https://www.romesentinel.com article Accessed January 2022

We are in a race for our lives and the choices we make, whether they are good or bad, will matter in the beginning, in the middle and at the end of our race. So, we have to make the right choices because it will affect our lives and the lives of others. Our goal in life should be to please God and put Him first above anyone else. If we can keep focus, we can have heaven here on earth.

DECLARATIONS

I will press toward the mark of the high calling in Christ Jesus.

I am called to be a mouthpiece of God and no matter what I go through, I will not give up.

I will press even when I do not want to because I know it is not even about me.

I know that there is a blessing in the pressing in Jesus' name.

I will press to see the Savior's face and hear Him say, "Well done thy good and faithful servant."

I am one of them from the chosen generation and a royal priest hood.

I will continue to move forward and I will not give up until I get to heaven.

September 28th

P SALM 68:19 (AMP), "BLESSED be the Lord, who bears our burdens day by day, The God who is our salvation! Selah."

Bears in the Merriam Webster Dictionary is defined as carrying the weight, support, or sustain.[231] The Greek word for bears is "Arkouda," which means bear a burden or be apt to.[232]

This scripture talks about God bearing our burdens by taking the weight and the load of our problems and storms off our shoulders and placing them on His shoulders to work them out in our favor. The Bible says that we are to cast our burdens on the Lord because He cares for us. God is our God of salvation and only through the perfect work of Jesus are we even able to receive eternal life by accepting the finished works of Jesus. When we reject Jesus, we are rejecting eternal life and peace here on this earth. It is only through Jesus we are even allowed to walk in peace.

---

231. Bears Merriam-Webster.com https://www.Merriam-Webster.com Accessed January 2022
232. "Arkouda" Greek word Bears https://www.biblehub.com Accessed January 2022

PRAYER

Father God, in the name of Jesus, we come to You today to thank You for bearing these heavy burdens that seem like it is crushing the life out of me in Jesus' name. Lord, give me the strength to overcome all the trials I am going through in Jesus' name. Lord, You daily load us with benefits and take care of our spiritual and natural needs in Jesus' name. Lord, thank You for sending Your Son to die on the cross for my sins so that I could one day receive Jesus in my heart and totally surrender my life unto Him. Lord, thank You for teaching me how to bear my burdens, but I thank You that I don't have to do it alone. You are with me to lead and guide me so I can get delivered in the areas that I need it in. Lord, thank You for Your faithfulness and truth in Jesus' name. Amen.

September 29th

*P*SALM 34:18 (AMP), "THE eyes of the LORD are toward the righteous (those with moral courage and spiritual integrity) And His ears are open to their cry."

Courage in the Merriam Webster Dictionary is defined as the ability to do something that you know is difficult or dangerous.[233] The Greek word for Courage is "Tharseo," which means to be of good courage and good cheer.[234]

The eyes of the Lord are turned toward the righteous, those that are in right standing with Him in their spiritual life. Those that have turned everything over to Him and have sold out totally. So, when we cry out for His help, He does not hesitate to send someone to help us. He often sends His angels to fight our battles, so we have nothing to be worried about. The righteous are taken under the special protection of the Lord. Many are the afflictions of the righteous, but the Lord will deliver them

233. Courage Merriam-Webster.com https://www.Merriam-Webster.com Accessed January 2022
234. "Tharseo" Greek word foe Courage Https://www.biblehub.com Accessed January 2022

out of them all. Our love for God will keep us from sinning because we want to please Him in everything that we do.

DECLARATIONS

I decree and declare that God will never leave or forsake us, but He will be with us until the end of this age.

I will get into His Presence daily to be refilled back up with His joy and peace in Jesus' name.

Lord, send a refreshing of Your consuming fire to my soul and spirit right now in Jesus' name.

Lord, I will cry out to You, and You will come to my rescue in Jesus' name.

Lord, Your Word declares that You are the healer of the brokenhearted, so Lord heal mine right now in Jesus' name.

Lord, I will walk in moral courage and will not be timid any longer in Jesus' name.

September 30th

PSALM 139:23-24 (AMP) "²³ *Search me (thoroughly), O God, and know my heart; and test me and know my anxious thoughts;* ²⁴· *"And see if there is any wicked or hurtful way in me and lead me in the everlasting way."*

Search in the Merriam Webster Dictionary is defined to investigate, look over carefully or thoroughly to find, or discover something.[235] The Greek word for Search is "Heurisko," which means to find, discover, learn, or searching.[236]

The Amplified Study Bible says that only when we are aware of our sins we can repent of them and be healed.[237] When God reveals something to you that needs changing or working on, do not walk in denial, saying that it is not you. Remember, God knows our hearts and thoughts, so we cannot slip anything past Him no matter how hard we try. I constantly ask God, "If there is anything in me that needs removing, reveal it to me." If it is

235. Search Merriam-Webster.com https://www.Merriam-Webster.com Accessed January 2022
236. "Heurisko" Greek word for Search https://www.biblehub.com Accessed January 2022
237. Amplified Study Bible Zondervan 2017 Accessed January 2022

something that I can do, I will adjust. If it is something that only He can do, I permit Him to do what He wants to in me. I give Him permission to remove anything in me that needs to go, so I can get healed in that area of my life. To make it to heaven, we cannot have unforgiveness, bitterness, or malice in our hearts against anyone and think we will have a close relationship with God. The consuming fire of God will burn anything in us out so we can be purified in our hearts and minds. Do not fight God when He wants to change areas in your life because He knows what you need better than you.

PRAYER

Father God, in the name of Jesus, I come to You today to ask that You create a clean heart within me and renew a right spirit in me in Jesus' name. Lord, I ask that You uproot anything like unforgiveness, bitterness, malice, or anger in my heart so I can be set free from what is hurting my relationship with You in Jesus' name. Lord, I will walk in forgiveness and get rid of anything that will hinder my walk with You in Jesus' name. Lord, you have my permission and cooperation to do whatever You want to in my life in Jesus' name. Lord, I forgive those who have intentionally hurt me and said all manner of evil against me in Jesus' name. Lord, heal my heart so I can walk in true forgiveness toward those who have intentionally hurt me in Jesus' name. Lord, teach me to give them the same type of grace that You have given me in Jesus' name. Lord, I thank You for a renewed spirit and a renewed mind in Jesus' name. Amen.

October 1st

PROVERBS 13:20 (AMP), "HE who walks (as a companion) with wise men will be wise, But the companions of fools of (conceited, dull-witted) fools (are fools themselves and) will experience harm."

Fool in the Merriam Webster Dictionary is defined as a person lacking in judgment or prudence.[238] The Greek word for Fool is "Moros," which means dull, stupid, or foolish.[239]

The scripture says that if you walk with wise men, you will remain wise. However, if you are wise and walk with fools, their foolishness will rub off on you and you will start doing foolish things. Wise people regulate their conduct and do not participate in everything that could harm their reputation. The wise have gotten their wisdom from God and His Word. They are not walking in worldly wisdom. A wise person has self-control and does not let their bodies dictate what they will do. They allow their spirits to lead them by partnering with God in all

238. Fools Merriam-Webster.com https://www.Merriam-Webster.com Accessed January 2022
239. "Moros" Greek word for Fool https://www.Merriam-Webster.com Accessed January 2022

that they do. A foolish person falls into mischief and does many things without thinking of the consequences to their actions. A fool says in his heart that there is no God. He is lost and wants other lost people to listen to him.

DECLARATIONS

I decree and declare that I will walk with the wise and not the foolish.

Lord, Your Word declares that if anyone needs wisdom, they are to ask You, and You will get it to them generously.

Lord, I choose to walk with people who are sold out for God just like I am.

I renounce all kinds of worldly wisdom in Jesus' name.

Lord, I will pray and think about a matter before acting on it.

Lord, remove the foolish people from around me and re-place them with people who have godly wisdom.

October 2nd

*P*SALM 119:165 (AMP), "THOSE who love Your law have great peace; Nothing makes them stumble."

Stumble in the Merriam Webster Dictionary is defined as to fall into sin or waywardness, or to make an error.[240] The Greek word for Stumble is "Ptaio," which means to cause to stumble, fall, sin, or transgress.[241]

Those who love God's Word will have great peace and will not allow anything to make them fall back into sin. They will not be offended by man because they do not want to break the law of God. They would rather endure the wrath of man than disappoint God in any way. Those that love the world are vexed by the things of the world and are walking in confusion and anxiety. Those that love God's Word are walking in perfect peace. They have put all their trust in God alone to do things for them. A person that is truly walking in the peace of God

---

240. Stumble Merriam-Webster.com Https://www.Merriam-Webster.com Accessed January 2022
241. "Ptaio" Greek Word for Stumble https://www.biblehub.com Accessed January 2022

will not take offense at their brethren because they love God's Word more than taking the bait of the enemy.

PRAYERS

Father God, in the name of Jesus, I come before You today to say that I love Your Word. I will continue to read and study the Word of God to get it into my heart so that I will not sin against thee. Lord, help me not to take the bait of the enemy and not walk in offense with my brothers and sisters in Jesus' name. Lord, help me to be able to extend each of them Your amazing grace in Jesus' name. Lord, I love You and Your Word, so I will not sin against thee and I will continue to walk in Your Word, love, and truth in Jesus' name. Amen.

October 3rd

*J*OHN 10:10 (AMP), "THE thief comes only in order to steal, kill, and destroy. I came that they may have and enjoy life, and have it in abundance (to the full, till it overflows)."

Overflow in the Merriam Webster Dictionary is defined as to flow over the brim of, to fill a space to capacity and spread beyond its limits.[242] The Greek word for Overflow is "Xecheilisma," which means outpouring, spill over, boil over, or bubble over.[243]

The enemy came to destroy God's people. He came to bring us hardship so that we would give up on God and not have the faith that God requires us to believe Him for what we need in our lives. His objective is to destroy our faith so we can turn our backs on God. Jesus came so that we could have abundant life, but the only way to have it is to give our lives to Him. We have to turn over our agenda and pick up God's plan concern-

242. Overflow Merriam-Webster.com https://www.Merriam-Webster.com Accessed January 2022
243. "Xecheilisma" Greek word for Overflow https://www.wordhippo.com Accessed January 2022

ing what He wants to do. If we stay with Jesus and obey Him, we will walk in abundance. We will never have to worry about living in lack again if we give our tithes and offerings to God. When we give Him that 10% that belongs to Him anyway, He will multiply everything that He gives back to us. It will come back to us press down, shaken together, running over, and shall men give unto our bosom. Once we release our seed, it never leaves our lives. It is just like the energizer bunny. It keeps going, going, going, and going by always bringing back a harvest.

DECLARATIONS

I decree and declare that God will give seed to the Sower.

I decree and declare that I am a Sower into the kingdom of God.

Jesus came so that we would have life and life more abundantly in Jesus' name.

Jesus is my source that keeps on giving.

The devil came to kill, steal, and destroy, but Jesus gives us life.

I will continue to give my tithes and offerings to be blessed in every area of my life.

I decree and declare that enemy is no match for God!

October 4th

*D*EUTERONOMY 28:1 (AMP), "NOW IT shall
be, if you diligently listen and obey the voice of the
LORD your God, being careful to do all of His commandments which I am commanding you today, the LORD your
God will set you high above all nations of the earth."

Listen in the Merriam Webster Dictionary is defined as to
pay attention to someone or something in order to hear what
is being said, sung, played, etc.[244] The Greek word for Listen is "Akouo," which means hear, listen, or comprehend by
hearing.[245]

This scripture talks about obeying the voice of the Lord when
He is talking to you audibly or in His Word. We are to obey
Him and if we do that then we will receive the blessings that are
in Deuteronomy. *Isaiah 1:19-20 (AMP)* *"19 If you are willing and
obedient, You shall eat the good of the land."* *20. "But if you refuse
and rebel, You shall be devoured by the sword."* When God tells

---

244. Listen Merriam-Webster.com Https://www.Merriam-Webster.com Accessed
January 2022
245. "Akouo" Greek Word for Listen https://www.biblehub.com Accessed January
2022

us to do something, we must obey Him instead of finding excuses as to why we can't do it. We may often be praying about a certain thing and nothing is happening in that area because we haven't moved and done what God said to do. He is waiting on our total obedience, not delayed disobedience or partial obedience. Partial obedience is still walking in disobedience.

PRAYER

Father God, in the name of Jesus, forgive me for all the times that I was disobedient to You. Lord, show it to me again so that I can complete the task this time without hesitation in Jesus' name. Lord, I will obey You, so that I can get back into alignment with Your will for my life in Jesus' name. Lord, I will obey and do what You tell me to do without questioning You in Jesus' name. Lord, I thank You for forgiving and reinstating me in Jesus' name. Amen.

October 5th

*D*EUTERONOMY 28: 4-5 (AMP), *"*4 *The off-spring of your body and the produce of your ground and the offspring of your animals, the offspring of your herd and the young of your flocks will be blessed."* 5. *"Your basket and your kneading bowl will be blessed."*

Offspring in the Merriam Webster Dictionary is defined as the immediate descendant of a person or animal, and individual born of a parent.[246] The Greek word for Offspring is "Genos," which means family, offspring, nation, or kind.[247]

If we would obey the voice of the Lord God, these blessings will not just be for us, but it will trickle down to our children, grandchildren, and to any animals that we may have. God is telling them that not only am I going to bless you, but I will bless your seed too. If we walked in disobedience, we wouldn't have anything for ourselves, our children, or grandchildren. It is easy to obey and do what God is requiring for us to do instead

246. Offspring Merriam-Webster.com https://www.Merriam-Webster.com Accessed January 2022
247 . "Genos" Greek word for Offspring https://www.biblehub.com Accessed January 2022

of leaning on our natural (carnal) mind. The carnal mind goes against God's instructions. God is going to bless everything that we put our hand to do.

DECLARATIONS

I decree and declare that I will be obedient to God so that my family and me can be blessed.

I decree and declare that the offspring of my body will be blessed because of my obedience.

I decree and declare that everything that I put my hand to do will be blessed and prosperous.

I decree and declare that my basket and kneading bowl will be blessed.

I decree and declare that I will always have food in my house and my refrigerator.

I decree and declare that the days of lack are over in my house and will never return.

October 6th

*D*EUTERONOMY 28:6-7 (AMP), *"⁶ You will be blessed when you come in and you will be blessed when you go out." ⁷· "The Lord will cause the enemies who rise up against you to be defeated before you; they will come out against you one way, but flee before you seven ways."*

Defeated in the Merriam Webster Dictionary is to win victory over or beat.[248] The Greek word for Defeated is "Nikise," which means defeated or conquered.[249]

These scriptures talk about hearing the voice of God and obeying Him. These are all the blessing that God has for His people if they obey Him and serve other gods. The same principles apply today. Will you listen and obey God? He will cause our enemies to flee right before our eyes and be defeated in our presence. Your enemies may get together to come against you, but they will not be successful in their attempts to harm or hinder you. If God is with you, He is better than the whole

248. Defeated Merriam-Webster.com https://www.Merriam-Webster.com Accessed January 2022

249. "Nikise" Greek word for Defeated https://www.wordhippo.com Accessed January 2022

world against you. Your enemies cannot curse who God says is blessed no matter how hard they try. God has His faithful servants covered under His blood and nothing by any means shall hurt them.

PRAYER

Father God, in the name of Jesus, I come before You today to let You know that it is a Yes down in my spirit. I will follow You and do what You are telling me to do. I have laid all excuses aside and I will not pick them back up again. I will move forward and do what You are telling me to do without hesitation. When I walk in disobedience, I am literally holding up my own blessing and the blessings of my offspring in Jesus' name. Lord, forgive me when I failed to do Your will for my life. Lord, I know now that I am never alone. You will be with me every step of the way. When my enemies rise up against me, You will hold up a standard against them and they will flee from my presence seven ways in Jesus' name. I do not have anything to fear because You are with me every step of the way in Jesus' name. Amen.

October 7th

EUTERONOMY 28:8 (AMP), "THE LORD will command the blessing upon you in your storehouses' and in all that you undertake, and He will bless you in the land which the LORD your God gives you."

Storehouses in the Merriam Webster Dictionary is defined as a building for storing goods, such as provisions, an abundant supply, or source.[250] The Greek word for Storehouses is "Apotheke," which means a place for putting away, a storehouse, or barn.[251]

God will bless you so good that you will have many storehouses that are full to capacity and not only that, but your finances will also be overflowing. Your finances will be so abundant that they will chase you down and overcome you. You will be living in the land of more than enough and the only thing that you have to do is obey God and do what He is telling you to do. Disobedient people will not receive the overflow. They will

250. Storehouses Merriam-Webster.com https://www.Merriam-Webster.com Accessed January 2022
251. "Apotheke" Greek word for storehouse https://www.biblehub.com Accessed January 2022

be living in the land of not enough or just enough. They will not make it to the land of more than enough because they are walking in disobedience. This is something that has to be done individually. Do you obey God or do you do what you want to do? Your future depends on you answering and doing the right thing. God will bless the land that He gives you to produce a bountiful harvest year after year.

DECLARATIONS

I decree and declare that I will obey God even if it means coming out of my comfort zone.

My storehouses will be overflowing with milk and honey in Jesus' name.

I will have more than enough. There will be seed to keep sowing and producing more harvests.

He will bless everything that I put my hand to do.

Everything that I touch or be a part of will be very successful and prosperous.

I decree and declare that I will sow more into the kingdom of God.

October 8th

*D*EUTERONOMY 28:9 (AMP) "THE Lord will establish you as a people holy (And set apart) to Himself, just as He was sworn to you, if you keep the commandments of the LORD your God and walk (that is, live your life each and every day) in His ways."

Establish in the Merriam Webster Dictionary is defined as growing or flourishing successfully.[252] The Greek word for Establish is "Sterizo," which means to make fast, establish, support, strengthen, or establish.[253]

God will establish His Body as a holy people. If we will be obedient and serve Him whole heartedly, He will take care of us because we are His people. We have to keep the Word of God and apply it to our lives to look like Jesus daily. We will live holy and righteous and will not practice sin because of Jesus's perfect sacrifice. He has redeem us from sin and it doesn't have any dominion over us because of what was done on the cross.

252. Establish Merriam-Webster.com https://www.Merriam-Webster.com Accessed January 2022
253. "Sterizo" Greek word for Establish https://www.biblehub.com Accessed January 2022

We are the righteousness of God in Christ Jesus, not of our own works. But through His perfect works, we can now be made righteous through His shed blood.

PRAYER

Father God, in the name of Jesus, we come before You today to acknowledge You as our Lord and Savior. Lord, we thank You for Your Word because Your Word is a lamp unto our feet. When we read, study, and apply the Word to our lives, we can then be called the righteousness of God. Lord, we thank You for giving us a choice to surrender our lives to You so that we can be adopted into the fold in Jesus' name. Lord, we thank You for being the Father that we didn't have in the natural realm. Thank You for making us feel wanted, loved and appreciated by a loving Father in Jesus' name. Lord, we will serve You with our whole hearts and surrender our lives to You in Jesus' name. Amen.

October 9th

*D*EUTERONOMY 28:11-12 (AMP) "11THE
LORD will give you great prosperity, in the offspring of your body and in the offspring of your
livestock and the produce of your ground, in the land which He
swore to your father to give you." 12. "The LORD will open for you
HIs good treasure house, the heavens, to give rain to your land in
its season and to bless all the work of your hand; and you will lend
to many nations, but you will not borrow."

Treasure in the Merriam Webster Dictionary is defined as
something valuable (such as money, jewels, gold, silver) that is
hidden or kept in a safe place.[254] The Greek word for Treasure
is "Thesauros," which means treasure or a store-house for precious things.[255]

God has a storehouse in heaven that is stocked up with treasures that He wants to give His obedient people. He wants to
rain down blessings upon His people, but they have to be in

254. Treasure Merriam-Webster.com https://www.Merriam-Webster.com Accessed
January 2022
255. "Thesaurus" Greek word for Treasure https://www.biblehub.com Accessed January 2022

right standing with Him and walking in alignment with His Word. He said that your offspring would be blessed because you are obedient to Him. If you own a farm and have different animals, they will be multiplied. Everything you own will be multiplied back to you good measure, press down, and running over. If you are farming, you will have a bumper crop after bumper crop. God will lavish the blessing of heaven down on His people. He said that God would open us His good treasure house full of things that we will need to help build up the kingdom of God. He will bless everything that you put your hand to do for your life and for the kingdom of God. People will see that you are blessed and it was God that did it. You will never have to borrow ever again. Money, finances, and everything will be so plentiful. It will never run out.

DECLARATIONS

I decree and declare that God will open up the windows of heaven and pour me out a blessing that I will not have room enough to receive.

I decree and declare that I will be living in the land of overflow in every area of my life in Jesus' name.

The Lord will open His good-treasure house to me.

I decree and declare that He will send rain to water the land so I can receive a bumper crop year after year.

I decree and declare that I will be a faithful tither and give as God blesses me to give.

I decree and declare that I will lend to many nations, but I will never borrow in Jesus' name.

October 10th

*D*EUTERONOMY 28:13-14 (AMP)" ¹³ *The LORD will make you the head(leader) and not the tail (follower); and you will be above only, and you will not be beneath, if you listen and pay attention to the commandments of the LORD your God, which I am commanding you today, to observe them carefully." ¹⁴ "Do not turn aside from any of the words which I am commanding you today, to the right or to the left, to follow and serve other gods."*

Head in the Merriam Webster Dictionary is defined as one in charge of a division or department in an office or institution.[256] The Greek word for Head is "Kephale," which means the head, a corner stone, ruler, or lord.[257]

God will make you the head. You will rise above your situation and stay above it if you listen and obey the voice of the Lord. We are to observe and do them. Apply them to our lives, so our lives will begin to line up with the Word of God. Do not

256. Head Merriam-Webster.com https://www.Merriam-Webster.com Accessed January 2022
257. "Kephale" Greek word for Head https://www.biblehub.com Accessed January 2022

turn to the left or the right. Continue to follow the Word of the Lord and everything will be well with you. Listen and pay attention to what the Word says. Hide the Word of God in your hearts so we will not sin against God. We will not put no other gods, people, places, and things before Him. Nothing or no one comes before God.

PRAYER

Father God, in the name of Jesus, we come before You today for making me the head and not the tail because I am obedient to Your commandments. I will be above only and not beneath. I will be a lender and not a borrower if I obey the commandments You have placed before me in Your Word in Jesus' name. I will not turn aside to any of the words that You are declaring over me today. I will live a life that is pleasing unto Your sight in Jesus' name. I will run this race with patience and surrender my whole life over to You in Jesus' name. Amen.

October 11th

*D*EUTERONOMY 28:15 *"BUT IT shall come about, if you do not listen to and obey the voice of the LORD you God being careful to do all which I am commanding you today, then all these curses will come upon you and overtake you."*

Curses in the Merriam Webster Dictionary is defined as a cause of trouble or bad luck.[258] The Greek word for Curse is "Katara," which means a curse, cursing, or a doomed one.[259]

The Amplified Study Bible states that the price of disobedience is always more than one can imagine in the beginning. It is not only the loss of peace or blessing, great as that might have been. In God's plan, the obedience is for the benefit of the follower of God, those watching and are influenced by this follower, and for the kingdom of God. If the follower disobeys, they may see how their actions affect themselves. They cannot know what other blessings are lost in the wider sphere of their

258. Curses Merriam-Webster.com https://www.Merriam-Webster.com Accessed January 2022
259. "Katara" Greek Word for Curse https://www.biblehub.com Accessed January 2022

own influence. It is a terrible thing to find oneself in the position of working against God. Disobedience brings suffering, which often spills over onto other people, even in future generations. The suffering is a wakeup call. It is meant to remind the disobedient that they are living against God and that they need to repent, turn to God, and ask for help. The problem is that often the disobedient have a skewed idea of who God is and what He desires, so they blame God and become more rebellious.[260]

DECLARATIONS

I decree and declare that I will obey the voice of the Lord.

I decree and declare that I will obey His commandments so that my life can be blessed.

I decree and declare that I will not work against God but work with God in Jesus' name.

I decree and declare that if I have been disobedient, I will repent and turn back to God.

I decree and declare that I will stay in right standing with God by walking in total obedience to Him.

260. The Amplified Study Bible by Zondervan @ 2017 Accessed January 2022

October 12th

MATTHEW 18:19 (AMP), "AGAIN I say to you, that if two believers on earth agree (that is, are of one mind, in harmony) about anything that they ask (within the will of God) it will be done for them by my Father in heaven."

Agree in the Merriam Webster Dictionary is defined as to achieve or be in harmony (as of opinion, feeling, or purpose).[261] The Greek word for Agree is "Sumphoneo," which means to call out with, to be in harmony, generally agree, or agree together.[262]

This scripture talks about if two people are praying and believing together and coming in agreement about what they are praying in the will of God for a matter and God will do what they are asking Him to do. There must be the power of agreement between the two believers. They both must have faith to believe that whatever they are praying for, God will answer them and touch their bodies or make things happen in their

261. Agree Merriam-Webster.com https://www.Merriam-Webster.com Accessed January 2022
262. "Sumphoneo" Greek word for Agree https://www.biblehub.com Accessed January 2022

lives. God hears His people's prayers when we pray to Him and He works things out for our good and their best interest.

PRAYER

Father God, in the name of Jesus, we come before you today. You said that if two agree on anything that You would move on their behalf according to Your will in Jesus' name. Lord, we are asking You to move and intervene on our behalf concerning_____ (the matter that we are bringing before You) in Jesus' name. Lord, we realize that we cannot make anything happen on our own in Jesus' name. We need You and Your spirit in us to do anything for the kingdom of God. Lord, there are two in agreement (me and the Holy Ghost), so Lord move mightily on my behalf in Jesus' name. Lord, I thank You for major breakthrough in my life today in Jesus' name. Amen.

October 13th

*M*ATTHEW 18:18 (AMP), "I assure you and most solemnly say to you, whatever you bind (forbid, declare to be improper and unlawful) on earth shall have (already) been bound in heaven, and whatever you loose (permit, declare lawful) on earth shall have (already) been loosed in heaven."

Bind in the Merriam Webster Dictionary is defined as to confine, restrain, or restrict as if with bonds.[263] The Greek word for Bind is "Deo" which means to tie to bind, fasten, declare to be prohibited and unlawful.[264] Loose in the Merriam Webster Dictionary is defined as having relative freedom of movement.[265] The Greek word for Loose is "Luo," which means to release, to dissolve, break, destroy, or untie.[266]

This is the key to the kingdom of how to pray effectively. God has given us the power to bind (tie up) and whatever we

263. Bind Merriam-Webster.com https://www.Merriam-Webster.com Accessed January 2022
264. "Deo" Greek word for Bind https://www.biblehub.com accessed January 2022
265. Loose Merriam-Webster.com https://www.Merriam-Webster.com Accessed January 2022
266. "Luo" Greek word for Loosed https://www.biblehub.com Accessed January 2022

bind on earth is bound in heaven. Whatsoever we loose in our prayers, God is loosing it from heaven to come to earth. So, this is a powerful tool in the hand of the believer. We do not have to keep getting beat up by the enemy and his minions because God has given us His Word to use against the attacks of the enemy. So, when we walk in the authority that God has given us, we can tear things up in the spiritual realm. The enemy cannot stand the Word of God. He will flee anytime that you use it. That is why he fights you so hard to get you to close your mouth and not speak. He knows that your mouth has the creative power to speak a thing and it shall be established. If you keep your mouth close and allow him to beat up on you, you will continue to feel defeated.

2 Timothy 1:7 (AMP) says, "God has not given us the spirit of fear but of power and love and a sound mind."

So, we will not fear what the enemy can do to us, but we will get our sword out, which is the Word of God. We must speak the Word over yourselves and situations, so we can come out victorious in Christ the way He wants us to be.

DECLARATIONS

I decree and declare that I will not have the spirit of fear but of power and love and a sound mind.

I decree and declare that I will not keep my mouth close but will say what God tells me.

I decree and declare that my mouth has creative power and I will speak what I want to see.

I decree and declare that I am victorious in Christ Jesus.

I decree and declare that whatever I bind on earth will be bound in heaven, and whatever I loose on earth will be loosed in heaven.

October 14th

2 CORINTHIANS 3:17 (AMP), "Now the Lord is the Spirit, and where the Spirit of the Lord is, there is liberty (emancipation form bondage, true freedom)."

Liberty in the Merriam Webster Dictionary is defined as the state or condition of people who are able to act and speak freely.[267] The Greek word for Liberty is "Eleutheria," which means freedom, liberty, or freedom from slavery.[268]

God is a Spirit and wherever His Spirit is, there is freedom there. We are free when we give our lives to Christ and allow Him to come and live on the inside of us. We must allow Him to take things out like wounds and trauma of our past. He cleans out our hard hearts and gives us a heart of flesh. He takes us through the process of perfecting us into the image of who we will be in our destiny as we continue to walk with Him. We are free from the law of sin and debt. You will never be truly free

267. Liberty. Merriam-Webster.com https://www.Merriam-Webster.com Accessed January 2022
268. "Eleutheria" Greek word for Liberty https://www.biblehub.com Accessed January 2022

until You have totally surrendered your life to a loving, compassionate, and graceful God.

PRAYER

Father God, in the name of Jesus, I come to You today to surrender my whole life to You. Lord, do what You want to do in me so I can be free in my mind, spirit, and body in Jesus' name. Lord, I give You permission to take anything that is in me out of me that is not like You. Lord, if there is anything in me that I need to do, reveal it to me so that it can be dealt with in Jesus' name. Lord, I desire to have a pure heart and clean hands when it pertains to anything or anyone that concerns You in Jesus' name. Lord, I know that the true freedom that I need is wrapped up in You Jesus. Lord, make me a clean and pure vessel to be used by You in this season in Jesus' name. Lord, I only want to do what Your will is for my life in Jesus' name. Lord, I will lay my will aside to pick up Yours in Jesus' name. Lord, refresh me with Your Spirit. Give me a fresh filling of Your Holy Ghost and fire in Jesus' name. Amen.

October 15th

MATTHEW 18:21-22 (AMP) " *²¹ Then Peter came to Him and asked, Lord, how many times will my brother sin against me and I forgive him and let it go? Up to seven times.*" *²². "Jesus answered him, "I say to you, not up to seven times, but seventy times seven.*"

Forgiveness in the Merriam Webster Dictionary is defined as to stop feeling anger toward (someone who has done something wrong) to stop blaming (someone).[269] The Greek word for Forgiveness is "Aphesis," which means dismissal, release, pardon, a sending away, a letting go, or complete forgiveness.[270]

These scriptures talk about how often we are to forgive people who have wronged us or done something to hurt us. Jesus told Peter that we are supposed to forgive not up to seven times but seventy times seven. We should be ready to forgive repeatedly. We have to consciously decide to forgive and let go of an old hurt again, seventy times seven. We are to forgive so

269. Forgiveness Merriam-Webster.com https://www.Merriam-Webster.com Accessed January 2022
270. "Aphesis" Greek word for Forgiveness https://www.biblehub.com Accessed January 2022

that our bodies can be healed because walking in unforgiveness caused arthritis, sinus infections, and certain kinds of cancers. We are actually forgiving because it will benefit us and keep our bodies healed. The enemy does not want us to forgive because He wants us bogged down in confusion, misery, and afflicted in our bodies. God wants us to forgive and the quicker we do it, the better and the happier we will be because we will walk in peace, joy, and in harmony with God.

PRAYER

Father God, in the name of Jesus, we come before You today to give all unforgiveness to You right now in Jesus' name. Lord, we release everyone who have hurt or injured us in Jesus' name. Lord, I forgive _____ _____so that my body can be healed and set free in Jesus' name. Lord, I surrender everything to You so that I can be filled back up in the areas that are lacking in my life in Jesus' name. Lord, we bind arthritis, sinus infections, and cancers. According to Your Word, You are bounding them in heaven in Jesus' name. Lord, we loose the healing virtue of Jesus to saturate our bodies and bring about healing and deliverance in our lives right now in Jesus' name. Lord, we thank You for total breakthrough and healing in our lives right now in Jesus' name. We will lay everything down in our lives that does not come into alignment with Your Will and Word for my life in Jesus' name. Amen.

October 16th

Proverbs 21:21 (AMP), "He who earnestly seeks righteousness and loyalty finds life, righteousness and honor."

Earnestly in the Merriam Webster Dictionary is defined as an earnest and serious manner, not lightly, orcasually.[271] The Greek word for Earnestly is "Epagonizomai," which means to contend with or earnestly for.[272]

The Amplified Bible Study Bible talks about how life, righteousness, and honor equal the abundant life. The pursuit of righteousness is its own reward, but added rewards are found in the fullness of life, achieving righteousness, and receiving honor. These are the gifts from the Lord.[273] We can only have abundant life in Christ Jesus. Jesus is the source of that abundant life. Abundant life is not just when we get to heaven, but God wants His children to have abundant life here on earth. Everything we may be seeking in our lives is wrapped up into

271. Earnestly Merriam-Webster.com https://www.Merriam-Webster,com Accessed January 2022
272. "Epagonizomai" Greek word for Earnestly https://www.biblehub.com Accessed January 2022
273. Amplified Study Bible by Zondervan Accessed January 2022

Jesus. Nothing that you can obtain outside of Jesus can hold a candle to what you can obtain with Jesus.

DECLARATIONS

I decree and declare that I will earnestly seek righteousness with Jesus.

I decree and declare that I will walk in loyalty with Jesus from this day forward in Jesus' name.

I decree and declare that there is life in righteousness because of the abundant life here on earth and the eternal life in heaven.

I decree and declare that righteousness and honor are rewards of the pursuit of righteousness.

I decree and declare that God declares that the abundant life is for all of His believers.

October 17th

❀

*P*SALM 73:26 (AMP), "MY flesh and my heart may fail, But God is my rock and strength of my heart and my portion forever."

Rock in the Merriam Webster Dictionary is foundation or support.[274] The Greek word for Rock is "Petra," which means a large mass or rock.[275]

Matthew Henry's Concise Commentary says that we must ascribe our safety in temptation, and our victory, not to our own wisdom, but to the gracious presence of God who is with us and Christ's intercession for us. All who commit themselves to God will be guided with the counsel of His Word and His Spirit.[276] God is our rock and strength. When we seek Him first, then all other things will be added unto us. It takes God to be first in our lives for us to be able to do anything that He asks us to do for Him.

---

274. "Rock" Merriam-Webster.com Https://www.Merriam-Webster.com Accessed January 2022
275. "Petra" Greek word for Rock https://www.biblehub.com Accessed January 2022
276. Matthew Henry's Concise Commentary https://www.biblehub.com Accessed January 2022

PRAYER

Father God, in the name of Jesus, I come before You today to say that You are my rock and the strength of my heart. Lord, You are my portion forever because I have chosen You as the Lord of my life in Jesus' name. Lord, You are more than able to help me with any situation that may arise in my life and home in Jesus' name. When my flesh and heart fail, You are right there to pick up the pieces in my life. With Your help, I can pick up and start all over again when I have messed up. Lord, thank You for your grace and mercy that has me covered when I lose my way in Jesus' name. Lord, I will draw all the strength from You that I will need for the tasks ahead of me.

October 18th

*J*OHN 16:33 (AMP), "I have told you these things, so that in Me you may have (perfect) peace. In the world you may have tribulation and distress and suffering, but be courageous (be confident, be undaunted, be filled with joy); I have overcome the world." (My conquest is accomplished, My victory abiding)."

Courageous in the Merriam Webster Dictionary is defined as very brave, having or showing courage.[277] The Greek word for Courageous is "Tharseo," which means to be of good courage or good cheer.[278]

God wants us to have perfect peace in Him regardless of what is going around us. We can walk in peace knowing that He is with us and will never leave us. He said, "In the world, you will have tribulation, distress and suffering, but be courageous because God has already overcome the world." Do not be afraid but be courageous because God has covered us no mat-

277. Courageous Merriam-Webster.com https://www.Merriam-Webster.com Accessed January 2022
278. "Tharseo" Greek word for Courageous https://www.biblehub.com Accessed January 2022

ter what we are going through. His Word declares that He will never leave or forsake us but will be with us until the end of the world. We are never alone. All we have to do is cry out to Him and He will come to see about us.

DECLARATIONS

I decree and declare that I will walk in perfect peace regardless of what is happening around me.

I decree and declare that through tribulation and distress, I will not give up but continue to move forward in God.

I decree and declare that in the midst of the suffering, I will continue to stay with the Lord.

I decree and declare that I will not fear but be courageous until the end in Jesus' name.

I decree and declare that the joy of the Lord is my strength and comfort in Jesus' name.

Lord, I can be courageous because You will never leave or forsake me.

October 19th

*J*EREMIAH 18:4 (AMP), "BUT the vessel that he was making from clay was spoiled by the potter's hand; so he made it over, reworking it and making it into another pot that seemed good to Him."

Potter in the Merriam Webster Dictionary is defined as one that makes pottery.[279] The Greek word for Potter is "Kerameus."[280] The Amplified Study Bible states that the potter's vessel was spoiled and thus unsuitable for its intended purpose. The potter remodeled the clay into an acceptable and unblemished work, symbolizing God's action in reforming Israel. The people had become marred, defiled, and had to be reformed into a vessel fit to be identified with the Lord.[281]

This is what God does to us. He places each of us on the potter's wheel to make and mold us all over again. When He finds a crack or chip in our exterior, He places us back on the potter's wheel to mold us. The molding gets out the things that

279. Potter Merriam-Webster.com https://www.Merriam-Webster.com Accessed January 2022
280. "Kerameus" Greek word for Potter https://www.biblehub.com Accessed January 2022
281. Amplified Study Bible Zondervan @2017 Accessed January 2022

have caused the chipping and the crack. It seals those areas in our hearts by leading us through healing and deliverance. He heals them with His love and compassion and makes us all over again so that we can be a whole vessel. He can use us for His glory in doing His will for our lives. God is the great potter that makes us look like we have never been marred. He will give us beauty for our ashes.

PRAYER

Father God, in the name of Jesus, we come before You today to offer our bodies as a living sacrifice, holy and acceptable unto You, which is our reasonable service. Lord, You are the Potter and we are the clay. Make and mold each of us into the men and women of God that You will have us to be in this world representing You. Lord, we know that when You put us on the wheel, it is to fix the chips and cracks that have gotten into our armor. Lord, we thank You that You are a concerned God that cares about Your children. Lord, make us into the masterpieces that You would have us to be to get the glory and honor out of our lives in Jesus' name. Lord, we know that when You are finished with us, the world will know that we are Your chosen vessels in Jesus' name. Amen.

October 20th

*N*UMBERS 22:12 (AMP), "GOD said to Balaam, "Do not go with them; you shall not curse the people (of Israel) for they are blessed."*

Blessed in the Merriam webster Dictionary is defined as having a sacred nature or connected with God.[282] The Greek word for Blessed is "Makarios," which means blessed, happy, or to be envied.[283]

The King Balak sent word for Balaam to curse the children of Israel God's people. God told Balaam in this verse that he could not curse who God is said to be blessed. Israel is God's chosen people and the blessing of Abraham resides on them. If you read more of the story, you will find that every time Balaam tried to curse Israel, he kept blessing them instead. God would not stand for anyone to curse His people. That is the same way that God feels today about His people. Nobody can curse who God says is blessed, no matter how hard they try. When you are

282. Blessed Merriam-Webster.com https://www.Merriam-Webster.com Accessed January 2022
283. "Markarios" Greek word for Blessed https://www.biblehib.com Accessed January 2022

fighting against God's people, you are actually fighting against God. Fighting against God is a dumb thing to do because you will not win over God or His people. Nobody can curse who God says is blessed no matter who they are, how rich and poor. No witch, warlock, or crystal ball reader can curse who God says is blessed. One thing about God is that He loves His people and He will fight for them in the spiritual realm where it counts the most.

No power is stronger than God's power. No familiar spirit has nothing on God's Spirit. God is all powerful and all knowing, and nothing or no one gets by God. Darkness cannot hide you from God. God got angry with Balaam because God told him not to go with them.

DECLARATIONS

I decree and declare that I will never open my mouth to curse anyone in Jesus' name.

I decree and declare that I am blessed by God and nothing can stop the blessings.

I decree and declare that nobody can curse who God says is blessed.

I thank the Lord for the blessings that are flowing over my life, business, ministry, marriage, and family in Jesus' name.

I decree and declare that I will obey the voice of the Lord.

I decree and declare that I will not fall for the temptations of the enemy because of financial gain.

October 21st

2 THESSALONIANS 3:3 (AMP), "BUT the Lord is faithful, and He will strengthen you (setting you on a firm foundation) and will protect and guard you from the evil one."

Faithful in the Merriam Webster Dictionary is defined as firm in adherence to promises or in observance of duty.[284] The Greek word for Faithful is "Pistos," which means faithful, reliable, trustworthy, or believing.[285]

We have to place our confidence in God and not man because man will let us down. God will not let you down. He will be there for us whenever we call Him. God is always faithful because that is who He is. Faithfulness is one of His attributes. He will strengthen you when you need to be strengthened, especially during the trials and tribulations that we go through in life. God will set you on a firm foundation if you let Him. He is the only One with a firm foundation because all other ground

284. Faithful Merriam Webster.com https://www.Merriam-Webster.com Accessed January 2022
285. "Pistos" Greek word for Faithful https://www.biblehub.com Accessed January 2022

is sinking sand. Nothing is sure, but God and He will protect us and hide us in His shadow away from the storms of life. We will go through them gracefully because we know that we are not alone doing it.

PRAYER

Father God, in the name of Jesus, I thank You for being faithful and never leaving me whenever I needed You. Lord, I thank You that whenever things are going right in my life, You are still there in Jesus' name. Lord, thank You for strengthening me when I need strengthening in Jesus' name. Thank You for the firm foundation that You have placed me on so that my feet will not slip, but I will have sure footing. Lord, thank You for Your hedge of protection surrounding my family and me like a shield in Jesus' name. Lord, I will trust You when I can't even trust anybody else in my circle and life. Lord, thank You for keeping Your promises and purposes that You have set up for my life in Jesus' name. Lord, I can confide in You when I can't confide in anyone else in Jesus' name. Amen.

October 22nd

*M*ALACHI 3:11 (AMP), "THEN I will rebuke the devourer (insects, plague) for your sake and he will not destroy the fruits of the ground, nor will your vine in the field drop its grapes (before harvest), "says the LORD of hosts.

Devourer in the Merriam Webster Dictionary is defined as to eat up greedily or ravenously, or to use to destroy as if by eating.[286] The Greek word for Devourer is "Katavrochthizo," which means gobble up, engorge, engulf, or consume.[287]

God will rebuke the devourer because we are giving our tithes back to Him. He will rebuke anything trying to eat up our seed so we cannot obtain it or sow it. Matthew Henry's Concise Commentary states that we must trust God for comfort and support because God has a blessing ready and waiting on us. When our faith is weak and the narrowness of our desires, we have no room to receive the blessings. He who makes it out

---

286. Devour Merriam-Webster.com https://www.Merriam-Webster.com Accessed January 2022
287. "Katavrochthizo" Greek word for Devour https://www.biblehub.com Accessed January 2022

of the trial will find nothing is lost by honoring the Lord with His substance.[288]

DECLARATIONS

I decree and declare that God will rebuke the devourer for His name's sake because I am a faithful tither.

I decree and declare that nothing will destroy the fruits of my ground.

I decree and declare that I am blessed beyond measure because I honor God with my first fruits.

I decree and declare that the vines in my field will not drop their grapes.

I decree and declare that I will always have an abundant harvest because my giving has come up as a memorial before God.

I decree and declare that God will cause men to give unto my bosom.

---

288. Matthew Henry's Concise Commentary https://www.biblehub.com Accessed January 2022

October 23rd

Corinthians 9:8 (AMP), "And God is able to make all grace (every favor and earthly blessing) come in abundance to you, so that you may always (under all circumstances, regardless of the need) have complete sufficiency in everything (being completely self-sufficient in Him), and have an abundance for every good work and act of charity."

Abundance in the Merriam Webster dictionary is defined as an ample quantity and abundant amount, or plentifulness.[289] The Greek word for Abundance is "Perissos," which means more, greater, excessive, abundant, or exceedingly.[290]

The Amplified Study Bible states that there is no better indicator of growth in the new life than in the area of giving. The person who fails to honor God with his money actually robs God. God will see to it that a generous giver will not suffer want. Instead, God generously provides for those who give so that they can continue to do so. So, it is a win, win situation to

---

289. Abundance Merriam-Webster.com https://www.Merriam-Webster.com Accessed January 2022
290. "Perissos" Greek word for Abundance https://www.biblehub.com Accessed January 2022

give back to God because He will multiply what He gives back to you every time. Don't miss your blessing because you cannot out give God no matter how hard you try.

PRAYER

Father God, in the name of Jesus, I come before You today to thank You for giving me the privilege to give my tithe back to You. Lord, I thank You for opening doors that no man can close and closing the ones that You don't want me to go through in Jesus' name. Lord, I give my 10% back to You because, in reality, all of my income belongs with You. Lord, thank You for rebuking the devourer for Your name's sake, so it cannot be able to eat up my seed. Lord, I trust you will all of my finances. Lord, Your Word declares that You will open the windows of heaven and pour us out a blessing that we will not have room enough to receive in Jesus' name. Lord, we thank You for the increase and the overflow in our lives in Jesus' name. Lord, Your Word declares that You will give seed to the Sower and bread to the eater in Jesus' name. Amen.

October 24th

2 CORINTHIANS 9:11 (AMP), "YOU will be enriched in every way so that you may be generous, and this (generosity, administered) through us is producing thanksgiving to God (from those who benefit)."

Generous in the Merriam Webster Dictionary is marked by abundance or ample proportions.[291] The Greek word for Generous is "Eumetadotos," which means ready to impart, willingly, sharing, or generous.[292]

We are still talking about tithing in this scripture. It states that we will be enriched in every way because we gave God back 10% of our total earnings. God will make sure that we will have the overflow. Everything that our hands touch will be blessed. He gives us the power to get wealth and He maketh rich and adds no sorrow with it. The Blessings of God will overtake us and run us down because we are cheerful givers that will not hold anything back from God. When God knows that

---

291. Generous Merriam-Webster.com https://www.Merriam-Webster.com Accessed January 2022
292. "Eumetadotos" Greek word for Generous https://www.biblehub.com Accessed January 2022

He can trust us with our finances, He doesn't mind giving us more because He knows that we will not turn our back on Him when He gives us more than enough. If He can trust you with your finances, He will lavish them on you. If He can't trust you with them, He will not give you an abundance of them.

DECLARATIONS

I decree and declare that I will be enriched in every area of my life because God can trust me with my finances.

I decree and declare that I will release my seed so there can be a harvest.

I decree and declare that God has given me seed because I am a Sower into His kingdom.

I decree and declare that God will give me more than enough. I will have a huge deluge of finances.

I decree and declare that God will give me the power to get wealth.

I decree and declare that God will give me blessings that will not add any sorrow with it.

October 25th

1CHRONICLES 16:8 (AMP), "O give thanks to the LORD, call on His name; Make His deeds known among the peoples."

Thanks in the Merriam Webster Dictionary is defined as a good feeling that you have towards someone who has helped you or given something to you.[293] The Greek word for Thanks is "Eucharistia,"which means thankfulness, giving thanks, or thanksgiving.[294]

We thank the Lord, the Maker of heaven and earth. We are to always have a heart of gratitude, thanking Him for whatever He has done in our lives. God doesn't have to do anything for us. He wants to because He loves us so much that He does what He does for us. He loves it when we thank Him for the things that He has done in our lives. He doesn't mind giving us His best when we can have an attitude of gratitude instead of complaining all the time. We are to tell of the goodness of the Lord and let people know just how good God is. When we show the

293. Thanks Merriam-Webster.com https://www.Merriam-Webster.com
294. "Eucharistia" Greek word for Thanks https://www.biblehub.com Accessed January 2022

love of God, people will want the God that we know and love who has provided everything for us. Lord, Your praise will forever be in our mouths. Lord, we will praise you when things are bad and not going the way that we feel like they should in Jesus' name. Lord, only You deserve the praise. Only You deserve the honor. Glory and honor are Your name and we praise You for all that You have done in our lives in Jesus' name.

PRAYER

Father God, in the name of Jesus, we come before You today to lift Your name on high. Lord, we thank You for everything that You have done in our lives in Jesus' name. Lord, we thank You for waking me up this morning and opening doors that no man can close. Lord, if we had 10,000 tongues, we couldn't thank You enough for all You do for us daily in Jesus' name. Lord, we thank You for our going out and our coming in. Lord, we thank You for giving us food to eat in Jesus' name. Lord, we thank You for the clothes on our backs. Lord, we thank You that we can dress and feed ourselves. Lord, we will not take what You do for us for granted in Jesus' name. Amen.

October 26th

PROVERBS 4:27 (AMP), "Do not turn away to the right nor to the left (where evil may lurk); Turn your foot from (the path of) evil."

Evil in the Merriam Webster Dictionary is defined as morally bad, causing harm or injury to someone.[295] The Greek word for Evil is "Kakos," which means bad, evil, in the widest sense.[296]

Gill's Exposition of the Entire Bible states not to turn to the right nor to the left. Neither will we walk into the road of immorality, profaneness, error, superstition, and false worship. We will attend to the way of holiness and truth, directed in the Word of God. We will not walk in the evil ways with evil men. We are to abstain from all appearances of evil and keep a distance from it. The evil of the sin brings on the evil of punishment.[297] We will not run to evil but will continue to walk in holiness and righteousness. We bind all evil things in our lives

295. Evil Merriam-Webster.com https://www.Merriam-Webster.com Accessed January 2022
296. "Kakos" Greek word for Evil https://www.biblehub.com Accessed January 2022
297. Gill's Exposition of the Entire Bible https://www.biblehub.com Accessed January 2022

right now in Jesus' name. We will not practice evil but practice holiness and righteousness.

DECLARATIONS

]

I decree and declare that I will not turn away to the left or right but stay on the narrow path.

I decree and declare that I will not intentionally walk into evil.

I decree and declare that I will run from evil and run to righteousness in Jesus' name.

I decree and declare that God has me hedged in His arms of protection, covering me from anything that the enemy may send against me.

I decree and declare that I will not practice evil but will walk in holiness.

I decree and declare that my level of discernment will be keener and sharper so that I will see evil before it comes near my dwelling.

October 27th

1JOHN 4:4 (AMP), "LITTLE children (believers, dear ones), you are of God and you belong to Him and have (already) overcome them (the agents of the antichrist); because He who is in you is greater than he (Satan) who is in the world (of sinful mankind)."

Overcome in the Merriam Webster Dictionary is defined as to get the better of or to gain the superiority.[298] The Greek word for Overcome is "Nikao," which means to conquer to prevail, victorious, or conquer.[299]

We are of God and His family because we have embraced the truth and are imbibed in His Spirit. We have overcome the agents of the enemy. He uses false prophets or teachers to draw us into error and sin. They will not turn us away from the truth of the Word of God. God and the Holy Spirit are in us. We will weigh all counsel with the Word of God. We will not take anyone's word but study the Word for ourselves to see what

298. Overcome Merriam-Webster.com https://www.Merriam-Webster.com Accessed January 2022
299. "Nikao" Greek word for Overcome https://www.biblehub.com Accessed January 2022

it says. We are victorious through the finished works of Jesus on the cross. We will allow the Holy Spirit to rule our hearts. The enemy rules in the hearts of the people of the world and leads them in the path of unrighteousness. If we have the Holy Spirit dwelling in our hearts, we are yet indeed more powerful than the enemy Satan. We are victorious in Christ through His finished works on the cross. The enemy has been defeated. He is trying to make you think that he has the same power as God. Not so. The only power that the enemy has is what you have given him. Snatch back the power you gave him and watch him flee from you.

PRAYER

Father God, in the name of Jesus, I come before You today to thank You for sending Your Son so that I could have the right to the tree of life. Lord, I thank You that I am in the Body of Christ and totally sold out to You. Lord, thank You for the intimate relationship that we have with each other in Jesus' name. Lord, thank You for Your hedge of protection that surrounds me like a shield. Lord, because I am of You and You are in me, the enemy cannot have any control over me. I have the Holy Spirit living inside me who is leading and guiding me in all truth. I belong to You, so there is nothing that the enemy can do to me. Lord, You have me hedged in Your arc of safety. I have already overcome the tricks and schemes of the antichrist spirit in Jesus' name. I will only hear the voice of the Lord louder than I will hear my own voice and the voice of the enemy. I will only listen to the voice of the Shepherd and follow Him. The God in me is greater than the enemy's power in Jesus' name. Amen.

October 28th

1John 4:8 (AMP), *"The one who does not love had not become acquainted with God (does not and never did know Him), for God is love.) He is the originator of Love, and it is an enduring attribute of His nature)."*

Acquainted in the Merriam Webster Dictionary is defined as having personal knowledge of something, having seen or experienced something.[300] The Greek word for Acquainted is "Historeo," which means to inquire about or visit.[301]

The person who does not love his fellow man or neighbor does not know and love God. God is love. That is who He is and if you do not love, you do not belong to God. God is the One who will teach you how to love yourself and others. We don't really know how to love anyone the right way unless we have a love relationship with God. We cannot say that we love God but hate your brother. You are a liar and the truth is not in you.

300. Acquainted Merriam-Webster.com https://www.Merriam-Webster.com Accessed January 2022
301. "Historeo" Greek word for Acquainted https://www.biblehub.com Accessed January 2022

To know God is to love Him, and to know people is to love like God loves them unconditionally.

DECLARATIONS

I decree and declare that I will love God with all my heart, mind, and soul.

I decree and declare that If I do not have love for my brother, I do not belong to God.

I decree and declare that I will walk in love just like God does.

I decree and declare that God is the originator of love, so we can learn to love like God loves.

I decree and declare that the love of God is running strong through my life in Jesus' name.

I decree and declare that I will love people with God's agape love, never-ending love, never leaving love in Jesus' name.

October 29th

1 JOHN 4:13 (AMP), "BY this we know (with confident assurance) that we abide in Him and He is us, because He has given to us His (Holy) Spirit."

Abide in the Merriam Webster Dictionary is defined as to endure without yielding or to wait for.[302] The Greek word for Abide is "Meno," which means to stay, remain, abide, wait, or await.[303]

The Amplified Study Bible states that the mutual abiding refers to the fellowship we have with God due to our salvation. The evidence that God abides in us, and we in Him is the experience of the Holy Spirit in us. We should be able to know that the Spirit is working in our lives to bring everything good to us.[304] To be a Christian, a person must believe that Jesus is the Son of God when we put our trust in Jesus' finished works.

302. Abide Merriam-Webster.com https://www.Merriam-Webster.com Accessed January 2022
303. "Meno" Greek word for Abide Https://www.biblehub.com Accessed January 2022
304. The Amplified Study Bible by Zondervan @ 2017 Accessed January 2022

DECLARATIONS

I decree and declare I will receive the finished works of Jesus.

I decree and declare that I will abide in Jesus so that He can abide in me.

I believe that Jesus is the Son of God.

I thank God for filling me with the Holy Spirit.

I have assurance and comfort knowing that Jesus is with me.

I decree and declare that I will have fellowship with God daily.

October 30th

*H*EBREWS *13:5 (AMP),* "*L*ET *your character (your moral essence, your inner nature) be free from the love of money (shun greed, be financially ethical) being confident with what you have, being content with what you have; For He has said, I will never (under any circumstances desert You)(nor give up on nor leave you without support, nor will I in any degree leave us helpless), Now Will I forsake or let you down or relax My Hold on You(assuredly not)!"*

Confident in the Merriam Webster Dictionary is defined as having a feeling or belief that you can do something well or succeed at something, or having confidence.[305] The Greek word for Confident is "Pepoithesis," which means confident, trust, or reliance.[306]

Jesus lets us know that He will never leave or forsake us and will be with us until the end of this world. He told us to walk in moral essence and to be free from the love of money. It is okay

---

305. Confident Merriam-Webster.com https://www.Merriam-Webester.com Accessed January 2022
306. "Pepoithesis" Greek word for Confident https://www.biblehub.com Accessed January 2022

to have money but it shouldn't make you turn your back on God the first chance you get. He will support us and be there for us no matter what we are going through. We can count on Jesus to always be there for us. He will never let us down. He will never turn His back on us when we are calling and crying out to Him. He will never leave us on earth, nor will He leave us when we get to heaven.

PRAYER

Father God, in the name of Jesus, I come before You to thank You for never leaving me and never turning Your back on me when I have messed up. Lord, thank You for holding my hand and guiding me close back to Your side in Jesus' name. Lord, thank You for Your continued support when other people have walked away from me in Jesus' name. As long as I got You by my side, it doesn't matter who doesn't stay in Jesus' name. Lord, thank You for coming to my rescue time after time in Jesus' name. Lord, thank You for coming to refresh me in my spirit man in Jesus' name. Amen.

October 31st

*J*AMES 1:6-7 (AMP), "BUT he must ask (for wisdom) in faith, without doubting (God's willingness to help)., for the one who doubts is like a billowing surge of the sea that is blown about and tossed by the wind." 7. "For such a person ought not to think or expect that he will receive anything (at all) from the Lord."

Wisdom in the Merriam Webster Dictionary is defined as a knowledge that is gained by having many experiences in life, knowledge of what is proper, or reasonable.[307] The Greek word for Wisdom is "Sophia," which means skill, wisdom, insight, skill divine, or intelligence.[308]

The starting point for wisdom is the genuine reverence for the Almighty and a steadfast confidence that God controls all circumstances, guiding us to His good purposes. The Word of God states that if we need wisdom, we are to ask of God, who will give us as much as we need. We definitely need the wisdom of God and not worldly wisdom. We need to know how to make

307. Wisdom Merriam-Webster.com https://www.Merriam-Webster.com Accessed January 2022
308. "Sophia" Greek for Wisdom https://www.biblehub.com Accessed January 2022

the right decisions that would benefit our walk with God. We never need to be leaning to our own understanding about anything. If we do that, we will end up making many bad decisions. It is best to consult God before making any major decisions that could change your life. We cannot be double minded, because a double minded person is unstable in all of their ways. Those types of people are called flaky or wavering minded. They can never make a decision and stand on it. They are steadily changing their minds. Either you will believe that God can do everything that He has said concerning you or don't. There is no way in between that you can get.

Declarations

I decree and declare that if I need wisdom, I will ask God for it.

I decree and declare that I will not be waverly minded in Jesus' name.

I decree and declare that I will ask God to rain down His Godly wisdom on me.

I decree and declare that I will not be double minded because if I do, I will not expect to receive anything from the Lord.

I decree and declare that my faith is strong, so that I can believe God at His Word for my life.

November 1st

*J*AMES 1:3 (AMP), "BE assured that the testing of your faith (through experience), produces endurance (leading to spiritual maturity, and inner peace."

Testing in the Merriam Webster Dictionary is defined as requiring maximum effort or ability.[309] The Greek word for Testing is "Peirazo," which means to make proof, to attempt to test, or try.[310]

The Amplified Study Bible states the aim of trying is not to destroy or afflict, but to purge and refine. Patience transcends the idea of bearing affliction, and it includes the idea of standing fast. Standing under pressure with staying power turns adversities into opportunities. God doesn't afflict our bodies with sicknesses. Sicknesses come from the enemy Satan. He comes to steal, kill, and destroy. He is definitely at his post doing his job. We must get the Word of God in our hearts and speak it

309. Testing Merriam-Webster.com Htps://www.Merriam-Webster.com Accessed January 2022
310. "Peirazo" Greek Word for Testing https://www.biblehub.com Accessed January 2022

over our lives so that healing with manifest. When our faith is tested, it should be stronger and not weaker. If you are getting weaker, you have taken your eyes off the Lord by focusing on the problem that you are going through instead. When we are going through anything we need to rely on Jesus. All we have to do is cry out to Him and He will see about us to make sure that we are all right. Through adversity, we can build up our endurance, learn how to pray effectively, lay before the Lord and cry out to Him so that He can come and strengthen us.

<u>PRAYER</u>

Father God, in the name of Jesus, thank You for teaching me how-to walk-in endurance because I know that trials come to make us strong in Jesus' name. Lord, thank You for Your Word that teaches our hand for battle and our fingers to war with the enemy when he tries to come against us. We will put on the full armor of God every day. The enemy tends to fight us in our minds. We will put on the mind of Christ, walk in a sound mind, and not let anything stop us from being all that God has called us to be. We will war with the Word of God, resist the enemy, and he will flee from us in Jesus' name. Lord, the trials and tribulations that I have gone through has strengthened my faith. Now I have that bulldog tenacity where I will not turn loose of my faith, believing, and trusting in God no matter what comes against me in Jesus' name. Amen.

November 2nd

JAMES 1:19-20 (AMP), " *[19] Understand this, my beloved brothers and sisters. Let everyone be quick to hear (be careful, thoughtful listener), slow to speak (a speaker of carefully chosen words and), slow to anger (patient, reflective, forgiving); [20.] "For the (resentful, deep-seated) anger of man does not produce the righteousness of God (that standard of behavior which He requires from us)."*

Understand in Merriam Webster Dictionary is to know the meaning of (something, such as the words that someone is saying or a language.[311] The Greek word for Understand is "Nous," which means mind, understanding, reason, or intellect.[312]

Matthew Henry's Concise Commentary states instead of blaming God during our trials, let us open our ears and hearts to learn what He teaches us through our trials. If we would govern our tongues, we can govern our passions. The worst thing we can bring to any dispute is anger. We must take off everything

311. Understand Merriam-Webster.com https://www.Merriam-Webster.com Accessed January 2022
312. "Nous" Greek Word for Understand https://www.biblehub.com Accessed January 2022

that is corruptible and yield to the Word of God with humble and teachable minds. Be willing to hear about our faults, talking not only patiently, but thankfully. Walking in anger does not produce righteousness, especially if you allow the anger to control you and what comes out of your mouth. Let our speech be seasoned with salt and teach us how to answer one another in love.[313]

DECLARATIONS

I decree and declare that I will remain teachable and not get offended when God shows me myself.

I decree and declare that I will not blame God while I am going through my trials.

I decree and declare that I will call out to God to help me through my trials and tribulations.

Lord, help me to walk in humility so that I can be found worthy to be used for Your glory.

Lord, help me to be slow to answer anyone who is trying to attack me.

I decree and declare that I will fast to get the spirit of anger in control, so it does not rule my life.

---

313. Matthew Henry's Concise Commentary https://www.biblehub.com Accessed January 2022

November 3rd

❧

*P*SALM 119:143 (AMP), "TROUBLE *and anguish have found me, Yet Your commandments are my delight and my joy."*

Commandments in the Merriam Webster Dictionary is defined as the act of power of commanding.[314] The Greek word for Commandment is "Entole," which means an injunction, order, command, law, or ordinance.[315]

Trouble and anguish have found me, but yet will I trust in Your Word because Your Word declares, "Let the weak say that I am strong." I will continue to read the Word of God when I am having troubles so it can strengthen and guide me. Matthew Henry's Concise Commentary states that sorrows are often the lot for God's people, but they will delight in the Word of the Lord, which strengthens them when they are in trouble or anguish. May we live the life of faith and grace here and be removed to the life of glory hereafter in Jesus' name. Amen.[316]

314. Commandments Merriam-Webster.com https://www.Merriam-Webster.com Accessed January 2022
315. "Entole" Greek for Commandments https://www.biblehub.com Accessed January 2022
316. Matthew Henry's Concise Commentary Psalm 119:143 https://www.biblehub.

PRAYER

Father God, in the name of Jesus, I come before You today to thank You for giving us Your Word. We need Your Word when we are going through troubles and trials. We are in sorrow when someone we love dies and leave this earth. We know according to Your Word to be absent from the body is to be present with the Lord. So, we know as the people of God that when a saint leaves this earth, they enter into heaven in a peaceful place where they will never have to worry about the cares of this world again. Your Word also declares in *Isaiah 53:5 (KJV)* ,*"But He was wounded for our transgressions, he was bruised for our iniquities; the chastisement of our peace was upon him, and with his stripes we are healed."* So, Lord I am believing You to move in the bodies of everyone that is reading this prayer. Heal every sickness and disease that is attacking their bodies in Jesus' name. Amen.

com Accessed January 2022

November 4th

*P*SALM 130:5 (AMP), "I wait (patiently) for the LORD, my soul (expectantly) waits. And in His Word do I hope."

Hope in the Merriam Webster Dictionary is defined as to want something to happen or be true and thinking that it could happen or be true.[317] The Greek word for Hope is "Elpis," which means expectation, trust, or confidence.[318]

I will wait patiently for the Lord, no matter how long it takes Him to come to my rescue or the rescue of someone who I know needs a miracle in their body and life. Lord, I will continue to pray and trust that You will answer on our behalf. Lord, I know that without a shadow of a doubt that You can do all things but fail. I will wait and trust You to do what is best for us in the long run. Lord, You are a miracle worker and you have been working miracles for centuries and I know that You can do it now. Move mightily God in this situation. Correct every-

317. Hope Merriam-Webster.com https://www.Merriam-Webster.com Accessed January 2022
318. "Elpis" Merriam-Webster.com https://www.Merriam-Webster.com Accessed January 2022

thing that needs correcting. Restore everything that needs restoring in Jesus' name.

DECLARATIONS

I decree and declare that I will keep all of my trust in the Lord.

I decree and declare that God will move mightily on our behalf.

I decree and declare that I will pray and worship as I wait on God to move.

Lord, we thank You and praise You for what You are getting ready to do in our lives and bodies in Jesus' name.

Lord, we surrender our will for your will in this matter.

I decree and declare a creative miracle in the bodies of people who have missing or default organs in Jesus' name.

November 5th

*P*SALM 119:45 (AMP), "AND *I will walk at liberty, For I seek and deeply long for your precepts."*

Precepts in the Merriam Webster Dictionary is defined as a command or principle intended especially as a general rule of action.[319] The Greek word for Precepts is "Entalma," which means an injunction, a religious precept, or ordinance.[320]

The Amplified Study Bible states that many think laws, instructions, and commandments as limiting and restricting, but the law of God paradoxically frees us. It frees us from sin and gives us peace from following the Lord's instructions.[321] The truth in the Word of God free our minds and hearts from the excuse of staying and walking in sin habitually. There is no excuse to keep doing something that you know would be driving a wedge between you and God. Jesus came to set us free from the law of sin and death, and if we just accept the finished works of Jesus and surrender our lives to Him. Then everything else

319. Precepts. Merriam-Webster.com https://www.Merriam-Webster.com Accessed January 2022
320. "Entalma" Greek word for Precepts https://www.biblehub.com Accessed January 2022
321. The Amplified Study Bible by Zondervan @ 2017 Accessed January 2022

would fall into place for our lives. When we are resting in Jesus, then we will have freedom.

PRAYER

Father God, in the name of Jesus, I come before You today to thank You for giving me Your liberty (freedom). Without your freedom from sin, I would be confused and not know where I need to be. Because of Your love, grace and mercy, I know that living a life with You will be better than living a life without You. Lord, thank You for Your Word that speaks life to all of my dead situations. Lord, thank You for Your Word that gives me hope to keep going forward in what You have told me to do. Lord, thank You for the wisdom so that I can apply the Word of God to my life to be in alignment with You. Lord, I just thank You for being God and someone I can lean on and depend on in Jesus' name. Amen.

November 6th

*M*ATTHEW 6:8 (AMP), "So do not be like them (praying as they do); for your Father knows what you need before you ask Him."

Praying in the Merriam Webster Dictionary is defined as entreat or making a request in a humble manner.[322] The Greek word for Praying is "Euche," which means prayer, a vow, or comprising a vow.[323]

This scripture talks about how you don't have to pray long, drawn-out prayers because they do not impress God. We can pray a prayer from the heart and God will understand what we are saying without using big words. He hears the prayer from the righteous and already knows what we need before we ask Him for it. He wants us to have a close personal relationship with Him. God heard Hannah's prayer and supplication, even when no sound came out of her mouth. He gave her what she wanted, which was her promised son.

322. Praying Merriam-Webster.com https://www.Merriam-Webster.com Accessed January 2022
323. "Euche" Greek word for Praying https://www.biblehub.com Accessed January 2022

<u>DECLARATIONS</u>

I decree and declare that I will pray from my heart and not use vain words.

Lord, thank You for knowing what I need before I ask You.

I decree and declare that I will continue to move closer to You God.

I decree and declare that praying big words do not impress God or others.

I decree and declare that God hears the prayers of the righteous.

I decree and declare God knows what we need before we even ask, and He knows why we want it.

November 7th

Romans 8:37 (AMP), "Yet in all these things we are more than conquerors and gain an overwhelming victory through Him who loved us (so much that He died for us)."

Overwhelming in the Merriam Webster Dictionary is defined as tending or serving to overwhelm, extreme, or great.[324] The Greek Word for Overwhelm is "Synklonismenoi," which means deluge, overrun, inundate, shower, or flush.[325]

We are victorious in Christ Jesus as long as we stay rooted and grounded in the Word of God and keep a close relationship with Jesus. We are more than conquers. We do not have to fight alone because God is with us. We will beat our enemies with their own weapons. No weapon formed against us shall prosper. The devil brings suffering to our lives to get us to leave and walk away from Jesus. We are victorious when we stay with God and obey Him despite the confusion around us.

324. Overwhelming Merriam-Webster.com https://www.Merriam-Webster.com Accessed January 2022
325. "Synklonismenoi" Greek word for Overwhelming https://www.biblerhub.com Accessed January 2022

PRAYER

Father God, in the name of Jesus, I am more than a conquer in Christ Jesus because I am a part of your family. Regardless of what is coming against me, I know that I can walk in the authority that You have given me. I know that God is fighting for me and I don't have to fight alone. God has His band of angels surrounding me, and keeping me covered under His precious blood. God is my battleax and we are going to fight and win this battle together in Jesus' name. Amen.

November 8th

ROMANS 8:26 (AMP), "IN the same way the Spirit (comes to us and) helps us in our weakness. We do not know what prayer to offer or how to offer it as we should, but the Spirit Himself (knows our need and at the right time) interceded on our behalf with signs and groanings too deep for words."

Intercede in the Merriam Webster Dictionary is defined as to intervene between parties with a view to reconciling differences, or mediate.[326] The Greek word for Intercede is "Huperentugchano," which means to intercede or to make petition for.[327]

Matthew Henry's Concise Commentary states that the infirmities of Christians are many and great. They would be overpowered if left to themselves, yet the Holy Spirit supports them. The Spirit, as a enlightened Spirit, teaches us what to pray for; as a sanctifying Spirit, works and stirs up praying graces;

---

326. Intercede Merriam-Webster.com https://www.Merriam-Webster.com Accessed January 2022
327. "Hyperentugchano' Greek word for Intercede https://www.biblehub.com Accessed January 2022

as a comforting Spirit, silences our fears; and helps us over all discouragements. The Holy Spirit is the spring of all desires toward God, which are often more than words can utter. The Spirit searches the heart, can perceive the mind and will of the spirit, the renewed mind, and advocates His cause. The Spirit makes intercession to God, and the enemy prevails not.[328]

DECLARATIONS

I decree and declare that the Spirit comes and helps us in our weakness.

I decree and declare that when I do not know how to pray, the Holy Spirit prays through me.

I decree and declare that I have support from the Holy Spirit because I am in partnership with Him.

I decree and declare that pray will silence my fears and help me over discouragements.

I decree and declare that the prayers of the righteous availeth much and produces wonderful results.

I decree and declare that the Spirt searched the heart, and helps me renew my mind in Jesus' name.

---

328 Matthew Henry's Concise Commentary https://www.biblehub.com Accessed January 2022

November 9th

ROMANS 8:34 (AMP), "WHO is the one who condemns us? Christ Jesus is the One who died (to pay our penalty), and more than that, who was raised (from the dead), and who is at the right hand of God interceding (with the Father) for us."

Condemns in the Merriam Webster Dictionary is defined as to say in a strong and definite way that someone or something is bad or wrong.[329]   The Greek word for Condemns is "Katakrima," which means punishment following condemnation, penal, or penalty.[330]

Matthew Henry's Concise Commentary states that we have a friend sitting at the right hand of God interceding for us. All power has been given to Jesus, the author and finisher of our faith. We are not to doubt it, for we know, according to the Word of God, Jesus is interceding and praying for us to make it. God gave His own Son, so we could be redeemed back to God.

329. Condemn Merriam-Webster.com https://www.Merriam-Webster.com Accessed January 2022
330. "Katakrima" Greek word for Condemn https://www.biblehub.com Accessed January 2022

We are redeemed through Christ's shed blood on the cross. This shows how much God loves us. Nothing can take Christ and the believer from each other. We are partners and we work together to achieve a common purpose.[331]

PRAYER

Father God, in the name of Jesus, we come before You today to thank You for sending Your Only Begotten Son to die for our sins. Without You sending Him, we wouldn't be able to be borne again out of this world of sin. Lord, we thank You and bless Your name because You came and did what the Father told You to do for me. Lord, I praise You and thank You for a new life in God through Your shed blood. Thank You for that cleansing blood that has washed me clean from every one of my sins. Lord, I thank You for choosing me to be in Your family. I appreciate everything that You have done for me up until this present time in my life. Lord, I do not take anything for granted because without You, I am nothing. In You, I am everything because of Your Will for my life in Jesus' name. Amen.

---

331. Matthew Henry's Concise Commentary https://www.biblehub.com Accessed January 2022

November 10th

❧

2TIMOTHY 4:2 (AMP), "PREACH the word (as an official messenger); be ready when the time is right and even when it is not) keep your sense of urgency, whether the opportunity seems favorable or unfavorable, whether convenient or inconvenient, whether welcome or unwelcome, correct (those that err in doctrine or behavior), warn (those who sin), exhort and encourage (those who are growing toward spiritual maturity, with inexhaustible patience and (faithful) teaching."

Preach in the Merriam Webster dictionary is defined as to deliver (something such as a sermon) publicly.[332] The Greek word for Preach is "Kerusso," which means to herald, proclaim, or preach.[333]

The Amplified Study Bible states that patience and doctrine are two necessary components of an effective ministry. True Spiritual growth occurs over time through consistent teaching and application of God's Word.[334] In other words, the more we

332. Preach Merriam-Webster.com https://www.merriam-Webster.com Accessed January 2022
333. "Kerusso" Greek word for Preach https://www.biblehub.com Accessed January 2022
334. The Amplified Study Bible by Zondervan @2017 Accessed January 2022

study and listen to the Word of God and apply it to our lives, the more we can grow. God wants us to grow into mature believers and stop walking around idling. Allow the Word to change you, so you can be delivered. God has given His people the Word to keep us on track. Many of us cannot trust Him to be there for us because we are always looking back on our pasts instead of looking ahead with God. We need to be walking in full spiritual maturity before God releases us in an area.

DECLARATIONS

I decree and declare that I will preach the Word in season and out of season.

I decree and declare that God has an urgent message for His People.

I decree and declare that I am growing spiritually and God has me right where He wants me.

I will not walk in err or sin against God in any way.

I will trust God to do what is best for me.

November 11th

1 Thessalonians 5:16-17 (AMP), "16 Rejoice always and delight in your faith." 17. "Be unceasing and persistent in prayer."

Persistent in the Merriam webster Dictionary is defined as continuing to do something or to try to do something even though it is difficult or other people want you to stop.[335] The Greek word for Persistent is "Anaideia," which means shamelessness or persistence.[336]

These scriptures tells you to rejoice always regardless of the difficult circumstances that you are going through. A Christian always has grounds for rejoicing. The Lord is a sovereign Ruler and will accomplish His purpose. Christian joy is not based on circumstances, but a growing awareness of God and a certain future of eternal life with Christ." Sometimes, you don't see the need to rejoice because the things that you are going through seems so bad. God wants us to rejoice in knowing that there is

335. Persistent Merriam-Webster.com https://www.Merriam-Webster.com Accessed January 2022
336 ."Anaideia" Greek word for Persistent https://www.biblehub.com Accessed January 2022

a place that has been prepared for us. One day we will go to live in harmony with the Lord. We have struggles and trials here on earth and they really get us down sometimes. It is hard to see the silver lining when your heart hurts, especially during the loss of a loved one or a divorce. I speak the joy of the Lord over everyone reading this paragraph. Let it fall down on you and consume you in Jesus' name.

PRAYER

Father God, in the name of Jesus, we come before You today because You have reminded us to rejoice in the midst of sorrow and pain. Lord, we are asking that You send Your supernatural joy, strength, and comfort to touch our lives like never before. Lord, show us where we need to be rejoicing at instead of complaining. Lord, we know that there is a cause to rejoice because there is a place that has been prepared for us and it is called heaven. Lord, why must we go through so much pain to reach heaven? Lord, I know that there is a purpose and a plan for the pain that we have been going through. I know that it is tied to my destiny in You. Lord, teach us to overcome hardships through Your Word in Jesus' name. Amen.

November 12th

1 Thessalonians 5:24 (AMP), "Faithful and absolutely trustworthy is He who is calling you (to Himself for your salvation), and He will do it (He will fulfill His call by making you holy, guarding you, watching over you, and protecting you as His own)."

Trustworthy in the Merriam Webster Dictionary is defined as worthy of confidence.[337] The Greek word for Trustworthy is "Pistikos," which means trustworthy, genuine, or pure.[338]

Barnes Notes of the Bible states that our sanctification depends on God and He has begun a work of grace in your hearts and He is faithful to complete it.[339] God knows all about us and He knows that we are a work in progress, so He works with us to get us to full maturity so we can be powerhouses in His kingdom by advancing it. He knows what steps to take with us to make us complete in Him. It would be better for us if we

337. Trustworthy Merriam-Webster.com https://www.Merriam-Webster.com Accessed January 2022
338. "Pistikos" Greek word for Trustworthy https://www.biblehub.com Accessed January 2022
339. Barnes Notes on the bible https://www.bibblehub.com Accessed Janauary 2022

cooperate with the process instead of trying to fight what God is doing in our lives.

DECLARATIONS

I decree and declare that God is calling us to be faithful and absolutely trust in Him.

God is calling all those to Himself who are willing to go through the process He wants to take us through.

Jesus is the source of our salvation. We have to go through Jesus to get to God.

He will fulfill His call in me by making me holy in Him.

God is guarding, watching, and protecting us to make us Him own.

God knows my future and has promised to give me a future and an expected end.

November 13th

*L*UKE 10:19 (AMP), "LISTEN *carefully; I have given you authority (that you now possess) to tread on serpents and scorpions, and (the ability to exercise authority) over all the power of the enemy Satan); and nothing will (in any way) harm you."*

Authority in the Merriam Webster Dictionary is defined as the power to give others or make decisions; the power or right to direct or control someone or something.[340] The Greek word for Authority is "Exousia," which means power, authority, especially moral authority, or influence.[341]

According to the Amplified Study Bible, this verse talks about the transfer of Jesus' power to His immediate circle of disciples.[342] Jesus is the Son of God and the same power that raise Jesus from the dead is living on the inside of us. That power is the Holy Ghost. So, we are walking in that Dunamis power. So we have the same power to lay hands on the sick and they

340. Authority Merriam-Webster.com https://www.Merriam-Webster.com Accessed January 2022
341. "Exousia" Greek word for Authority https://www.biblehub.com Accessed January 2022
342. The Amplified Study Bible by Zondervan @2017 Accessed January 2022

shall recover. We have the same power to cast out demons and devils that Jesus used when He walked this earth. It takes great faith to do the things that Jesus did and even greater things. Jesus has given us the authority because we have become partakers with Him in the kingdom. He is with us and for us. He is fighting for us and He will not allow anything or anyone hurt His children.

PRAYER

Father, we come to You today to thank You for giving us authority to tread on serpents and scorpions. I will speak the Word of God in authority and say to that mountain that it has to move from one place to the other. I will resist the devil and He will flee from me because I am using the Word of God at him. God has given us all the power over the enemy and the only power he comes up with is what we give him. Lord, I will snatch all the power that I have given Him unconsciously in Jesus' name. Lord, I will always refer to Your Word when I have an issue with the enemy. I will read and study the Word and get it on the inside of my heart so I will not sin against thee. I will not fear what the enemy can do to me because of Jesus' finished works on the cross. I break the spirit of fear off our lives. I decree and declare that you have a sound mind and the mind of Christ in Jesus' name. I will not let fear stop me any longer in Jesus' name. Amen.

November 14th

*E*PHESIANS 2:3 (AMP), "AMONG these (unbelievers) *we all once lived in the passions of our flesh (our behavior governed by the sinful self), indulging the desires of human nature (without the Holy Spirit) and (the impulses) of the (sinful) mind. we were, by nature, children (under the sentence) of (God's) wrath, just like the rest (of mankind)."*

Unbelievers in the Merriam Webster Dictionary is defined as one that does not believe in a particular religious faith.[343] The Greek word for Unbelievers is "Apistos," which means unbelieving or unchristian.[344]

This scripture says that before we got saved, we were once unbelievers and living in the passions of our flesh (sin) indulging in whatever we were big or bad enough to do because we weren't being led by the Holy Spirit. We were governed by our flesh. We were children under the sentence of God's wrath because we refused to accept Jesus and continue to refuse salva-

343Unbeliever Merriam-webster.com https://www.Merriam-Webster.com Accessed January 2022
344. "Apistos" Greek word for Unbeliever https://www.biblehub.com Accessed January 2022

tion. We were headed to a devil's hell and thinking we were okay because the devil had us spiritually blind. Once we surrendered our lives to Jesus, we were no longer under God's wrath because now we are His children and not His enemy. If you haven't given your life to Jesus, now is the time before it is too late.

DECLARATIONS

I decree and declare that I am not an enemy of God.

I decree and declare that I am not an unbeliever but a believer of Christ.

I decree and declare that I surrender all to Jesus from this day forward in Jesus' name.

I decree and declare that the spiritual blinders have been taken off of my eyes in Jesus' name.

I decree and declare that I believe that Jesus Christ is the Son of God.

I decree and declare that I am no longer an orphan but a son/daughter of God.

November 15th

*E*PHESIANS 3:16 (AMP), "MAY He grant you out of the riches of His glory, to be strengthened and spiritually energized with power through His Spirit in your inner self, (indwelling your innermost being and personality)."

Energized in the Merriam Webster Dictionary is defined as to make energic, vigorous, or active.[345] The Greek word for Energized is "Energes," which means work, active, productive, or production of due work.[346]

God's rich grace can never be exhausted. God has an abundance of grace for us and He will powerfully strengthen His children. We need abundant strength to bear trials that come our way and to do the things God has told us to do for Him. We will find that great strength in glorifying His name as well. Our inner man, the heart, mind, and soul need constant supplies of grace daily. Every Christian needs God's grace continuously to bear whatever comes up against them. They can resist tempta-

---

345. Energized Merriam-Webster.com Https://www.Merriam-Webster.com Accessed January 2022
346. "Energes" Greek word for Energized https://www.biblehub.com Accessed January 2022

tion and walk in a new level of faith. As long as we live on this earth, we will need His unmerited favor and grace operating in our lives.

PRAYER

Father God, in the name of Jesus, I come before You today, thanking You for Your never-ending grace. I don't know what I would do without Your unmerited favor. It is the ability to do what I couldn't do on my own. It is the ability to love someone who is hard to love. It is the ability to help someone who is down on their luck and not looking for anything back from them. It is the ability to love someone who doesn't like you in spite of. Lord, thank You for giving me Your amazing Grace because it is definitely needed in this world today. Lord, thank You for strengthening me spiritually and physically to make it through yet another year in Jesus' name. Amen.

November 16th

*E*PHESIANS 3:20 *(AMP), "Now to Him who is able to (carry out His purpose and) do superabundantly more than all that we dare ask or think (infinitely beyond our greatest prayers, hopes, or dreams), according to His power that is at work within us,"*

Superabundantly in the Merriam Webster Dictionary is defined as an amount or supply more than sufficient to meet one's needs.[347] The Greek word for Superabundantly is "Huperekperissou," which means superabundantly, far more, or more earnestly.[348]

God can do anything but fail. God can carry out the most elaborate dreams, visions, and ideas you have so He can get the glory. God can do more than we could think or imagine. God has an infinite mind. His thoughts are not our thoughts. When we ask Him to do a thing, He will do exceedingly more than we

---

347. Superabundantly Merriam-webster.com https://www.Merriam-Webster.com Accessed January 2022
348. "Hyperrkperissou" Greek word for Superabundantly https://www.biblehub.com Accessed January 2022

have asked all the time. Most of the time with God, we are not even dreaming big enough. God is able.

DECLARATIONS

I decree and declare that God can do anything but fail.

God will carry out His purpose in my life according to His Word.

God wants His children to dream bigger than we have ever imagined for our lives.

God is not slack concerning His promises. If He has said it, then that settles it.

God is not an almost God, but He is an On Time God.

Lord, give Your children many witty ideas and dreams that would be a blessing to our homes and the Kingdom of God.

November 17th

*E*PHESIANS 4:30 (AMP), "AND do not grieve the Holy Spirit of God (but seek to please Him) by whom you were sealed and marked (branded as God's own) for the day of redemption (the final deliverance from the consequences of sin)."

Sealed in the Merriam Webster Dictionary is defined as something that confirms, ratifies, makes secure, guarantee, or assurance.[349] The Greek word for Sealed is "Sphragizo," which means seal, set, or a seal upon.[350]

We are not supposed to be doing anything to grieve the Holy Spirit who lives on the inside of us like lying, corrupt communication that stirs up evil desires, and lusts. Corrupt passions of bitterness, wrath, anger, clamour, and malice also grieve the Holy Spirit. Provoke not the Holy Spirit to withdraw His presence and His gracious influences. We do not want God to take His Holy Spirit away from us. Avoid evil at all costs.

349. Sealed Merriam-Webster.com https://www.Merriam-Webster.com Accessed January 2022
350. "Sphragzo" Greek word for Sealed https://www.biblehub.com Accessed January 2022

PRAYER

Father God, in the name of Jesus, we come before You to-day to repent for letting anything evil come out of our mouths when we were mad at someone. Lord, forgive us for cussing, trash talking, and acting ghetto in Jesus' name. Lord, we do not want You to take Your Holy Spirit away from us. If we lack self-control and fail to let You come inside our hearts, clean us up in Jesus' name. Lord, I am not going to deny it any longer. I need Your help, so I will no longer operate in my flesh. Lord, heal me from rejection, so I will not let the things in my past destroy my future. Lord, give me the strength to fast to get that destiny stealing spirit out of me to be made whole. Lord, I am tired of going around the same mountain yearly in Jesus' name. Amen.

November 18th

PROVERBS 10:22 (AMP), "THE blessing of the LORD brings (true) riches, And He adds no sorrow to it (for it comes as a blessing from God)."

Blessings in the Merriam Webster Dictionary is defined as a thing conducive to happiness or welfare.[351] The Greek word for Blessings is "Makarios," which means blessed, happy, or to be envied.[352]

The blessings that the Lord gives us are numerous and they will not bring any sorrow. When God gives you and your family a house or car, He will make sure that you can afford to pay for it. He will cause someone to give you a car or house so you can be debt free. That is how my God works. He will not give you something for it to be repossessed. We serve a rich and plentiful God, who owns everything. God can pay your household bills. All He has to do is speak the word to someone and they will write you a check for the total bill and more. God always

351. Blessing Merriam-Webster.com https://www.Merriam-Webster.com Accessed January 2022
352. "Makarios" Greek Word for Blessing https://www.biblehub.com Accessed January 2022

does exceedingly above more than we can ask or think. When you are a citizen of the kingdom you need to always have a figure in your head of how much it would cost to be debt free. You may never know when it is your day to become debt free. Take God out of the box that you have Him in because He is bigger than that. Quit thinking small and start thinking bigger because you serve a bigger, mega, and a major God.

DECLARATIONS

I decree and declare that the Lord will make me rich and add no sorrow with it.

I decree and declare that God will supply my every need, such as His riches in glory by Christ Jesus.

I decree and declare that God will give me several witty ideas and dreams to be a blessing to me and the kingdom of God.

I decree and declare that my expectations will go to another level in God.

I decree and declare that the blessings of the Lord are for every area of my life in Jesus' name.

November 19th

❦

*P*ROVERBS 10:27 (AMP), "THE (reverent) fear of the LORD (worshiping, obeying, serving, and trusting Him with awe-filled respect) prolongs one's life."

Reverent in the Merriam Webster's Dictionary is defined as expressing or characterized by reverence or worshipful.[353]The Greek word for Reverent is "Eulabeia," which means caution, fear of God, piety, or reverence.[354]

When we fear God, we will be secured in life here on earth and when we get to heaven. Also, worshiping brings joy to the heart and produces a long, healthy, prosperous life. When we have that reverential fear of Him, we will not do anything to grieve His Spirit or bring shame to His name. Our loyalty is in God and not man.

---

353. Reverent Merriam-Webster.com https://www.Merriam-Webster.com Accessed January 2022
354. "Eulabeia" Greek for Reverent https://www.biblehub.com Accessed January 2022

PRAYER

Father God, in the name of Jesus, I will forever have reverential fear towards You. Not the fear that shakes in my boots when I want to talk or spend time with You. Having reverential fear means I don't want to do anything to hurt You or tarnish Your name in the world. I will no longer walk in the flesh, fulfilling the lust of my eye and the pride of life. I will allow the Holy Spirit to lead and guide me to reverence who You are God. I will obey You and lean not to my own understanding. I want what You desire for my life God. Lord, I love You and praise Your holy name in Jesus' name. Amen.

November 20th

Proverbs 11:14 (AMP), "*Where there is no (wise, intelligent) guidance, the people fall (and go off course like a ship without a helm.*"

Guidance in the Merrian Webster Dictionary is defined as the direction provided by a guide.[355] The Greek word for Guidance is "Hodegeo," which means to lead, guide, teach, or instruct.[356]

The Word of God states, "If anyone needs wisdom, He is to ask of God who will give it generously to those that ask Him." Wisdom is something that every believer needs because operating in worldly wisdom is not a good thing. Saved people only need to get their wisdom from God. They may talk to someone full of God. In turn, they are full of wisdom. Age doesn't determine if you have wisdom. There are old and young fools. If a saved person allows God to come into their heart to teach things that they need to know, and not lean on their own un-

355. Guidance merriam-Webster.com https://www.Merriam-Webster.com Accessed January 2022
356. "Hodegeo" Greek word for Guidance https://www.biblehub.com Accessed January 2022

derstanding, they can walk in the wisdom of God. The wisdom of God will not tell you to do crazy, off the wall things that don't line up with God's Word. The flesh not under submission to the Holy Spirit will tell you to do crazy things. Fasting is vital so we can bring our bodies under subjection.

DECLARATIONS

I decree and declare that I will only listen to sound wisdom and sound doctrine.

I decree and declare that if I need wisdom, I will ask God for it.

I decree and declare that the best kind of wisdom to have is godly wisdom.

I decree and declare that I will not be a fool or listen to a fool, but stay in alignment with God.

I decree and declare that I will not keep leaning to my own understanding and making a mess of my life.

I decree and declare that I will submit my will to God's will to obtain wisdom.

November 21st

JOSHUA 1:5 (AMP), "*No man will (be able to) stand before you (to oppose you) as long as you live. Just as I was (present) with Moses, so I will be with you; I will not fail you or abandon you.*"

Oppose in the Merriam Webster Dictionary is defined as to place over against something so as to provide resistance, counterbalance, or contrast.[357] The Greek word for Oppose is "Anthistemi," which means to set against, withstand, resist, or oppose.[358]

God reminded Joshua that he was not alone in this passage. Just like God was with Moses, He would be with him. God was urging him to obey all of the laws. This is the same for us today. God wants His people to obey Him and His Word. When we are in right standing with God and in proper alignment, He will not withhold anything from us. He will rain down His blessings upon us. We must walk in total obedience to Him.

357. Oppose Merriam-Webster.com Https://www.Merriam-Webster.com Accessed January 2022

358. "Anthistemi" Greek word for Oppose https://www.biblehub.com Accessed January 2022

PRAYER

Father God, in the name of Jesus, we come before you today to thank You for being with us and never leaving us, just like You were with Moses and Joshua. If we do the same things they did, we will get the same results in our lives in Jesus' name. Lord, I know You will not fail or abandon me because You have been with me all these years and You haven't left me yet. Even when I walked off, You were right where I left You when I picked you back up. Lord, thank You for never giving up on me and loving me past my mess. Lord, thank You for being with me through thick and thin. Lord, when my enemies tried to rise up against me, You protected me. Lord, thank You for fighting the battles that I was not even aware of in Jesus' name. Amen.

November 22nd

2 TIMOTHY 3:16 (AMP), "ALL scripture is God-breathed (given by divine inspiration) and is profitable for instruction, for conviction (of restoration to obedience), for training in righteousness (learning to live in conformity to God's will, both publicly and privately —behaving honorably with personal integrity and moral courage."

God breathed defined by www.biblehub.com means to be inspired by God.[359] The Greek word for God-breathed is "Theopneustos," meaning God breathed, inspired by God, or due to the inspiration of God.[360]

The Word of God was inspired by the Holy Ghost and God —breathed so everything in the Word is true, regardless of who disagrees with it. It doesn't matter what denomination says about it. It is still God's Word. Many denominations subtract and add to the Word. It is definitely true without adding or taking anything away from it. It is inspired by God and it is the road map to help all Christians live Christ like lives. Every-

359. God-Breathed https://www.biblehub.com Accessed January 2022
360. "Theopheastes" Greek for God breathed https://www.biblehub.com Accessed January 2022

thing we will ever go through is in the Bible. It has so many stories and parables to help you understand what you are reading. Many translations of the Bible help you understand what you are reading so you can apply it to your life. I like the Amplified Study Bible and the New Living Translation Bible. The New International Version is missing many scriptures about fasting, so you have to be careful. Many of the authors had taken parts of it out when they translated it. The King James Version is a good Bible. Ask the Holy Spirit what Bible would be better for you to get a better understanding. Now that we have established that everything in the Bible is true, nothing should stop you from learning more about who Jesus is.

DECLARATIONS

Now that I know the Word of God is true, I will start to study it more.

I will study to show myself approve to rightly divide the word of truth.

I will take the Word of God and apply it to my life in Jesus' name.

I will walk in honesty and integrity for the rest of my days as I apply the Word to my life.

All Scriptures are God-breathed, given by divine inspiration.

The Word is profitable for instruction, conviction, correction, or training in righteousness.

November 23rd

SAMUEL 2:2 (AMP), "THERE is no one holy like the LORD, There is no one besides You, There is no Rock like our God."

God in the Merriam Webster Dictionary is defined as a spirit or being that has great power, strength, knowledge, etc., and that can affect nature and the lives of people.[361] The Greek word for God is "Theos," which means creator of all things.[362]

No one is Sovereign or Holy like You God. You are the Creator of the universe and everything that we know was made by You. You brought all the animals of the earth to Adam to name. You are the All-Supreme One. You are the Alpha and Omega, the beginning and the end, the first and the last. You are Jehovah Rapha or healer and Jehovah Jireh, our provider. You are the Great I Am. You are everything that we need wrapped up into One. Nothing on this earth cannot happen without You knowing it. You are the Great Physician, who has never lost a case.

---

361. God Merriam-Webster.com https://www.Merriam-Webster.com Accessed January 2022
362. "Theos" Greek word for God https://www.biblehub.com Accessed January 2022

PRAYER

Father God, in the name of Jesus, we come before You today as humbly as we know how. Lord, we thank You that You are the Most Holy One. You are the Creator of this universe and in six days, You made the world and all of its inhabitants. Lord, You are the ruler over all life on this earth in Jesus' name. Lord, You are my rock and I have my roots wrapped around and anchored in You Jesus. You are the Great I Am. It is You who move and have my being. It is You who I call on in the time of my need in Jesus' name. It is You who I call on when I am overwhelmed with the cares of this world. It is You who will put Your loving arms around me and hold me close. It is You who will wipe all of my tears from my eyes. It is You who loves me unconditionally even when I don't feel lovable. It is You Lord who holds my hand when I feel afraid and alone in this world. Lord it is You who says, "Come on, my child. Rest in my presence from the stress and the strain of this world." Lord, we thank You for Your never ending love and presence in our lives in Jesus' name. Lord, thank You for being God of my life in Jesus' name. Amen.

November 24th

COLOSSIANS 3:15 (AMP), "LET the peace of Christ *(the inner calm of one who walks daily with Him) be the controlling factor in your hearts (deciding and settling questions that arise). To this peace indeed you were called as members in one body (of believers), And be thankful (to God always)."*

Peace in the Merriam Webster Dictionary is defined as free from civil distrubances.[363] The Greek word for Peace is "Eirene," which means one, peace, quietness, rest, peace of mind, or invocation of peace.[364]

Matthew Henry's Concise Commentary states to let the peace of God rule in your hearts; it is of His working in all who are His. Thanksgiving to God helps to make us agreeable with all men. The Gospel is the Word of Christ. Many have the Word, but it dwells in them poorly. It has no power over them. The soul prospers when we are full of scriptures and the grace

363. Peace Merriam-Webster.com Https://www.Merriam-Webster.com Accessed January 2022
364. "Eirene" Greek word for Peace https://www.Biblehub.com Accessed January 2022

of Christ. When we sing, we sing psalms. We must be affected by what we sing. Let us do everything in the name of the Lord Jesus and in believing dependence on Him.[365]

Why are, we as the people of God. not walking in peace? It is because we refused to let the Word of God take root in our spirits to bring a change in our lives. Wow! Help us all Lord to die to the carnal mind and pick up the new regenerated mind in Jesus.

Declarations

I decree and declare that the carnal mind will die and I will pick the new regenerated mind of Christ.

I decree and declare that I will let the peace of God rule in my heart.

I will not let people and situations stress me out any longer in Jesus' name.

Lord, give us Your peace that surpasseth all understanding in our lives in Jesus' name.

I decree and declare that I will not let demonic people steal my peace.

I decree and declare that peace is a gift and I will not give mine up so freely in Jesus' name.

365. Matthew Henry's Concise Commentary Accessed January 2022

November 25th

*C*OLOSSIANS 3:1 (AMP), "THEREFORE IF you have been raised with Christ (to a new life, sharing in His resurrection from the dead) keep seeking the things that are above, where Christ is, seated at the right hand of God."

Resurrection in the Merriam Webster Dictionary is defined as the rising of Christ from the dead.[366] The Greek word for Resurrection is "Anastasis," which means a standing up, a resurrection, or an arising up.[367]

Set your mind on things above (heavenly things), the eternal realities of heaven. We have been raised with Christ and sit with Him in heavenly places with Christ Jesus. He said to keep seeking things from the heavenly realm instead of the temporal things on this earth. We are to catch the spirit of the things above.

---

366. Resurrection Merriam-Webster.com https://www.Merriam-Werbster.com Accessed January 2022
367. "Anastasis" Greek word for Resurrection https://www,biblehub.com Accessed January 2022

Ellicott's Commentary states being heavenly minded is already anticipating heaven, not only in hope, but in tone and temper, seeing things as God sees them and seeing all things that are in relation to Christ. From where our treasure is, that is where our treasure will be also. God is preparing a place for us and is drawing us there to be with Him.[368]

PRAYER

Father God, in the name of Jesus, I come before You today to do according to what Your word declares. I will think about things in heaven more than things on this earth. Lord, we will lay up more treasure in heaven because that eternal treasure will be greater than this earthly treasure in Jesus' name. Lord, I realize You will give us some earthly treasures here on earth, but the earthly treasures cannot have us. Lord, when You tell us to release some of those earthly treasures, we cannot close up our bowels of mercy for other people. Lord, You told us in Your Word to be heavenly minded by thinking on the things of heaven and storing our treasures up there in Jesus' name. Lord, we thank You for having us sit with You in heavenly places to walk from victory and not walking to victory in Jesus' name. Lord, help us all to stay heavenly minded that we would keep You first and seek You, then all other things will be added unto us in Jesus' name. Amen.

---

368. Ellicott's Commentary for English Readers' https://www.biblehub.com Accessed January 2022

November 26th

COLOSSIANS 3:23-25 (AMP), "²³ Whatever you do (whatever you task may be), work from the soul (that is, put in your very best effort), as (something done) for the Lord and not for men, ²⁴· "Knowing (with all certainly) that it is from the Lord (not from men) that you will receive the inheritance which is your (greatest) reward. It is the Lord Christ whom you (actually) serve." ²⁵· "For he who does wrong will be punished for his wrongdoing, and (with God) there is no partiality (no special treatment based on a person's position in life)."

Lord in the Merriam Webster Dictionary is defined as God or Jesus.[369] The Greek word for Lord is "Kuriakos," which means of the Lord or special to the Lord.[370]

There is a future reward that Christ gives to faithful people in His service. We normally think we receive an eternal reward for spiritual practices like reading the Bible, prayer, or evangelism. All work done in the honor of Christ will bring an eternal

---

369. Lord Merriam-Webster.com https://www.Merriam-Webster.com Accessed January 2022
370. "Kuriakos" Gree word for Lord https://www.biblehub.com Accessed January 2022

reward. Only what you do for Christ will last. He has to get the glory out of the situation. That is why we are to put our best effort inti doing what He has told us to do here on this earth so He can be glorified. Nothing that I will ever do should be to please men, but to please God is the ultimate goal for everything. Pleasing God, being obedient, and advancing His Kingdom is the key to it all. According to verse 25, when you do wrong, you are punished by God with no special treatment. We will all get the same reward, whether we do good or bad. Do good and please God with your life, ministry, career, marriage, etc.

DECLARATIONS

I decree and declare above all else, I will seek to please God over man.

In my service to the Lord, I will work whole heartedly, so God can get the glory out of it.

I will receive the eternal reward for the Lord and not from man.

Receiving the inheritance of eternal life is the greatest reward for me.

I will serve the Lord God with happiness and gladness for the rest of my days.

I will strive to please God, be obedient to Him, advance the kingdom, and live a holy and righteous lifestyle.

November 27th

PSALM 32:7 (AMP), "You are my hiding place; You LORD, protect me from trouble; You surround me with songs and shouts of deliverance."

Hiding in the Merriam Webster Dictionary is defined as to conceal for shelter or protection.[371] The Greek word for Hiding is "Kruptos," which means hidden, secret, inward nature, or character.[372]

God is our refuge in the time of trouble. We run and cry out to Him. We are safe from the cares of this world. God will surround me with the songs of deliverance to heal me from hurts, wounds, and scars from the past so that I can walk in wholeness. We can get into the presence of God in the secret place and allow God to build us back up when we are weary and heavy laden with the cares of this world. Jesus said to cast our cares on Him because He cares for me. He wants us to empty and dump everything on our hearts and minds on Him.

371. Hiding Merriam-Webster.com https://www.Merriam-Webster.com Accessed January 2022
372. "Kruptos" Greek word for Hiding https://www.biblehub.com Accessed January 2022

He didn't mean for us to carry all of our problems and other people's problems. After you pray or minister to them, lay their troubles at Jesus' feet because it is His job to take care of their needs not ours. Jesus, it is your job to heal and my job is to pray. God wants to deliver us from everything that has us bound and weighed down in our lives. Release it to Him and release people to Him. Only He can change hearts, minds, and save souls.

PRAYER

Father God, in the name of Jesus, I come to You today to lay all of my burdens and the burdens of others at Your feet right now in Jesus' name. Lord, it is Your will for people to be healed, delivered, and set free, so I lay them at Your feet so You can do just that. Lord, do Your will in their lives in Jesus' name. Lord, if it is Your will to heal them on this side of heaven, let it be done in Your timing. Lord, strengthen their bodies and make death loose it holds over them now in Jesus' name. Lord, let the supernatural healing come directly from the hem of your garment so that they can be made whole in their minds and bodies in Jesus' name. Amen.

November 28th

SALM 42:1 (AMP), "AS THE deer pants (longingly) for the water brooks, So my soul pants (longingly) for You, O God."

Longingly in the Merriam Webster Dictionary is defined as
a strong desire especially for something unattainable.[373] The
Greek word for Longingly is "Orego," which means to stretch
out, to reach after, to yearn for, or am eager for.[374]

Matthew Henry's Concise Commentary states that a gracious soul can take little satisfaction in God's courts if it does
not meet with God. The living never can take up their rest any-
where short of living with God. To appear before the Lord is
the desire of the upright as it is the dread of the hypocrite.[375]
The upright loves to spend quality time in the presence of the
Lord, communing with the Spirit of God in the secret place.
That is where we should all want to be as much as possible in

---

373. Longingly Merriam-Webster.com https://www.Merriam-Webster.com Accessed
January 2022
374. "Orego" Greek for the Word Longingly https://www.biblehub.com Accessed
January 2022
375. Matthew Henry's Concise Commentary https://www.biblehub.com Accessed
January 2022

the face of the Lord —soaking up His presence like never before because we need His presence to be effective in anything.

DECLARATIONS

I decree and declare that as the deer pants for the water brooks, my soul longs for You.

I decree and declare that I need God's presence daily.

Lord, help me to come into Your presence to find comfort for my weary soul.

Lord, I love to spend quality time in Your presence to soak up Your love.

Lord, protect me in the secret place from the troubles of this world.

Lord, I give You my first fruits in the morning before starting my day.

November 29th

*R*OMANS 12:12 (*AMP*), "*C*ONSTANTLY *rejoicing in hope (because of our confidence in Christ) steadfast and patient in distress, devoted in prayer (continually seeking wisdom, guidance, and strength.*"

Devoted in the Merriam Webster Dictionary is defined by being characterized by loyalty and devotion.[376] The Greek word for Devoted is "Proskartereo," which means to attend constantly, persevere, continue, steadfast, or wait on.[377]

Matthew Henry's Concise Commentary states God is honored by our hope and trust in Him, especially when we rejoice in that hope. He is served by not only working for Him but sitting still quietly when He wants us to suffer. Patience for God's sake is true piety. Those that rejoice in hope are likely to be patient in tribulation. We should not be cold in the duty of prayer, nor soon weary of it.[378] But we must (P.U.S.H.) pray until some-

376. Devoted Merriam-Webster.com https://www.Merriam-Webster.com Accessed January 2022
377. "Proskartereo" Greek word for Devoted https://wwwbiblehub.com Accessed January 2022
378. Matthew Henry's Concise Commentary https://www.Biblehub.com Accessed January 2022

thing happens, even when it seems like nothing is changing in the natural realm. Remember God is a Spirit and things form in the Spirit realm before they manifest in the natural realm. We must pray without ceasing because fervent prayer is the key to all breakthroughs.

PRAYER

Father God, in the name of Jesus, we come before You today to ask You to give me more patience when I am praying for something to manifest in my life or the life of others in Jesus' name. Lord, help me to lean and depend on You to make whatever I have been praying for come to pass in my life and in the life of others in Jesus' name. Lord, help us to see things the way You see them so we will know what to expect in the end. Lord, we are praying and have been praying a long time for healing in bodies in Jesus' name. Lord, we know that according to Your Word, we are healed by Your stripes in Jesus' name. Lord, reveal anything that may be holding up our healing and deliverance in Jesus' name. Amen.

November 30th

1 Corinthians 13:9-10 (AMP), "For we know in part, and we prophesy in part (for our knowledge is fragmentary and incomplete). 10. "But when that which is complete and perfect comes, that which is incomplete and partial will pass away."

Prophesy in the Merriam Webster Dictionary is defined as to utter by or as if by divine inspiration.[379] The Greek word for Prophesy is "Propheteia," which means prophecy, prophesying, the gift of communicating and enforcing revealed truth.[380]

We prophesy in part and we know in part because our knowledge is only what God shows us. He doesn't always give us all the information we need at one time. He will give us just enough to encourage us to keep holding on. When we make it to heaven, we will not need to know in part because everything will be revealed to us. Prophesy comes to edify, encourage, warn, instruct, and rebuke. We must know the timing and

379. Prophesy Merriam-Webster.com Https://www.Merriam-Webster.com Accessed January 2022
380. "Propeteia" Greek for Prophesy https://www.Biblehub.com Accessed January 2022

seasons of God so we can be in proper alignment with Him. We want to be at the right place at the right time to get the right results. That is why it is so important to have an intimate relationship with God so He can tell us what we need to know to stay in position and alignment with Him.

DECLARATIONS

I decree and declare that I will stay in position and in alignment with God.

I will prophesy to edify the church by foretelling the future and speaking a message from God to the people.

I will write down my prophecies and pray over them.

I will not let the enemy steal what God has promised me through prophecy.

I will stay in close fellowship with God to hear what He is telling me.

I will decree and declare over my prophecies until they manifest in my life.

December 1st

*J*AMES 4:7 (AMP), "So submit to (the authority of) God, Resist the devil (stand firm against him) and he will flee from you."

Resist in the Merriam Webster dictionary is defined as to withstand the force or effect of.[381] The Greek word for Resist is "Anthistemi," which means to set against, oppose, or resist.[382]

When we submit to God and His Word, we resist sin and temptation, then use the Word of God against the enemy when he comes to bother you. That is why it is so important to know the Word and have it in your heart. So, you can use it when the enemy comes to assault you, by speaking the Zoe life over your situation. The enemy will not stay around when He hears God's Word. You can see that happening when Jesus fasted 40 days in the wilderness before going into ministry. The enemy came to Him to get Him to change some stones into bread. Jesus told the enemy that it was written that man should not live by bread alone, but by every word that proceed out of the mouth of God.

---

381. Resist Merriam-Webster.com https://www.biblehub.com Accessed January 2022
382. "Anthistemi" Greek word for Resist https://www.biblehub.com Accessed January 2022

God's Word is life and it is power. It is fire and like a hammer that breaks the rock into pieces. The Word will repel the enemy's advances toward you.

DECLARATIONS

I decree and declare the Word of God over my life and body in Jesus' name.

I will resist the devil by using the Word of God on Him.

Resist the devil and he will flee from you.

Knowing the Word of God is beneficial to my breakthrough in Jesus' name.

I will hide the Word of God in my heart, so I do not sin against God by falling into unrepented sin.

The Word of God is like a consuming fire and a hammer that breaks the rock into pieces.

December 2nd

PSALM 19:7-8 (AMP), "⁷ *The law of the LORD is perfect (flawless), restoring and refreshing the soul; The statutes of the LORD are reliable and trustworthy, making the wise simple.*"⁸. "*The precepts of the LORD are right, The commandment of the LORD is pure, enlightening the eyes.*"

The Law of the Lord is when we draw near to God, He promises to draw near to us. His Word is perfect, true, reliable, and fair.[383] The Greek word for the Law of the Lord is "Nomos," which means divine laws, that which is assigned, or custom.[384]

These scriptures are full of adjectives used to describe what God's Word is. All of these can give His Word new meaning to you. God's Word covers every aspect of our lives and the things that we need. God's Word is not lacking in any way. So, if we have issues in our lives, it has nothing to do with His Word. Could it be that we have something wrong with our understanding of the Word, where we don't get what we need from it when we

383. Law of the Lord https://www.lovegodgreatly.com Accessed January 2022
384. "Nomos" Greek word for Law of the Lord https://www.biblehub.com Accessed January 2022

read and study it? The Word of God reveal God's saving grace. God's law is perfect and complete. God uses His Word for conversion. God's Word is true and can be trusted because He is faithful. The truth is hidden to those who are wise (proud) in their own eyes. But for those who are humble, the Word give them wisdom and leads to salvation and repentance.[385]

PRAYER

Lord, we pray for everyone reading this devotional on today. Open up their understanding, so they can see that the Word of God has everything that they need in it. Lord, help them to see that the Your Word is reliable and trustworthy. Lord, help them to see that the Word of God is true and it was written by the leading and guiding of the Holy Spirit. Lord, help them to see that Your Word is flawless. You didn't leave anything out. Everything concerning their lives is covered in certain chapters in the Bible. Lord, help them to see that the Words in these pages are life and power. It will restore them when they have been broken in their hearts and spirits. Lord, teach and help them know that the Word of God is right, stands strong, and will not fail them. If they would only put their full trust in You and in Your Word, they can walk in peace in the midst of what is going on around them. Lord, help them to realize that the Word of God is eye-opening to those who don't try to lean to their own understanding, but they trust God to make things happen in their lives. Lord, help them to know that true wisdom is found in the Word of God and not in worldly wisdom. Lord, show them if they hide the Word of God in their hearts, they will not

385. Wisdom Merriam-Webster.com https://www.Merriam-Webster.com Accessed January 2022

sin against You. Lord, let them know that You need total sur-render from them to walk in this level of peace in their lives. Lord, most of all, let them know that a life apart from You will lead them in the wrong direction. Lord, touch their hearts so they can surrender right now to You, and be called a son or daughter of God in Jesus' name. Amen.

December 3rd

ROVERBS 4:7-8 (AMP), "⁷ The beginning of wisdom is: Get (skillful and godly) wisdom (it is preeminent)! And with all your acquiring, get understanding (actively seek spiritual discernment, mature comprehension, and logical interpretation). ⁸ "Prize wisdom (and exalt her), and she will exalt you; She will honor you if you embrace her."

Wisdom in the Merriam Webster Dictionary is defined as knowledge that is gained by having many experiences in life.[386] The Greek word for Wisdom is "Sophia," which means wisdom, insight, skill (human or divine), or intelligence.[387]

We need Godly wisdom more than anything else because with it, we are being led by the Holy Spirit and not doing anything in our own strength. We are leaning and relying on God for everything. God will lead us on the right path if we ask Him what we need to do in our lives and the lives of others. The wisdom of God doesn't go against His Word. Godly wisdom comes

---

386. Wisdom Merriam-Webster.com https://www.Merriam-Webster.com Accessed January 2022
387. "Sophia" Greek word for Wisdom https://www.biblehub.com Accessed January 2022

directly from the Word of God and you will not go wrong if you stick to it about everything. If we need wisdom, we are to ask God for it and He will give us as much as we need. Just like King Solomon asked for wisdom and God gave it to Him. Wisdom is worth more than any amount of money. We are to teach our children and grandchildren what the Word of God declares, which is true wisdom. If we don't teach them from home, the world will teach them the twisted version of it. That is why we must train them up while they are young. Teach them before they get introduced to the twisted version of wisdom.

DECLARATIONS

I decree and declare that I will ask God for wisdom, so I will know the right thing to do at all times.

I decree and declare that wisdom is the principal thing and, in all things, I will get an understanding.

Getting Godly wisdom early in life is important and must not be neglected.

I will train up my child while they are young in the Word of God, so when they get old, they will not depart from the faith.

I decree and declare that it is my job to train my child and grandchild about God and His Word.

I will not lean on my own understanding (worldly wisdom) about anything in my life.

December 4th

PROVERBS 8:13 (AMP), "THE (reverent) fear and worshipful awe of the LORD includes the hatred of evil; Pride and arrogance and the evil way, And the perverted mouth, I hate."

Reverent in the Merriam-Webster Dictionary is formal: honor or respect that is felt for or shown to someone or something.[388] The Greek Word for Reverent is "Eulabeia," which means fear of God, piety, or holy caution.[389]

The offer for wisdom is held out to those who fear God. Coming to wisdom requires coming to God and turning away from all God hates, such as evil, pride, and arrogance. There should not be all types of communication coming out of our mouths. Bitter and sweet water should not be coming from the same fountain. We have to give up our old man and the deeds of him to receive the new man, the one that has been born again and full of the Holy Ghost. We have often grieved

388. Reverent Merriam-Webster.com Https://www.Merriam-Webster.com Accessed January 2022
389. "Eulabeia" Greek word for Reverent https://www.biblehub.com Accessed January 2022

the Holy Spirit that lives inside us because we fail to practice self-control and put a bridle on our tongues. A person with a perverted mouth will say all manner of evil out their mouth with little or no conviction about it. If the Holy Spirit is leading you, there should be no way that your soul or body should be leading unless you have overridden the Holy Spirit. The red flags are flying high, and all the bells are ringing, but you refuse to be silenced at this point when you know that you are out of control. True repentance is needed if you have gone too far in perverted speech. Wisdom is holding your peace. Let God deal with the situations and people.

PRAYER

Father God, in the name of Jesus, we come before You today to ask that You forgive me for overriding the Holy Spirit when He told me to hush and leave the room the other day. I allowed the enemy to goad me on and did something that I am totally ashamed of. Lord, help me to hold my tongue and be obedient when I know I am being tricked by the enemy. I will not grieve the Holy Spirit and do something that will dishonor God. Lord, create in me a clean heart and renew a right spirit in me. Lord, forgive me for going to that lady's house, calling her out, fighting her, and calling her everything but a child of God. I allowed the enemy to pull me far below the snake line and now have hurt my witness with those standing around. Lord, please forgive me and help me control the spirit of anger that wants to rob me of my Destiny in You. Lord help me to apologize and humble myself so I can be delivered from my past mistakes in Jesus' name. Amen.

December 5th

*P*ROVERBS 10: 3 (AMP), *"The LORD will not allow the righteous to hunger (God will meet all his needs). But He will reject and cast away the craving of the wicked."*

Wicked in the Merriam Webster Dictionary is defined as disposed to or marked by mischief, causing or likely causing harm, distress, or trouble.[390] The Greek word for Wicked is "Poneroteros,"which more wicked.[391]

Matthew Poole's Commentary says though the righteous may be poor, the Lord will not suffer him to want what is needful for spiritual life. Those who are fervent in spirit, serving the Lord, are likely to be rich in faith, and rich in good works. Those that fear the Lord shall not want any good thing and at least while they suffer, it does not arise from the wrath of God. Nor can it separate them from the Love of God and Christ Jesus.[392]

---

390. Wicked Merriam-Webster.com https://www.Merriam-Webster.com Accessed January 2022
391. "Poneros" Greek word for Wicked https://www.biblestudytool.com Accessed January 2022
392. Matthew Henry's Concise Commentary https://www.biblehub.com Accessed January 2022

DECLARATIONS

I decree and declare that the Lord will not allow the righteous to hunger spiritually.

He will reject and cast away the craving of the wicked.

I decree and declare that I will not be listed among the wicked in Jesus' name.

I decree and declare that I am fervent in spirit in Jesus' name.

I decree and declare that I will serve the Lord all the days of my life in Jesus' name.

I decree and declare that I will always be rich in faith and will walk in extraordinary faith.

December 6th

ISAIAH 38:21 (AMP), "NOW Isaiah had said, "Have them take a cake of figs and rub it (as an ointment) on the inflamed spot, that he may recover."

Ointment in the Merriam Webster Dictionary is defined as a salve or unguent for application to the skin.[393] The Greek word for Ointment is "Muron,"which means anointing-oil, or ointment.[394]

The Prophet Isaiah was sent to Hezekiah by God. Hezekiah was sick and at the point of death. The Prophet Isaiah gave him a message from God, "For the Lord says this, "Set your house in order and prepare a will, for you shall die and will not live." Hezekiah turned his face to the wall, prayed, reminded God how he had walked before Him in faithfulness and truth with a whole heart devoted to Him. God gave the Word again to Isaiah and he went back and told Hezekiah that God had heard his prayer, seen his tears, and would add fifteen years to his life.

393. Ointment Merriam-Webster.com https://www.Merriam-Webster.com Accessed January 2022
394. "Muron" Greek word for Ointment https://www.biblehub.com Accessed January 2022

Also, Isaiah told the servants what kind of ointment to put on the sores on his body to heal and dry them up.

PRAYER

Father God, in the name of Jesus, we come before You today to ask that You would prolong the life of your daughter or son. They have served You for many years, being faithful and walking in your truth which is the Word of God. God, give them many more years so they can live to a ripe old age in Jesus' name. Lord, we bind premature death off of their lives right now in Jesus' name. Lord, You made their bodies and know how they are supposed to function in Jesus' name. Lord, let the Balm of Gilead saturate their hearts and minds and bring about newness in their bodies and lives in Jesus' name. Lord, we command their bodies to align with the Word of God on today in Jesus' name. Lord, whatever is broken in their bodies and lives, we ask that You fix it and make them complete in Jesus' name. Lord, we depend on You to bring them through this sickness that they are going through in Jesus' name. Lord, let Your will be done in their lives and bodies in Jesus' name. Lord, speak life over them now and let the resurrecting power of God saturate them and make them new from this day forward in Jesus' name. Amen.

December 7th

*I*saiah 40:31 (AMP), "But those who wait for the LORD (who expect, look for, and hope in Him). Will gain new strength and renew their power; They will lift up their wings (and rise up close to God) like eagles (rising toward the sun); They will run and not become weary, They will walk and not grow tired."

Strength in the Merriam Webster Dictionary is defined as the quality that allows someone to deal with problems in a determined and effective way.[395] The Greek Word for Strength is "Ischus," which means strength, power, might, force, or ability.[396]

Where God has begun the work of grace, He will perfect it and help those who are humble and dependent on Him. They shall run the way of God's commandments cheerfully. Let us watch against unbelief, pride, and self-confidence. If we go forth in our own strength, we shall faint and utterly fall; but having

395. Strength Merriam-Webster.com https://www.Merriam-Webster.com Accessed January 2022
396. "Ichus" Greek word for Strength https://www.biblehub.com Accessed January 2022

our hearts and hopes in heaven, we shall be carried above all difficulties. We shall lay hold of the prize of our high calling in Christ Jesus. Waiting on the Lord means waiting for His help and trust in Him and putting our hope and confidence in Him. God will renew our strength as we lean and trust in Him.

The people of God should trust in the Lord and in turn, they will become strong in faith. They will gain the knowledge to contend with their spiritual foes and gain victory over their sins. God gives us the strength to be able to do it all when we ask Him to.

DECLARATIONS

I decree and declare that God has begun a great work in me and He will complete it.

I decree and declare that I will walk in humility and be totally dependent on Him.

I decree and declare that I shall lay hold of the prize of the High calling in Christ Jesus.

I decree and declare that God will renew our strength as we lean and trust in Him.

I decree and declare that as I trust the Lord, my faith will continue to get stronger and stronger.

I decree and declare that I will use the Word of God against the enemy and he will flee from me seven ways.

December 8th

ISAIAH 41:10 (AMP), "Do not fear (anything), for I am with you; Do not be afraid, for I am your God. I will strengthen you, be assured I will help you. I will certainly take hold of you with my righteous right hand (a hand of justice, of power, of victory, of salvation)."

Fear in the Merriam Webster Dictionary is defined as false evidence appearing real. It is also an unpleasant emotion caused by being aware of danger or a feeling of being afraid.[397] The Greek Word for Fear is "Phobos," which means panic, flight, fear, the causing of fear, terror, alarm, or cause of fear.[398]

Matthew Henry's Concise Commentary states that God speaks with tenderness; Fear thou not, for I am with thee; not only within call, but present with thee. Art thou weak? I will strengthen thee. Art thou in want of friends? I will help thee in the time of need. Art thou ready to fall? I will uphold thee

---

397. Fear Merriam-Webster.com https://www.Merriam-Webster.com Accessed January 2022
398. "Phobos" Greek word for fear https://www.biblehub.com Accessed January 2022

with the right hand which is full of righteousness, dealing forth rewards, and punishments.[399]

Fear is false evidence appearing real, meaning it is not real. The enemy has played it up in our minds and imaginations and we overreact before anything has happened. The enemy brings fear in the people of God, so they will remain stuck in one place instead of moving toward their destinies. The Word of God declares that we will not have the spirit of fear but of power, love, and a sound mind. So, we curse fear at the root in Jesus' name. Amen.

<u>PRAYER</u>

Father God, in the name of Jesus, we come before You today to cast down the spirit of fear and all of its symptoms of torment in Jesus' name. We bind the tricks of Satan, and we loose the resurrecting power of Jesus to build low self-esteem until they have confidence in God's ability to help them with anything that they need help in. I decree we will not let fear stop us from moving forward in God and doing what we are supposed to be doing in Jesus' name. We send fear back to the pit of hell from where it came from in Jesus' name. We loose the peace of God over this person's life and ministry in Jesus' name. Lord, let them know that they are not alone because they have the Holy Spirit living on the inside of them in Jesus' name. Lord, let them know that all they have to do is call upon the name of Jesus and You will assist them in whatever they need to be done so You can get the glory out of the situation in Jesus' name.

399. Matthew Henry's Concise Commentary https://www.biblehub.com Accessed January 2022

Lord, help us to get healed and delivered from things that are from the unknown and just keep all our trust in You Jesus from this day forward in Jesus' name. Amen.

December 9th

*H*EBREWS 4:11 (AMP), "LET us therefore make every effort to enter that rest (of God, to know and experience it for ourselves), so that no one will fall by following the same example of disobedience (as those who died in the wilderness)."

Rest in the Merriam Webster Dictionary is defined as a peace of mind or spirit.[400] The Greek Word for Rest is "Anapauo," which means to give rest, give intermission labor, or take my ease.[401]

God wants us to rest in Him by giving Him everything that is troubling us and allowing Him to work it out in His own timing. We must walk in obedience and do what He is telling us to do while waiting instead of being distracted from our tasks. The enemy has many distractions to get us off focus, so we must be very careful and not allow distractions to keep us off task.

400. Rest Merriam-Webster.com https://www.Merriam-Webster.com Accessed January 2022
401. "Anapauo" Greek word for Rest https://www.biblehub.com Accessed January 2022

DECLARATIONS

I decree and declare that I will not lose focus on what is important in this season of my life.

I decree and declare that I will walk in obedience to what God has told me to do.

I decree and declare that I will rest and trust God to work everything out for my good.

I decree and declare that I will move forward in the finishers anointing toward victory.

I decree and declare that I will get busy about my Father's business.

I put all of my complete trust in God to move on my behalf.

December 10th

*H*EBREWS 4:12(AMP), "FOR THE word of God is living and active and full of power (making it operative, energizing, and effective). It is sharper than any two-edged sword, penetrating as far as the division of soul and Spirit (the completeness of a person), and of the joints and marrow (the deepest parts of our nature), exposing and judging the very thoughts and intentions of the heart."

Power in the Merriam Webster Dictionary is defined as the ability to act or produce an effect.[402] The Greek word for Power is "Dunamis," which means miraculous power, might, strength, or marvelous works.[403]

The Holy Scriptures are the Word of God. The Spirit of God is in His Word, and when someone hears the Word of God, it convicts them of sin in their lives and leads them to repentance. The Word convinces powerfully, converts, and comforts powerfully. It makes a soul that has long been proud become

402. Power Merriam-Webster.com https://www.Merriam-Webster.com Accessed January 2022
403. "Dunamis" Greek word for Power https://www.biblehub.com Accessed January 2022

humble and a perverse spirit become meek and obedient. Sinful habits a person has been rooted in are separated and cut off by this sword. The Word will show the sinner all that is in their heart. Our lives should reflect the Word; if it is not, then we are not allowing the Word to change us. We are supposed to be applying the Word of God to our lives so that our lives can start lining up with the Word of God. If it is not, we are trying to hold onto some unconfessed sin that separates us from a true relationship with Jesus.

PRAYER

Father God, in the name of Jesus, we come before You today to release every sin that so easily besets us. So that the Word of God can change us as we read and hear it in Jesus's name. Lord, forgive us for getting comfortable in our sin, that the enemy makes it seems like something that we will miss when we surrender our lives to You, Jesus. Lord, I take the sword of the Spirit and cut anything from my life that does not need to be there in Jesus's name. Lord, I will allow You to deliver me from any perverse thinking or talk in Jesus's name. Lord, I will take God's Word and apply it to my life every day in Jesus' name. Lord, I will trust You to do what You need to do in me to perfect me for Your purpose for my life in Jesus's name. Amen.

December 11th

PSALM 18:39-40 (AMP), "*[39] For you encircled me with strength for the battle; You have subdued under me those who rose up against me.*" *[40.] "You have also made my enemies turn their backs to me (in defeat), And I silenced and destroyed those who hated me.*"

Encircled in the Merrian Webster Dictionary is defined as to form a circle around.[404] The Greek Word for Encircled is "Kukloo," which means to encircle, besiege, or surround.[405]

David was girthed in strength, courage, and valor from the Lord. So is the Spirit of love, power, and a sound mind which we have because of Christ. The Lord has subdued those that have risen up against David. And His enemies turn their backs because they were defeated with the help of the Lord. The same things go for us today. We are victorious because we are in Christ and He has already won the battle. We can have courage because of who we represent and belong. We do not have to

404. Enriched Merriam-Webster.com https://www.Merriam-Webster.com Accessed January 2022
405. "Kukloo" Greek word for Enriched https://www.biblehub.com Accessed January 2022

sit back in fear and timidity because the Lion of Judah resides in each of us. We have nothing to fear because God has us all hedged in and covered under His blood. So, we can be bold prayer warriors, speaking thus said the Lord without the fear of retaliation from the enemy. We will not just lay down and play dead but walk and operate in the authority God has given us.

DECLARATIONS

I decree and declare that we are victorious in Christ Jesus.

I decree and declare that I will not fear, but do what God has told me to do for the Kingdom.

I decree and declare that no weapon formed against me shall prosper in Jesus' name.

I decree and declare that You have encircled me with strength through the battles I am going through.

Lord, thank You for subduing all those that have risen up against me in Jesus's name.

Lord, thank You for making my enemies flee before me seven ways. They have turned their backs on me and fled.

December 12th

ATTHEW 16:26 (AMP), "*FOR what will it profit a man if he gains the whole world (wealth, fame, success) but forfeits his soul? Or what will a man give in exchange for his soul?*"

Forfeits in the Merriam Webster Dictionary is defined as to lose or lose the right to, especially by some error, offense, or crime.[406] The Greek Word for Forfeits is "Zemioo," which means to damage or suffer loss.[407]

What would profit a man if he puts everything in the things of the world but died without God and went to hell. There is no redemption in hell. A true disciple of Christ follows Him in duty and glory. He is the one that walks in the same way Christ walked in, is led by his Spirit, and treads in His steps whithersoever He goes. We must take up our cross and place every trouble that bothers us there. Barnes Notes of the Bible states that thousands lose their soul for the most trifling gain or

406. Forfeit Merriam-Webster.com https://www.Merriam-Webster.com Accessed January 2022
407. "Zemioo" Greek word for Forfeit https://www.biblehub.com Accessed January 2022

the most worthless indulgences in the world. One soul is worth more than all the world. Let us learn rightly to value our souls; Christ is their only Savior.[408]

PRAYER

Father God, in the name of Jesus, I come today to give my life to You. Lord, I know according to Your Word that if I leave this world without You, in hell I will lift up my eyes. So, Lord, I don't want to spend eternity in hell, so I am giving my life over to You so that when I stop breathing, I will wake up in glory with Jesus. Lord, forgive me of all of my sins. Knowingly and unknowingly, though, and deed, omission, and commission God. Lord, save me from a place where there will be gnashing of teeth throughout eternity in Jesus' name. Lord, I do not want what the world has to offer, but I want everything You have to offer me. So, Lord, I ask You into my heart to live and reside in me from this day forward in Jesus's name. Lord, thank You for saving me and bringing me into the sheepfold in Jesus's name. Lord, I give up wealth, fame, and success to have an intimate relationship with You in Jesus' name. Amen.

408. Barnes Noted of the Bible, https://www.biblehub.com Accessed January 2022

December 13th

✣

*R*OMANS 6:23 (AMP), "FOR *the wages of sin is death, but the free gift of God (that is, He remarkable, overwhelming gift of grace to believers) is eternal life in Christ Jesus our Lord."*

Grace in the Merriam Webster Dictionary is defined as unmerited divine assistance given to humans for their regeneration or sanctification.[409] The Greek word for Grace is "Charis," which means grace, kindness, blessing brought to man by Jesus Christ, gratitude, or favor.[410]

For the payment of sin is death. God gives us His grace and we have to activate it by our faith. Grace is more than unmerited favor. It is the ability to do what we couldn't do in the flesh. God gives us His unmerited ability to love those who are unlovable or hard to get along with. God gives us His unmerited power to treat our neighbors right regardless of the color of their skin. Grace is for the believer and helps the believer to believe God at His Word concerning a matter.

409. Grace Merriam-Webster.com Https://www.Merriam-Webster.com Accessed January 2022
410 "Charis" Greek for Grace https://www.biblehub.com Accessed January 2022

DECLARATIONS

I decree and declare that the wages of sin are still death.

Lord, I thank You for Your amazing grace that saved a wretch like me.

Lord, Your Word declares that Your grace is sufficient. It is strength that is made perfect in our weakness.

Lord, Thank You for giving me Your never-ending grace so I can love people the right way.

Grace is more than unmerited favor.

I will use the Grace of God to treat people right and with respect regardless of their skin color in Jesus' name.

December 14th

ROMANS 9:15-16 (AMP), "15 For He says to Moses, "I WILL HAVE MERCY ON WHOMEVER I HAVE MERCY, AND I WILL HAVE COMPASSION ON WHOMEVER I HAVE COMPASSION." 16. "So then God's choice is not dependent on human will, nor on human effort (the totality of human striving), but on God who shows mercy (to whomever He chooses it is His sovereign gift)."

Sovereign in the Merriam Webster Dictionary is defined as one possessing or held to possess supreme political power or sovereignty.[411] The Greek Word for Sovereign is "Pantokrator," which means ruler of all, ruler of the universe, or the almighty.[412]

God does not owe any of us salvation. He has mercy on us despite the way we act, not because of how we act. The Lord does not wish for us to perish but for all of us to come to repentance. But He also says that no one comes to Jesus unless His

411. Sovereign Merriam-Webster.com https://www.Merriam-Webster.com Accessed January 2022
412."Pantokrator" Greek word for Sovereign https://www.biblehub.com Accessed January 2022'

Father draws them. He has mercy on whomever He desires and hardens whom He desires. God has a right to do as He pleases, God both draws and hardens, and God is worthy to be praised and worshiped are made known in creation, so man is without an excuse. Why are some saved and some condemned? Everyone deserves condemnation; it is only by God's grace that anyone is saved. A person must want to be saved because God will not force them to serve Him. It has to be their choice to serve Him and give their lives to Him.

PRAYER

Father God, in the name of Jesus, I come before You today to thank You for Your mercy and for not giving me what I deserve. Lord, thank You for having compassion on me when I have made mistakes and walked away for You. Lord, I thank You for drawing me back close to You by Your Spirit. Lord, I ask You to forgive me of sins knowingly and unknowingly, in thoughts and deeds in Jesus' name. Lord, I don't want anything holding me back from a close relationship with You. Lord, I thank You for not leaving me out from under Your covering in Jesus' name. Lord, I thank You for Your amazing grace that has saved a wretch like me. Lord, thank You for redeeming me back to You because of Your perfect sacrifice in Jesus' name. Amen.

December 15th

*R*OMANS 13: 11 (AMP), *"Do this, knowing that this is a critical time. It is already the hour for you to awaken from your sleep (of spiritual compla-cency); for our salvation is nearer to us now than when we first believed (in Christ)."*

Critical in the Merriam Webster Dictionary is defined as being or relating to or being the stage of disease at which an abrupt change for the better or worse may be expected.[413] The Greek Word for Critical is "Kritikos," which means able to judge or discern.[414]

Matthew Henry's Concise Commentary says that we are to wake up out of our sleep and slumber now. We must wake up from carnality, security, sloth, negligence, and spiritual death. Consider the time that we are in. These are busy times and per-ilous times. Salvation is right at hand. There is no need to wait because we are nearing our journey's end. We are to make our-

413. Critical Merriam-Webster.com Https://www.Merriam-Webster.com Accessed January 2022
414. "Kritikos" Greek word for Critical https://www.biblehub.com Accessed January 2022

selves ready the night is far spent and the day is at hand. We must cast off the sinful works of darkness. We must dress our souls and put on the armor of light. If we are unarmed, then we are undressed. Put on Christ that includes all.[415]

DECLARATIONS

I decree and declare that I will get ready and stay ready with Christ.

Lord, I give my life to You and ask that You would live inside of me and make me a new creature in You.

Lord, I cast off all the sinful works of darkness out of my life.

Lord, I close every door I have opened to the sinful works of darkness.

Lord, we all need to hurry because we are nearing our journey's end.

Lord, I wake up out of carnality, slothfulness, negligence, and spiritual deadness to be set on fire by Your Spirit.

---

415. Matthew Henry's Concise Commentary https://www.biblehub.com Accessed January 2022

December 16th

*P*SALM 24:1 (AMP), "THE EARTH is the LORD'S and the fullness of it. The world, and those who dwell in it."

Earth in the Merriam Webster Dictionary is defined as the planet on which we live that is third in order from the sun.[416] The Greek word for Earth is "Ge," which means the earth, land, soil, region, country, and inhabitants of a region.[417]

The Amplified Study Bible states we should have a heightened sense of stewardship to care for God's creation. We should look to God to understand what is important and what is not important. Seeing God's creation every day should help make praise and thanksgiving a way of life. It should also help us desire to understand God's redemptive acts in history and our lives.[418]

416. Earth Merriam-Webster.com https://www.Merriam-Webster.com Accessed January 2022
417. "Ge" Greek word for Earth https://www.biblehub.com Accessed January 2022
418. The Amplified Study Bible by Zondervan @ 2017 Accessed January 2022

God also made everyone in the world, regardless of race, nationality, creed, color, big, small, short, or tall.

PRAYER

Father God, in the name of Jesus, I come before You today to thank You for creating and knowing me before I was even formed in my mother's womb. Lord, thank You for the trees and everything around me. Lord, thank You for the air that we breathe. Lord, thank You for gravity, so everything in the earth is not floating around weightless. Lord, thank You for food to eat, clothes on my back, and shoes on my feet. Lord, I thank You for being closed in my right mind. Lord, thank You for everything that I have. I Thank You for being able to feed myself, dress, bathe, and drive myself where I need to go. Lord, I have so much to thank You for in Jesus' name. Thank You for making man in Your own image and likeness in Jesus' name, Amen.

December 17th

MATTHEW 24:4-5 (AMP), " ⁴ *Jesus answered, "Be careful that no one misleads you (deceiving you and leading you into error)."* ⁵· *"For many will come in MY name (misusing it, and appropriating the strength of the name which belongs to Me), say, "I am the Christ (the Messiah, the Anointed), and they will mislead many."*

Misusing in the Merriam Webster Dictionary is defined as to use incorrectly, abuse, or mistreat.[419] The Greek Word for Misuse is "Apochresis," which means using up, abuse, or misuse.[420]

Here is a warning from the Word of God, to be careful that no one deceives and misleads you, causing you to err in your walk with God. Many false prophets and teachers will say that they are the Messiah and mislead many with their itching ears and those running to see signs and lying wonders. That is why we must study the Word to show ourselves approved so we can rightly divide the Word of truth. So, you will not be fooled or

---

419. Misusing Merriam-Webster.com https://www.Merriam-Webster.com Accessed January 2022
420. "Apochresis" Greek word for Misuse https://www.biblehub.com Accessed January 2022

misled by lying wonders. If it doesn't line up with the Word of God, then it is not true because God will not contradict His Word.

DECLARATIONS

I decree and declare that I will test the spirit by the Spirit so I will not be fooled or deceived.

I decree and declare that I will read and study the Bible so I will not be fooled by any lying wonders.

I decree and declare that I will not believe everything I see and hear without consulting the Holy Spirit about it.

I decree and declare that if the Holy Spirit gives me a red flag, I will not pursue a matter.

I will not ignore the red flags but take heed that I enter not in deception.

I will not have itching ears to follow any doctrines that sound like the truth but is not the truth

December 18th

*M*ATTHEW 24:35-36 (AMP), "³⁵ Heaven and earth (as now know) will pass away, but My words will not pass away." ³⁶· "But of that (exact) day and hour no one knows, not even the angels of heaven, nor the Son (in His humanity), but the Father alone."

Humanity in the Merriam Webster Dictionary is defined as compassionate, sympathetic, or generous, behavior or disposition, the state of being humane.[421] The Greek Word for Humanity is "Anthropos," which is a man, human, mankind, or one of the human races.[422]

Jesus does not know the exact time He shall return to earth for the second time. The Father knows the exact time that will be, so we need to get ready and stay ready because we don't know when He is coming. Nor do we know when death will come knocking on our doors, and we may not have time to get ready. So, if you are ready, do not allow anything or anyone to

421. Humanity Merriam-Webster.com https:/www.Merriam-Webster.com Accessed January 2022
422. "Anthroos" Greek word for Humanity Https://www.biblehub.com Accessed January 2022

pull you out of our Savior's arms. If you are not yet surrendered to Him, now is the time to take where you will spend eternity seriously because we can't mess this up. We got to get this right because after our hearts stop beating and our tongues are glued to the roof of our mouths, there will be no second chances to repent and get into right standing with God. So now is the time to run and not walk. Surrender your all to Jesus while there is still time.

PRAYER

Father God, in the name of Jesus, I come before You today just making sure that I am in right standing with You because after I leave this world, my fate will have been already sealed in heaven. Lord, I ask that You would forgive and reinstate me and place my name in the Lambs' Book of Life. I surrender everything unto You right now in Jesus' name. I have no more time to keep saying that I am not ready because no one knows for certain where death may strike. I want to be ready to see Jesus because it could be any day now. Lord, I bind premature death. I decree and declare that I will live a long and healthy life by leaning and depending on You, God. Lord, I know Your Word will not pass away because it is forever settled in heaven in Jesus' name. Amen.

December 19th

*M*ARK 4:22-23 (AMP), "²² *For nothing is hidden, except to be revealed; nor has anything been kept secret, but that it would come to light (that is, things are hidden only temporarily, until the appropriate time comes for them to be known.* ²³· "*If anyone has ears to hear, let him hear and heed my words.*"

Temporarily in the Merriam Webster Dictionary is defined as during a limited time.[423] The Greek Word for Temporarily is "Proskarios," which means for a season, temporary, or a limited time of opportunity.[424]

The teaching of Jesus always reveals the motives of the human heart. He is saying here that nothing is hidden and everything that we think is hidden will eventually come to the light. When things are hidden, they are only hidden temporarily until the appropriate time comes for them to be known. Matthew Henry's Concise Commentary states that this is the parable of

423. Temporarily Merriam-Webster.com https://www.Merriam-Webster.com Accessed January 2022
424. "Proskairos" Greek word for Temporarily https://www.biblehub.com Accessed January 2022

the good seed and it shows the manner in which the Kingdom of God makes progress in the world. Let the Word of Christ have the place it ought to have in a soul. The seed grows gradually: first the blade, then the ear, and after that, the full corn in the ear. When it is sprung up, it will go forward.[425]

DECLARATIONS

I decree and declare that for nothing that is hidden, except to be revealed in Jesus' name.

I decree and declare that if anyone has ears, let him hear and heed my words.

Everything hidden will eventually come to the light at the right time.

The Kingdom of heaven is at hand.

The good seed parable shows how the Kingdom of God makes progress in the world.

I decree and declare that I will hide the Word of God in my heart, so I will not sin against thee.

I decree and declare that the Word of God and the Kingdom of God are going forward on the earth.

---

425. Matthew Henry's Concise Commentary https://www.biblehub.com Accessed January 2022

December 20th

ARK 5: 23, 41-42 (AMP), "²³ And begged anxiously with Him, saying, "My little daughter is at the point of death; (please) come and lay Your hands on her, so that she will be healed and live. ⁴¹· "Taking the child's hand, He said (tenderly) to her, "Talitha Kum!" which translated (from Aramaic) means, "Little girl, I say to you, get up! ⁴²· "The little girl immediately got up and began to walk, for she was twelve years old. And immediately they (who witnessed the child's resurrection) were overcome with great wonder and utter amazement."

Anxiously in the Merriam Webster Dictionary is defined as afraid or nervous, especially about what may happen, feeling anxiety.[426] The Greek Word for anxiously is "Merimnao," which means to be anxious, to care for, to be over-anxious, or distracted.[427]

426. Anxiously Merriam-Webster.com https://www.Merriam-Webster.com Accessed January 2022
427."Merimnao" Greek word for Anxious https://www.biblehub.com Accessed January 2022

Jairus had a need and he had heard about Jesus. He believed that Jesus could heal his daughter. He came to Jesus to ask Him to come and pray for His daughter so that she would be healed. Jesus was going with Jairus when He ran into the lady with the issue of blood. She was healed of her blood flow in an instance. Before Jesus could get to Jairus's house, the mourners came to tell him that his daughter had already died and there was no reason to trouble the Master any longer. Jesus told him only to believe and have faith that she was asleep and not dead. Jesus put everyone out of the room except Peter, James, and John, and the child's parents. He called the young girl and she awakened and was healed from her sickness. Jesus is performing the same miracles today. Whatever sickness that is plaguing you, Jesus is well able to heal you of every manner of sickness and disease there is. All you have to do is call out to Him and He will come and heal you of your infirmities.

PRAYER

Father, God, in the name of Jesus, we come before You today asking that You heal all manner of sickness and diseases plaguing Your people right now in Jesus's name. Lord, we ask that You would heal the COVID-19 virus, Delta Variant, and Omicron Variant. Wipe it out from our land. Lord, heal bodies from the top of their heads to the soles of their feet in Jesus' name. Lord, we command cancer to dry up by the root in Jesus' name. Lord, we command lupus and autoimmune diseases to dry up at the root in Jesus' name. Lord, we pray that You would go deep down in our immune systems and give us a greater immune system so that our bodies can fight off any foreign substance that will try to bring any illnesses to Your people in Jesus' name. Lord, we pray that You would heal our land of all chemical warfare right now in Jesus' name. Amen.

December 21st

TIMOTHY 1:7 (AMP), "*FOR God did not give us a spirit of timidity or cowardice or fear, but (He has given us a spirit) of power and of love and of sound judgment and personal discipline (abilities that result in a calm, well-balanced mind and self-control).*"

Timidity in the Merriam Webster Dictionary is defined as lacking in courage, self-confidence, or shy.[428] The Greek Word for Timidity is "Delia," which means cowardice.[429]

God did not give us the Spirit of fear. Fear comes from the enemy Satan because he wants you to focus on things that don't even matter. He begins to talk to you and tell you lie after lie until you start to believe them. God wants you to have a stable mind. That is why we need to put on God's full armor every morning, from head to toe. We will first put on the helmet of Salvation. It covers our minds and thoughts. We have to pray, decree, and declare over our minds. Say something like this: I

---

428. Timidity Merriam-Webster.com https://www.Merriam-Webster.com Accessed January 2022
429. "Delia" Greek word for Timidity Https://www.biblehub.com Accessed January 2022

have the mind of Christ. I have a sound mind. I have the mind of a genius. I can think of many witty ideas and dreams that will be a blessing to my family and me and the Kingdom of God. I have a photographic memory; I can remember anything at any given time. Keep speaking the Word of God over your mind and you will have a good mind. Fear is false, evidence, appearing, real the enemy wants to shut you up before you can reach your full potential in God. That is why he is fighting you so hard that you will lose your faith. If you lose your faith, there is no way that you can believe God for anything. Faith is the currency for the Kingdom and for getting prayers answered, so don't fall for the enemy's bait. Believe God at His Word because He is a God that cannot lie no matter how hard He tried.

DECLARATIONS

I decree and declare that I will believe God at His Word.

The devil is a liar and the truth is not in him.

Anything that the enemy is saying about me or speaking to me is a lie because he can't tell the truth.

I am all that God has said I am and I will do what God has said I can do as I walk out in faith.

I bind the spirit of fear, timidity, and cowardice off of the people of God and they will let the lion roar through them.

I decree and declare that I have a sound mind and the mind of Christ in Jesus' name.

I loose the God kind of confidence on the people of God right now in Jesus' name.

December 22nd

MATTHEW 28:19 (AMP), "Go therefore and make disciples of all nations (help the people learn of Me, believe in Me, and obey My words), baptizing them in the name of the Father and of the Son and of the Holy Spirit."

Disciples in the Merriam Webster Dictionary is Christianity. According to the Gospel accounts, one of the twelve in the inner circle of Christ's followers.[430] The Greek Word for Disciples is "Mathetes," which means a disciple, a learner, or pupil.[431]

The Amplified Study Bible gives six compelling reasons for sharing our faith in Christ with those who have not experienced new life in Christ.

1. Because God has commanded us to do so. (Acts 1:8)

---

430. Disciples Merriam-Webster.com https://www.Merriam-Webster.com Accessed January 2022
431. Mathetes" Greek word for Disciples https://www.biblehub.com Accessed January 2022

2. Because it demonstrates our love for God. If we truly love Him, then we will keep His commandments. (John 14:15).

3. Because all are lost without Christ. (Romans 3:10,23)

4. This is God's chosen method: He could use angels, but He only uses redeemed sinners to tell lost sinners about Christ. (Romans 10:14-17, 1 Timothy 1:15)

5. Because God desires to save all people. (Acts 4:12, 1 Timothy 2:4, 2 Peter 3:9)

6. Because faith grows best when each generation conscientiously strives to pass it on to the next.[432]

PRAYER

Father God, in the name of Jesus, we come before You today asking if You would give us Your kind of confidence so we can further Your Kingdom so that You can get the glory out of everything that we do in Jesus' name. Lord, help us to always be in sync with Your will and Your way for our lives in Jesus' name. I bind the spirit of fear, intimidation, anxiety, and confusion off of Your people and loose the healing Balm of Gilead to everyone You have called into the ministry to be a disciple in Jesus' name. Lord, remove all of their fears and let them know that they will not have to try to do anything You have called them to do on their own. Lord, let them know that You are with them and have been with them from day one in Jesus' name. Lord, we ask that You would give them peace in the midst of the confusion in Jesus' name. Lord, help Your Son or daughter to know without a shadow of a doubt that You have their backs in Jesus' name. Lord, let them know that You are with them

432. The Amplified Study Bible by Zondervan @ 2017 Accessed January 2022

wherever they go in Jesus' name. Lord, let them know that You have called them for such a time as this in Jesus' name. Amen.

December 23rd

ECCLESIASTES 5: 19 (AMP), "Also, every man to whom God has given riches and possessions, He has also given the power and ability to enjoy them and to receive (this as) his (allotted) portion and to rejoice in his labor this is the gift of God (to him)."

Allotted in the Merriam Webster Dictionary is defined as assigned or distributed as a portion, share, or lot.[433] The Greek Word for Allotted is "Proskleroo," which means assign, by lot, allot, associate with, or follow as a disciple.[434]

God has given His people riches and possessions and the power and ability to enjoy them. So, this scripture lets you know that God wants His people to be blessed. We are blessed to be a blessing to others and not keep it all for ourselves. God will abundantly bless those whom He can trust with their finances. God can trust you to do what is right concerning your finances. He can trust you to give when He tells you to without

433. Allotted Merriam-Webster.com https://www.Merriam-Webster.com Accessed January 2022
434.   "Proskleroo" Greek Word for Allotted https://www.biblehub.com Accessed January 2022

questioning Him. He will tell you to give a large amount and you are so blessed in that area that you will not even miss that sizable offering. God's wish for His people is not for us to be poor, broke, busted, and disgusted. That is the route that the enemy wants for the people of God, but that is not God's will for our lives. Broke people can't help build up the Kingdom of God. Well off, wealthy, and those living in the abundance can. Amen.

DECLARATIONS

I decree and declare that the blessing of God maketh it rich and addeth no sorrow with it.

I decree and declare that I will be a lender and not a borrower in Jesus' name.

I decree and declare that I will have more than enough.

I decree and declare that I am walking in the overflow and victory in Jesus' name.

I decree and declare that my Father is rich and so are His children.

I decree and declare that I have a fortune 500 company in the making.

December 24th

*E*CCLESIASTES 7:9 (AMP), "Do not be eager in your heart to be angry, For anger dwells in the heart of fools."

Angry in the Merriam Webster Dictionary is defined as filled with anger, having a strong feeling of being upset or annoyed.[435] The Greek Word for Anger is "Orge," which means impulse, wrath, passion, punishment, vengeance, or anger.[436]

Do not continue to be angry. The Word of God declares be angry but sin not. Do not act out on your anger by hitting others or cussing people out. Anger is a destructive flood, working all kinds of havoc in our lives. It often leads us somewhere that we don't want to be. The enemy wants us to have periods of uncontrolled anger so we can act in our flesh. The acts of the flesh do not produce righteousness. If you are having issues with anger, then deliverance is needed in that area for you to get free of that spirit. Anger disrupts and disunites families and

435. Angry Merriam-Webster.com Https://www.Merriam-Webster.com Accessed January 2022
436. "Orge" Greek word for Angry https://www.biblehub.com Accessed January 2022

may even lead to murder. So, you have to be careful with this spirit because it could destroy many lives in the blink of an eye.

If you are dealing with this spirit, one of the sure ways to get rid of it is through fasting and prayer. You would fast from food for several days and drink liquids. Get some scriptures based on self-control and decree and declare them over your life. Be real with yourself about things in the past that you haven't been healed from. So true healing can take place in those areas as well. It will take some time, but you can get delivered from this spirit. Allow God to heal those wounded and painful areas in your heart so you can walk in total wholeness. It will take being honest with yourself to get healed from it.

PRAYER

Father God, in the name of Jesus, I come before You today to be real with You. God, I need help in this area of my life. I need to be rid of the past traumas, wounds, and pains of my past so I can get delivered from this spirit of anger that keeps gripping my life in Jesus' name. Lord, go deep down in my heart from my childhood and uproot all those weeds of bitterness from my parents. Lord, uproot the spirit of rejection from me because I felt like nobody wanted me and I was just a burden to my family in Jesus' name. Lord, uproot all the hurt and pain from losing my father at an early age through death or when he walked out and left us. Lord, help me to see myself as You see me in Jesus' name. Lord, help me walk in forgiveness toward those who hurt me. Lord, I release and forgive them so I can be free from this anger in Jesus' name. Amen.

December 25th

ISAIAH 1:18 (AMP), "COME now, and let us reason together, says the LORD, though your sins are like scarlet, they shall be as white as snow; Though they are red like crimson. They shall be like wool."

Scarlet in the Merriam Webster Dictionary is defined as grossly and glaringly offensive.[437] The Greek Word for Scarlet is "KoKKinos," which means crimson.[438]

We are a stiff-necked rebellious people who would rather do what we want when we want. Everybody wants the benefits of God's grace without accepting the accountability to God. Just as in the days of Isaiah, we ignore God's commands to care for the destitute and lose sight of God's requirements for justice and righteousness. The Amplified Study Bible states that each of us stands before God dirty and bloody, but we are still His people when we are clearly not ready to fellowship with a holy God. We need to be cleaned up first. Our God is a redeeming

---

437. Scarlet Merriam-Webster.com https://www.Merriam-Webster.com Accessed January 2022

438. "Kokkinos" Greek word for Scarlet https://www.biblehub.com Accessed January 2022

God who knows how to deal with sin. No rebellion goes beyond His reach. The remedy has to be on His terms. The first step in obedience is repentance, turning away from the direction we are going to see God.[439] God is there for us; He hasn't turned His back on us regardless of how many times we have messed up. He says as long as we walk with a repentant heart, He will forgive us and give us multiple chances to get it right. God is merciful to His creation, especially if He sees that You are making a conscious effort to live as close to Him as possible. He will help you grow into the man or woman of God that He has called you to be.

DECLARATIONS

I repent of all my sins knowingly and unknowingly, thought, deed, omission, and commission in Jesus' name.

Lord, forgive us for being a stiff-necked rebellious people instead of submitting to Your will.

Lord, forgive us for our sins so that You can heal our land of pestilences.

Lord, thank You for giving me multiple chances in Jesus' name.

Lord, thank You for being merciful to Your children in Jesus' name.

439. The Amplified Study Bible by Zondervan @ 2017 Accessed January 2022

Lord, I make a 180 degree turn from sin and turn back to righteousness in Jesus' name.

December 26th

ISAIAH 30:18 (AMP), "THEREFORE the LORD waits (expectantly) and longs to be gracious to you, And therefore He waits on high to have compassion on you. For the LORD is a God of justice; Blessed (happy, fortunate) are all those who long for Him (since He will never fail them)."

Expectantly in the Merriam Webster Dictionary is defined as one who is looking forward to something.[440] The Greek Word for Expectantly is "Apekdechomai," which means to expect eagerly, wait for eagerly, or look for.[441]

Those who make God their confidence will have comfort. God waits to be gracious to all who come to Him by faith and happy for those who wait upon Him. God will never fail us. Whenever we need Him all we have to do is reach out to Him and He comes to see about us. God loves His children and will move heaven and earth when they cry out to Him. He will never fail us; people will always fail us, but God will not fail us. Amen

---

440. Expectantly Merriam-Webster.com https://www.Merriam-Webster.com Accessed January 2022'
441. "Apekdechomai" Greek word for Expectantly https://www.biblehub.com Accessed January 2022

PRAYER

Father God, in the name of Jesus, I come before You today to thank You for never leaving or forsaking me but being with me until the end of this age. Lord, thank You for coming to see about me when I called out to You in Jesus' name. Lord, I can have the faith and the confidence that You are forever with me in this world. Lord, I get up every day expecting for You to move mightily in my life in Jesus' name. God, You are my source and resource for anything I need in my life. My job is not the answer, but You, God, are the answer for my every problem in Jesus' name. Amen.

December 27th

*D*ANIEL 6:16 (AMP), *"THEN the king gave a command, and Daniel was brought and thrown into the den of lions. The king said to Daniel, "May your God, whom you constantly serve, rescue you Himself."*

Rescue in the Merriam Webster Dictionary is defined as too free from confinement, danger, or evil; safe.[442] The Greek Word for Rescue is "Rhuomai," which means to draw to oneself, deliver, or rescue (from danger or destruction).[443]

King Darius wrote a decree that the people in his Kingdom couldn't pray to one God and that was him. But Daniel served the Creator of the Universe and refused to bow down to a statue made in King Darius' image. So, the decree stated that they could only bow down and pray when the flute blew. Daniel served the all-knowing God and refused to bow down to any statute. Daniel continued to pray three times a day as He had always done before the decree was written. The men that wanted

---

442. Rescue Merriam-Webster.com https://www.Merriam-Webster.com Accessed January 2022
443. "Rhuomai" Greek word for Rescue https://www.biblehub.com Accessed January 2022

to see Daniel harmed went and told King Darius that they saw Daniel praying to His God instead of bowing to King Darius's statue and so now King Darius had to make good on the decree. So now he has given orders for Daniel to be thrown in the lion's den. Daniel was thrown in the lion's dens, but nothing happened because God closed the mouth of the lions and when King Darius went out to see what had happened to Daniel, he found Daniel asleep on the lion's back. God had kept the lions from eating Daniel. The same applies to anyone reading this today. If you have a problem, just know that God can also solve your problems. God is no respecter of persons. What He has done for Daniel, He will do for you as well. God will close and shut the mouth of your enemies so that you will come out victorious again.

DECLARATIONS

I decree and declare that God was with Daniel in the Lion's den.

God closed the mouth of the lion's, so they didn't want to eat Daniel.

God came to Daniel's rescue, and he came out victorious.

If God be for you, then who can be against you?

I decree and declare that God hears the prayer of the righteous, and He answers them.

I decree and declare that God is no respecter of person. What He has done for one, He will do for the other one.

December 28th

ANIEL 6: 26-27 (AMP), "[26] I issue a decree that in all the dominion of my kingdom men are to (reverently) fear and tremble before the God of Daniel, For He is the Living God, enduring and steadfast forever; And His Kingdom is one which will not be destroyed. And His dominion will be forever. [27.] "He rescues and saves and performs signs and wonders in heaven and on earth. He who has rescued Daniel from the power of the lions."

Decree in the Merriam Webster Dictionary is defined as an order usually having the force of law.[444] The Greek Word for Decree is "Dogma," which is an opinion, ordinance, or decree.[445]

After King Darius went back to the lion's den and saw that Daniel was not harmed, he wrote a decree to serve the God that Daniel served because there was a demonstration that Daniel's God was indeed alive. The fear of the Lord fell upon the people

---

444. Decree Merriam-Webster.com https://www.Merriam-Webster.com Accessed January 2022
445. "Dogma" Greek word for Decree https://www.biblehub.com Accessed January 2022

because they knew that God had intervened in the situation without a shadow of doubt.

PRAYER

Father God, in the name of Jesus, thank You for opening the eyes of the unbelievers so they can be like King Darius and believe that You are real. Lord, show them without a shadow of a doubt the greatness of your mercy and grace toward us in Jesus's name. Lord, we know it had to be Your Spirit to shut the mouth of the lions while Daniel was in the lion's den all night in Jesus' name. Lord, help us believe You even more at Your Word in Jesus' name. Lord, we know that You have no respecter of persons. What You did for Daniel all those years ago, we know that You can do the same things for me in Jesus' name. Lord, we ask that You shut the mouths of all of my haters, the naysayers, and anybody else that has been coming up against me or my ministry, marriage, career, church, etc., in Jesus' name. Lord, I know I am victorious because of what Christ has done in my life in Jesus' name. Amen.

December 29th

*J*OEL 2:12 (AMP) "EVEN now, "says the LORD, Turn and come to Me with all of your heart (in genuine repentance), with fasting and weeping and mourning (until every barrier is removed and the broken fellowship is restored)."

Genuine in the Merriam Webster Dictionary is defined as an actual, real, or true, not false or fake.[446] The Greek Word for Genuine is "Alethinos," which means true, made of truth, real, or genuine.[447]

God told Israel to turn to Him with all of their heart and come in true repentance. We do not have time to be playing with God. We must be serious about every aspect of our Christian walk with God. We must turn to God with genuine repentance because He knows whether we mean it or not when we make vows to Him. We can never fool Him, so we might as well come clean and tell Him exactly where we are in our Christian

---

446. Genuine Merriam-Webster.com Https://www.Merriam-Webster.com Accessed January 2022

447. "Alethinos" Greek Word for Genuine https://www.biblehub.com Accessed January 2022

walk with Him. Life is too short not to be growing closer to God. The judgment of the Lord is upon the land. Make sure that you are in right standing with God when His judgment begins to fall. God is looking for genuine repentance for sin with fasting and sorrow. True repentance from the heart is life-changing, meaning you won't keep doing the same thing over and over if you know it grieves God. We can no longer use sin as a crutch to stay in a sinful lifestyle when God is calling His people to holiness and righteousness.

DECLARATIONS

I decree and declare that I will genuinely repent and live a holy and righteous lifestyle in Christ Jesus.

I decree and declare that I will not be trying to find excuses to stay in sin.

Lord, I am serious about my walk with You. I don't have time to keep playing church.

Lord, I surrender everything that is not like You in my life so that You can cleanse me in that area of my life.

Lord, create in me a clean heart and renew a right spirit in me in Jesus' name.

Lord, I desire to be pleasing in Your sight in Jesus' name.

December 30th

*H*AGGAI 2:4-5 (AMP) "BUT now be courageous, Zerubbabel, declares the LORD, "be courageous also, Johsua the son Jehozadak, the high
priest, and be courageous, all you people of the land, declares the
LORD, and work; for I am with you, declares the LORD of hosts."
5. "As for the promise which I made with you when you came out of
Egypt, My Spirit stands (firm and immovable) and continues with
you; do not fear!"

Courageous in the Merriam Webster Dictionary is defined
as very brave, having or showing courage.[448] The Greek Word
for Courageous is "Tharseo," which means to be of good courage and good cheer.[449]

God says to be of good courage. You are not alone; I am with
You. Do not fear because I got you and I am protecting you from
danger. God is saying the same thing to us today. His promises
are "Yes" and "Amen." We have nothing to fear because noth-

---

448. Courageous Merriam-webster.com https://www.Merriam-Webster.com Accessed January 2022
449. "Tharseo" Greek word for Courageous https://www.biblehub.com Accessed
January 2022

ing by any means shall hurt us. If God be for you, who can be against us? God is greater than anybody or anything. Immanuel is with us.

PRAYER

Father, we come before Your throne today, thanking You for being with us through the thick and thin in our lives. Lord, we can have faith and courage that You are with us. Lord, we know that You would never leave us but will be with us until the end of this world. Lord, help us keep confidence in Your ability instead of our abilities to help us through our troubles and trials in Jesus' name. Lord, we thank You for making way for us that we couldn't see with our natural eyes. Lord, thank You for always being there for us whenever we needed to cry out to You. Lord, just like You told Zerubbabel, we will be courageous and stand on Your Word and will for our lives in Jesus' name. Lord, thank You for being a friend that will stick closer to us than any brother in Jesus' name. Amen.

December 31st

MATTHEW 3:2 (AMP), "REPENT (change your inner self, your old way of thinking, regret past sins, live your life the way that proves repentance; seek God's purpose for your life), for the Kingdom of heaven is at hand."

Regret in the Merriam Webster Dictionary is defined as to mourn the loss or death of, and to miss very much.[450] The Greek Word for Regret is "Metamelomai," which means to regret, to repent, or change my mind.[451]

Repent, change your mind, and the old way you think. We are to have a total alternation in our minds. Change our judgment, disposition, and affections. True repentance is thinking of God, holiness, and righteousness. A change of mind produces a modification of the way that you are going. When we repent of our sins, we can, in turn, return to God for complete forgiveness of them. God gives us all mercy; He doesn't give us what

450. Regret Merriam-Webster.com https://www.Merriam-Webster.com Accessed January 2022
451. "Metamelomai" Greek word for Regret https://www.biblehub.com Accessed January 2022

we deserve. When we change our minds, we do a 180-degree turn from unrighteousness to righteousness in Christ Jesus.

DECLARATIONS

I decree and declare that I repent for all my sins, knowingly and unknowingly.

Lord, thank You for forgiving me of my past, present, and future sins in Jesus' name.

I will repent and change my mind about what I was doing in Jesus' name.

I will do a 180-degree turn from unrighteousness to righteousness in Jesus' name.

Lord, I thank You for saving a wretch like me and giving me a new heart.

Lord, I thank You for having mercy on me and not giving me what I deserved in Jesus' name.

About The Author

D r. LaRose Angela Richardson is the wife of Richard Richardson and the mother of Satar Cowan. She has one granddaughter, Allara Cowan. She has lived in Southeast Georgia all of her life. In May 2016, she graduated with a Doctor's Degree in Theology from Crossland Christian University in Orlando, Florida. She is the co-author of "It Cost Me Everything" written by Prophetess Kimberly Moses. She also has three other books that she has written. The first one is "Waking in Total Freedom after Healing from Deep Inner Wounds," and the second one is "Prayers That Availeth Much," and her third book is "180 days of Communing with God Daily devotional." She has also started a blog this year under the name of Grace Ministries Walking in Freedom, which can be found at ministerrich0628.blogspot.com. Her ministry pages can be found on Facebook, "Grace Ministries" and "Walking in Freedom." You can go on those pages weekly and hear a LIVE word from the Lord. All the teachings are words of encouragement that will inspire and to help you move forward in ministry. She can be contacted on Facebook on her ministry pages or her personal page "Angela Richardson." You can also email her at ministerrich0628@gmail.com.

References

1. Devotional Merriam-Webster.com 2019. https://www. Merriam-Webster.com accessed June 2021

2. "Proskartereo" The Greek word for devotional https:// www.biblehub.com accessed June 2021

3. Power Merriam-Webster.com 2019. https://www.Merriam-Webster.com Accessed June 2021

4. "Dumanis" The Greek Word for Power https://www.biblehub.com Accessed June 2021

5. Wind Merrian-Webster.com 2019. https://www.Merriam-Webster.com Accessed June 2021

6. "Pnuema" The Greek word for Wind https://www.biblehub.com Accessed June 2021

7. Strength Merriam-Webster.com 2019 https://www.Merriam-Webster.com Accessed June 2021

8. "Ischus" The Greek word for Strength https://www.biblehub.com Accessed June 2021

9. Shaking Merriam-Webster.com 2019 https://www.Merriam-Webster.com June 2021

10. "Saleuo" The Greek word for shaking https://www.biblehub.com Accessed June 2021

11. Matthew Henry's Concise Commentary. Volume 1 Zondervan Accessed June 2021

12. Obey Merriam-Webster.com 2019 https://www.Merriam-Webster.com Accessed June 2021

13. "Hypakoe" The Greek Word for Obey https://www.bible-hub.com Accessed June 2021

14. Paralyzed Merriam-Webster.com 2019 https://www.Mer-riam-Webster.com Accessed June 2021

15. "Paraluo" The Greek word for Paralyzed https://www.bi-blehub.com Accessed June 2021

16. Suddenly Merriam-Webster.com 2019 https://www.Merri-am-Webster.com Accessed June 2021

17. "Exaiphnes" The Greek Word for Suddenly https://www.biblehub.com Accessed June 2021

18. Ashamed Merriam-Webster.com 2019 https://www.Merri-am-Webster.com Accessed June 2021

19. "Aischune" The Greek Word for Ashamed https://www.biblehub.com Accessed June 2021

20. Matthew Henry's Concise Commentary book @1960 Zondervan Accessed June 2021

21. Salvation Merriam-Webster.com 2019 https://www.Merri-am-Webster.com Accessed June 2021

22. "Sozo" The Greek Word for salvation https://www.bible-hub.com Accessed June 2021

23. Matthew Henry's Concise Commentary Book Volume 1 @ 1960 Zondervan Accessed June 2021

24. Away Merriam-Webster.com 2019 https://www.Merriam-Webster.com Accessed June 2021.

25. "Apo" The Greek Word for Away https://www.biblehub.com Accessed June 2021

26. Persuaded Merriam-Webster.com https://www.Merriam-Webster.com Accessed June 2021

27. "Peitho" The Greek word for Persuaded https://www.biblehub.com Accessed June 2021

28. Unbelief Merriam-Webster.com https://www.Merriam-Webster.com Accessed June 2021

29. "Apistia" The Greek word for Unbelief https://www.biblehub.com Accessed June 2021

30. Matthew Henry's Concise Commentary Volume 1 @1960 Zondervan Accessed June 2021

31. Grace Merriam-Webster.com https://www.Merriam-Webster.com Accessed June 2021

32. "Charis" the Greek word for Grace https://www.biblehub.com Accessed June 2021

33. Matthew Henry's Concise Commentary Volume 1 Zondervan @ 1960 Accessed June 2021

34. Condemnation Merriam-Webster.com https://www.Merriam-Webster.com Accessed June 2021

35. "G2631 - katakrima - Strong's Greek Lexicon (kjv)." Blue Letter Bible. Accessed 6 Jun, 2022. https://www.blueletterbible.org/lexicon/g2631/kjv/tr/0-1/

36. Matthew Henry's Concise Commentary @ 1960 Zondervan Accessed June 2021

37. Carnal mind Merriam-Webster.com https://www.Merriam-Webster.com Accessed June 2021

38. "Sarkikos" the Greek word for carnal mind. https://www.biblehub.com Accessed June 2021

39. Spiritual Mind Merriam-Webster.com https://www.Merriam-Webster.com Accessed June 2021

40. "Pneumatikos" the Greek Word for Spiritual mind https://www.biblehub.com Accessed June 2021

41. Prayers that Availeth Much by LasRose A Richardson @2019 Accessed June 2021

42. Adoption Merriam-Webster.com https://www.Merriam-Webster.com Accessed June 2021

43. "Huiothesia" the Greek word for Adoption https://www.biblehub.com Accessed June 2021

44. https://www.dailyverse.kniwingjesus.com accessed June 2021

45. Perseverance Merriam-Webster.com https://www.biblehub.com Accessed June 2021

46. "Hupomone" The Greek word for Perseverance https://www.biblehub.com Accessed June 2021

47. Matthew Henry's Concise Commentary @1960 Zondervan accessed June 2021

48. Intercesssion Merriam-Webster.com https://www.Merriam-Webster.com Accessed June 2021

49. "Huperentugchano" the Greek word for Intercession https://www.biblehub.com Accessed June 2021

50. Matthew Henry's Concise Commentary Volume 1 @1960 Zondervan Accessed June 2021

51. https://www.kcm.org 5 benefits of speaking in tongues. Accessed June 2021

52. Callings Merrian-Webster.com https://www.Merriam-Webster.com Accessed June 2021

53. "Klesis" the Greek word for Calling Https://www.biblehub.com Accessed June 2021

54. Vengeance Merriam-Webster.com https://www.Merriam-Webster.com Accessed June 2021

55. "Ekidikesis" the Greek word for Vengeance https://www.biblehub.com Accessed June 2021

56. Abound Merrian-Webster.com https://www.Merriam-Webster.com Accessed June 2021

57. "Huperperisseuo" The Greek word for Abound https://www.bibleheub.com Accessed June 2021

58. www.bibleref.com https://www.bibleref.com June 2021

59. Speak Merriam-Webster.com https://www.Merriam-Webster.com Accessed June 2021

60. "Homologeo" the Greek for saying the same thing https://www.biblestudytool.com Accessed June 2021

61. Matthew Henry's Concise Commentary @1960 Zondervan Accessed June 2021

62. Hammer Merriam-Webster.com https://www.Merriam-Webster.com Accessed June 2021

63. "Maqqebeth" the Greek word for Hammer https://www.biblehub.com Accessed June 2021

64. Prepared Merriam-Webster.com https://www.Merriam-Webster.com Accessed June 2021

65. "Katartizo" The Greek Word for Prepared https://www.biblehub.com Accessed June 2021

66. Matthew Henry's Concise Commentary @1960 Zondervan Volume 1 Accessed June 2021

67. Kingdom Merriam-Webster.com https://www.Merriam-Webster.com Accessed June 2021

68. "Basileia" The Greek word for Kingdom https://www.biblehub.com Accessed June 2021

69. Matthew Henry's Concise Commentary Volume 1 @1960 Accessed June 2021

70. Joined Merriam-Webster.com https://www.Merriam-Webster.com Accessed June 2021

71. "Suzeugnumi" The Greek word for Joined https://www.biblehub.com Accessed June 2021

72. Matthew Henry's Concise Commentary Volume 1 @1960 Zondervan Accessed June 2021

73. Suffer Merriam-Webster.com https://www.Merriam-Webster.com Accessed June 2021

74. "Pascho" The Greek word for Suffer https://www.biblehub.com Accessed June 2021

75. Rejoice Merriam-Webster.com https://www.Merriam-Webster.com Accessed June 2021

76. "Sugchairo" Greek word for Rejoice https://www.biblehub.com accessed June 2021

77. Matthew Henry's Concise Commentary Volume 1 @1960 Zondervan Accessed June 2021

78. Fight Merriam-Webster.com https://www.Merriam-Webster.com Accessed June 2021

79. "Agonizomai" the Greek word for Fight https://www.biblehub.com Accessed June 2021

80. Matthew Henry's Concise Commentary Volume 1 @1960 Zondervan Accessed June 2021

81. Spirit Merriam-Webster.com https://www.Merriam-Webster.com Accessed June 2021

82. "Pneuma" The Greek Word for Spirit https://www.biblehub.com Accessed June 2021

83. Weapon Merriam-Webster.com https://www.Merriam-Webster.com Accessed June 2021

84. "Hoplon" The Greek word for Weapon https://www.biblehub.com Accessed June 2021

85. Woe Merriam-Webster.com https://www.Merrian-Webster.com Accessed June 2021

86. "Ouai" The Greek Word for Woe https://www.biblehub. com Accessed June 2021

87. Matthew Henry's Concise Commentary Volume 1 2 1960 Zondervan Accessed June 2021

88. Word Merriam-Webster.com https://www.Merriam-Webster.com Accessed June 2021

89. "Logos" Greek for the Word (WORD) https://www.biblehub.com Accessed June 2021

90. Jehovah Shammah https://www.jesusplusnothing.com Accessed August 2021

91. Light Merriam-Webster.com https://www.Merriam-Webster.com Accessed August 2021

92. "Phos" Greek word for Light https://www.biblehub.com Accessed August 2021

93. Matthew Henry's Concise Commentary https://www.biblehub.com Accessed August 2021

94. Everlasting Merriam-Webster.com https://www.Merriam-Webster.com Accessed August 2021

95. "Aionios" the Greek word for Everlasting https://www.biblehub.com Accessed August 2021

96. Benefits Merriam-Webster.com https://www.Merriam-Webster.com Accessed August 2021

97. "Ophelia" Greek word for Benefits https://www.biblehub. com Accessed August 2021

98. Blessed Merriam-Webster.com https://www.Merriam-Webster.com Accessed August 2021

99. "Markarios" the Greek word for Blessed https://www.biblehub.com accessed August 2021

100. Pour Merriam-Webster.com https://www.Merriam-Webster.com Accessed August 2021

101. "Spendo" The Greek Word for Pour https://www.biblehub.com Accessed August 2021

102. Fire Bible study Bible (KJV) Hendrick and Henderickson Bibles Accessed September 2021

103. Fountain Merriam-Webster.com https://www.Merriam-Webster.com Accessed September 2021

104. "Pege" the Greek word for Fountain. https://www.biblehub.com Accessed September 2021

105. Matthew Henry's Concise Commentary https://www.biblehub.com Accessed September 2021

106. Plowman Merrian-Webster.com https://www.Merriam-Webster.com Accessed September 2021

107. "Arotriao" the Greek word for Plowman https://www.biblehub.com Accessed September 2021

108. Fire Bible (KJV) Study Bible Hendrickson Publishing 2020 accessed September 2021

109. Laborers Merriam-Webster.com https://www.Merriam-Webster.com Accessed September 2021

110. "Kopos" The Greek Word for Laborers https://www.biblehub.com Accessed September 2021

111. Fire Study Bible (KJV) Hendrickson Publishing 2020 Accessed September 2021

112. Anointed Merriam-Webster.com https://www.Merriam-Webster.com Accessed September 2021

113. "Chrisma" The Greek word for Anointed https://www.biblehub.com Accessed September 2021

114. Fire bible study Bible (KJV) Hendrickson Publishing 2020 Accessed September 2021

115. Enemies Merriam-Webster.com Https://www.Merriam-Webster.com Accessed September 2021

116. "Echthros" the Greek Word for Enemies https://www.biblehub.com Accessed September 2021

117. Fire study Bible (KJV) Hendrickson Publishing 2020 Accessed September 2021

118. Good measure Merriam-Webster.com https://www.Merriam-Webster.com Accessed September 2021

119. "Metron" the Greek word for Good Measure https://www.biblehib.com Accessed September 2021

120. Deny Merriam-Webster.com https://www.Merriam-Webster.com Accessed September 2021

121. "Aparneomai" The Greek word for Deny https://www.biblehub.com Accessed September 2021

122. Fire study Bible Henderickson Publishing 2020 Accessed September 2021

123. Say Merriam-Webster.com https://www.Merriam-Webster.com Accessed September 2021

124. "Phemi" The Greek word for Say https://www.biblehib.com Accessed September 2021

125. Barnes Notes on the Bible Romans 8 :31 https://www.biblehub.com Accessed October 2021

126. Repentance Merriam-Webster.com https://www.Merriam-Webster.com Accessed October 2021

127. "Metanoeo" The Greek Word for Repentance https:///www.biblehub.com Accessed Octobeer 2021

128. Overcome Merriam Webster.com https://www.Merriam-Webster.com Accessed October 2021

129. "Nikao" The Greek word for Overcome https://www.biblehub.com Accessed October 2021

130. Barnes Notes on the Bible Commentary https://www.biblehub.com Accessed October 2021

131. Salvation Merriam-Webster.com https://www.Merriam-Webster.com Accessed October 2021

132. "Soteria" The Greek word for Salvation https://www.biblehub.com Accessed October 2021

133. Matthew Henry's concise Commentary https:/www.biblehub.com Accessed October 2021

134. Righteousness Merriam-Webster.com https://www.Merriam-Webster.com Accessed October 2021

135. "Dikaiosune" Greek word for Righteousness https://www.biblehub.com Accessed October 2021

136. Matthew Henry's Concise Commentary https://www.biblwehub.com Accessed October 2021

137. Father Merriam-Webster.com https://www.Merriam-Webster.com Accessed October 2021

138. "Pater" The Greek word for Father https://www.biblehub.com Accessed October 2021

139. Matthew Henry's Concise Commentary https://www.biblehub.com Accessed October 2021

140. Ordained Merriam-Webster.com https://www.Merriam-Webster.com Accessed October 2021

141. "Diatasso" The Greek Word for Ordained https://www.biblehub.com Accessed October 2021

142. Communion Merriam-Webster.com https://www.Merriam-webster.com Accessed October 2021

143. "Koinonia" The Greek word for Communion https://www.biblehub.com Accessed October 2021

144. Matthew Henery's Concise Commentary https://www.biblehub.com Accessed October 2021

145. Valor Merriam-Webster.com https://www.Merriam-Webster.com Accessed October 2021

146. "Andreia" Greek word for Valor https://www.biblehub. com Accessed October 2021

147. Matthew Henry's Concise Commentary https://www. biblehub.com Accessed October 2021

148. Rejoice Merriam-Webster.com https://www.Merriam-Webster.com Accessed October 2021

149. "Sugchairo" The Greek word for Rejoice httos://www. biblehub.com Accessed October 2021

150. Matthew Henry's Concise Commentary https://www. biblehub.com Accessed October 2021

151. Created Merriam-Webster.com https://www.Merriam-Webster.com Accessed October 2021

152. "Ktizo" Greek word for Created https://www.biblehub. com Accessed October 2021

153. Woman thou art Loosed Holy Bible by T.D. Jakes 1998 Accessed October 2021

154. Blesses Merriam-Webster.com https://www.Merriam-Webster.com Accessed October 2021

155. "Markarios" Greek Word for Blesses https://www.bi-blehub.com Accessed October 2021

156. Matthew Henry's Concise Commentary https://www. biblehub.com Accessed October 2021

157. Commandments Merriam-Webster.com https://www. Merriam-webster.com Accessed October 2021

158. "Entole" the Greek word for Commandment https:// www.biblehub.com Accessed October 2021

159. Matthew Henry's Concise Commentary https:// www,biblehub.com Accessed October 2021

160. Perfect Merriam-Webster.com https://www,Merriam-Webster.com Accessed October 2021

161. "Teleios" The Greek word for Perfect https://www.bi-blehub.com Accessed October 2021

162. Matthew Henry's Concise Commentary, https://www.biblehub.com Accessed October 2021

163. Fire Bible study Bible Zondervan @2012 Accessed October 2021

164. Characteristics of a true faithful and dependable God Fire Bible Study Bible Zondervan Accessed October 2021

165. Teacheth Merriam-Webster.com https://www.Merri-am-Webster.com Accessed October 2021

166. "Didasko" Greek Word for Teacheth https://www.bi-blehub.com Accessed October 2021

167. Wise Merriam-Webster.com https://www.Merriam-Webster.com Accessed October 2021

168. "Sophia" Greek word for Wise https://www.biblehub.com Accessed October 2021

169. Peace Merriam-Webster.com https://www.Merriam-Webster.com Accessed October 2021

170. "Eirene" Greek word for Peace https://www.biblehub.com Accessed October 2021

171. Valley Merriam-Webster.com https://www.Merriam-Webster.com Accessed October 2021

172. "Ikoiladu" Greek word for Valley https://www.word-hippo.com Accessed October 2021

173. Forgave Merriam-Webster.com https://www.Merriam-Webster.com Accessed October 2021

174. "Aphesis" Greek word for Forgave https://www.bible-hub.com October 2021

175. The Pulpit Commentary https://www.biblehub.com Accessed October 2021

176.   Meditation Merriam-Webster.com https://www.Merriam-Webster.com Accessed October 2021

177.   "Dalogismos" Greek Word for Meditation https://www.biblehub.com Accessed October 2021

178.   Call   Merriam-Webster.com   https://www.Merriam-Webster.com Accessed October 2021

179.   "Klesis" Greek word for Call https://www.biblehub.com Accessed October 2021

180.   Silent   Merriam-Webster.com   https://www.Merriam-Webster.com Accessed October 2021

181.   "Sigao" Greek word for Silent https://www.biblehub.com Accessed October 2021

182.   Fruitful Merriam-Webster.com https://www.Merriam-Webster.com Accessed October 2021

183.   "Karpos" Greek word for Fruitful https://www.biblehub.com Accessed October 2021

184.   Bubbling Merriam-Webster.com htttps://www.Merriam-Webster.com Accessed October 2021

185.   "Zelos" Greek word for Bubbling https://www.biblehub.com Accessed October 2021

186.   Matthew Henry's Concise Commentary https://www.biblehub.com Accessed October 2021

187.   Gladness Merriam-Webster.com https://www.Merriam-Webster.com Accessed October 2021

188.   "Euphrosune" Greek word for Gladness https://www.biblehub.com Accessed October 2021

189.   Saved Merriam-Webster.com Https://www.Merriam-Webster.com Accessed October 2021

190.   "Sozo" Greek word foe Saved https://www.biblehub.com Accessed October 2021

191. Matthew Henry's Concise Commentary https://www.biblehub.com Accessed October 2021

192. Opportunity Merriam-Webster.com https://www.Merriam-Webster.com Accessed October 2021

193. "Efkaina" Greek word for Opportunity https://www.wordhippo.com Accessed October 2021

194. Matthew Poole's Commentary https://www.biblehub.com Accessed October 2021

195. Praises Merriam-Webster.com https://www.Merriam-Webster.com Accessed October 2021

196. "Epainos" Greek word for Praises https://www.biblehub.com Accessed October 2021

197. Matthew Henry's Concise Commentary https://www.biblehub.com Accessed October 2021

198. Harvest Merriam-Webster.com https://www.Merriam-Webster.com Accessed October 2021

199. "Therismos" Greek word for Harvest https://www.biblehub.com Accessed October 2021

200. Learned Merriam-Webster.com https://www.Merriam-Webster.com Accessed October 2021

201. "Manthano" Greek word for Learned https://www.biblehub.com Accessed October 2021

202. Perfect Merriam-Webster.com https://www.Merriam-Webster.com Accessed October 2021

203. "Teleios" Greek for Perfect https://www.biblehub.com Accessed October 2021

204. Love Merriam-Webster.com https://www.Merriam-Webster.com October 2021

205. "Agape" Greek word for Love https://www.biblehub.com Accessed October 2021

206.   Matthew Henry's Concise Commentary https://www. biblehub.com Accessed October 2021

207.   Excellent Merriam-Webster.com https://www.Merriam-Webster.com Accessed October 2021

208.   "Arete" Greek word for Excellent https://www.biblehub.com Accessed October 2021

209.   Fear Merriam-Webster. https://www.Merriam-Webster.com Accessed October 2021

210.   "Phobos" Greek word for Fear https://www.biblehub. com Accessed October 2021

211.   Matthew Henry's Concise Commentary https://www. biblehub.com Accessed October 2021

212.   Renewed Merriam-Webster.com https://www.Merriam-Webster.com Accessed October 2021

213.   "Anakainoo" Greek word for Renewed https://www. biblehub.com Accessed October 2021

214.   Savior Merrriam-Webster.com https://www.Merriam-Webster.com Accessed October 2021

215.   "Soter" Greek word for Savior https://www.biblehub. com October 2021

216.   Matthew Henry's Concise Commentary https://www. biblehub.com Accessed October 2021

217.   Secret Merriam-Webster.com https://www.Merriam-Webster.com Accessed January 2022

218.   "Kruptos" Greek word for Secret https://www.biblehub.com Accessed January 2022

219.   Commandments Merriam-Webster.com https://www. Merriam-Webster.com Accessed January 2022

220.   "Entole" Greek word for Commandments https://www. biblehub.com Accessed January 2022

221. The Amplified Study Bible Zondervan 2017 Accessed January 2022

222. Doers Merriam-Webster.com https://www.Merriam-Webster.com Accessed January 2022

223. "Poietes" Greek word for Doers https://www.biblehub.com Accessed January 2022

224. Ungrateful Merriam-Webster.com https://www.Merriam-Webster.com Accessed January 2022

225. "Acharistos" Greek word for Ungrateful https://www.biblehub.com Accessed January 2022

226. Believe Merriam-Webster.com https://www.Merriam-Webster.com Accessed January 2022

227. "Pisteuo" Greek word for Believe https://www.blueletterbible.com Accessed January 2022

228. Goal Merriam-Webster.com https://www.Merrriam-Webster.com Accessed January 2022

229. "Telos" Greek word for Goal https://www.wikipedia.org Accessed January 2022

230. https://www.romesentinel.com article Accessed January 2022

231. Bears Merriam-Webster.com https://www.Merriam-Webster.com Accessed January 2022

232. "Arkouda" Greek word Bears https://www.biblehub.com Accessed January 2022

233. Courage Merriam-Webster.com https://www.Merriam-Webster.com Accessed January 2022

234. "Tharseo" Greek word foe Courage Https://www.biblehub.com Accessed January 2022

235. Search Merriam-Webster.com https://www.Merriam-Webster.com Accessed January 2022

236. "Heurisko" Greek word for Search https://www.bible-hub.com Accessed January 2022

237. Amplified Study Bible Zondervan 2017 Accessed January 2022

238. Fools Merriam-Webster.com https://www.Merriam-Webster.com Accessed January 2022

239. "Moros" Greek word for Fool https://www.Merriam-Webster.com Accessed January 2022

240. Stumble Merriam-Webster.com Https://www.Merriam-Webster.com Accessed January 2022

241. "Ptaio" Greek Word for Stumble https://www.bible-hub.com Accessed January 2022

242. Overflow Merriam-Webster.com https://www.Merriam-Webster.com Accessed January 2022

243. "Xecheilisma" Greek word for Overflow https://www.wordhippo.com Accessed January 2022

244. Listen Merriam-Webster.com Https://www.Merriam-Webster.com Accessed January 2022

245. "Akouo" Greek Word for Listen https://www.biblehub.com Accessed January 2022

246. Offspring Merriam-Webster.com https://www.Merriam-Webster.com Accessed January 2022

247. "Genos" Greek word for Offspring https://www.bible-hub.com Accessed January 2022

248. Defeated Merriam-Webster.com https://www.Merriam-Webster.com Accessed January 2022

249. "Nikise" Greek word for Defeated https://www.word-hippo.com Accessed January 2022

250. Storehouses Merriam-Webster.com https://www.Merriam-Webster.com Accessed January 2022

251. "Apotheke" Greek word for storehouse https://www. biblehub.com Accessed January 2022

252. Establish Merriam-Webster.com https://www.Merri- am-Webster.com Accessed January 2022

253. "Sterizo" Greek word for Establish https://www.bible- hub.com Accessed January 2022

254. Treasure Merriam-Webster.com https://www.Merri- am-Webster.com Accessed January 2022

255. "Thesaurus" Greek word for Treasure https://www. biblehub.com Accessed January 2022

256. Head Merriam-Webster.com https://www.Merriam- Webster.com Accessed January 2022

257. "Kephale" Greek word for Head https://www.biblehub. com Accessed January 2022

258. Curses Merriam-Webster.com https://www.Merriam- Webster.com Accessed January 2022

259. "Katara" Greek Word for Curse https://www.biblehub. com Accessed January 2022

260. The Amplified Study Bible by Zondervan @ 2017 Ac- cessed January 2022

261. Agree Merriam-Webster.com https://www.Merriam- Webster.com Accessed January 2022

262. "Sumphoneo" Greek word for Agree https://www.bi- blehub.com Accessed January 2022

263. Bind Merriam-Webster.com https://www.Merriam- Webster.com Accessed January 2022

264. "Deo" Greek word for Bind https://www.biblehub.com accessed January 2022

265. Loose Merriam-Webster.com https://www.Merriam- Webster.com Accessed January 2022

266. "Luo" Greek word for Loosed https://www.biblehub. com Accessed January 2022

267. Liberty. Merriam-Webster.com https://www.Merriam-Webster.com Accessed January 2022

268. "Eleutheria" Greek word for Liberty https://www.biblehub.com Accessed January 2022

269. Forgiveness Merriam-Webster.com https://www.Merriam-Webster.com Accessed January 2022

270. "Aphesis" Greek word for Forgiveness https://www.biblehub.com Accessed January 2022

271. Earnestly Merriam-Webster.com https://www.Merriam-Webster,com Accessed January 2022

272. "Epagonizomai" Greek word for Earnestly https://www.biblehub.com Accessed January 2022

273. Amplified Study Bible by Zondervan Accessed January 2022

274. "Rock" Merriam-Webster.com Https://www.Merriam-Webster.com Accessed January 2022

275. "Petra" Greek word for Rock https://www.biblehub. com Accessed January 2022

276. Matthew Henry's Concise Commentary https://www.biblehub.com Accessed January 2022

277. Courageous Merriam-Webster.com https://www.Merriam-Webster.com Accessed January 2022

278. "Tharseo" Greek word for Courageous https://www.biblehub.com Accessed January 2022

279. Potter Merriam-Webster.com https://www.Merriam-Webster.com Accessed January 2022

280. "Kerameus" Greek word for Potter https://www.biblehub.com Accessed January 2022

281. Amplified Study Bible Zondervan @2017 Accessed January 2022

282. Blessed Merriam-Webster.com https://www.Merriam-Webster.com Accessed January 2022

283. "Markarios" Greek word for Blessed https://www.biblehib.com Accessed January 2022

284. Faithful Merriam Webster.com https://www.Merriam-Webster.com Accessed January 2022

285. "Pistos" Greek word for Faithful https://www.biblehub.com Accessed January 2022

286. Devour Merriam-Webster.com https://www.Merriam-Webster.com Accessed January 2022

287. "Katavrochthizo" Greek word for Devour https://www.biblehub.com Accessed January 2022

288. Matthew Henry's Concise Commentary https://www.biblehub.com Accessed January 2022

289. Abundance Merriam-Webster.com https://www.Merriam-Webster.com Accessed January 2022

290. "Perissos" Greek word for Abundance https://www.biblehub.com Accessed January 2022

291. Generous Merriam-Webster.com https://www.Merriam-Webster.com Accessed January 2022

292. "Eumetadotos" Greek word for Generous https://www.biblehub.com Accessed January 2022

293. Thanks Merriam-Webster.com https://www.Merriam-Webster.com

294. "Eucharistia" Greek word for Thanks https://www.biblehub.com Accessed January 2022

295. Evil Merriam-Webster.com https://www.Merriam-Webster.com Accessed January 2022

296. "Kakos" Greek word for Evil https://www.biblehub.com Accessed January 2022

297. Gill's Exposition of the Entire Bible https://www.biblehub.com Accessed January 2022

298. Overcome Merriam-Webster.com https://www.Merriam-Webster.com Accessed January 2022

299. "Nikao" Greek word for Overcome https://www.biblehub.com Accessed January 2022

300. Acquainted Merriam-Webster.com https://www.Merriam-Webster.com Accessed January 2022

301. "Historeo" Greek word for Acquainted https://www.biblehub.com Accessed January 2022

302. Abide Merriam-Webster.com https://www.Merriam-Webster.com Accessed January 2022

303. "Meno" Greek word for Abide Https://www.biblehub.com Accessed January 2022

304. The Amplified Study Bible by Zondervan @ 2017 Accessed January 2022

305. Confident Merriam-Webster.com https://www.Merriam-Webester.com Accessed January 2022

306. "Pepoithesis" Greek word for Confident https://www.biblehub.com Accessed January 2022

307. Wisdom Merriam-Webster.com https://www.Merriam-Webster.com Accessed January 2022

308. "Sophia" Greek for Wisdom https://www.biblehub.com Accessed January 2022

309. Testing Merriam-Webster.com Htps://www.Merriam-Webster.com Accessed January 2022

310. "Peirazo" Greek Word for Testing https://www.biblehub.com Accessed January 2022

311.   Understand Merriam-Webster.com https://www.Merriam-Webster.com Accessed January 2022

312.   "Nous" Greek Word for Understand https://www.biblehub.com Accessed January 2022

313.   Matthew Henry's Concise https://www.biblehub.com Accessed January 2022

314.   Commandments Merriam-Webster.com https://www.Merriam-Webster.com Accessed January 2022

315.   "Entole" Greek for Commandments https://www.biblehub.com Accessed January 2022

316.   Matthew Henry's Concise Commentary Psalm 119:143 https://www.biblehub.com Accessed January 2022

317.   Hope Merriam-Webster.com https://www.Merriam-Webster.com Accessed January 2022

318.   "Elpis" Merriam-Webster.com https://www.Merriam-Webster.com Accessed January 2022

319.   Precepts. Merriam-Webster.com https://www.Merriam-Webster.com Accessed January 2022

320.   "Entalma" Greek word for Precepts https://www.biblehub.com Accessed January 2022

321.   The Amplified Study Bible by Zondervan @ 2017 Accessed January 2022

322.   Praying Merriam-Webster.com https://www.Merriam-Webster.com Accessed January 2022

323.   "Euche" Greek word for Praying https://www.biblehub.com Accessed January 2022

324.   Overwhelming Merriam-Webster.com https://www.Merriam-Webster.com Accessed January 2022

325.   "Synklonismenoi" Greek word for Overwhelming https://www.biblerhub.com Accessed January 2022

326. Intercede Merriam-Webster.com https://www.Merriam-Webster.com Accessed January 2022

327. "Hyperentugchano' Greek word for Intercede https://www.biblehub.com Accessed January 2022

328. Matthew Henry's Concise Commentary https://www.biblehub.com Accessed January 2022

329. Condemn Merriam-Webster.com https://www.Merriam-Webster.com Accessed January 2022

330. "Katakrima" Greek word for Condemn https://www.biblehub.com Accessed January 2022

331. Matthew Henry's Concise Commentary https://www.biblehub.com Accessed January 2022

332. Preach Merriam-Webster.com https://www.merriam-Webster.com Accessed January 2022

333. "Kerusso" Greek word for Preach https://www.biblehub.com Accessed January 2022

334. The Amplified Study Bible by Zondervan @2017 Accessed January 2022

335. Persistent Merriam-Webster.com https://www.Merriam-Webster.com Accessed January 2022

336. "Anaideia" Greek word for Persistent https://www.biblehub.com Accessed January 2022

337. Trustworthy Merriam-Webster.com https://www.Merriam-Webster.com Accessed January 2022

338. "Pistikos" Greek word for Trustworthy https://www.biblehub.com Accessed January 2022

339. Barnes Notes on the bible https://www.bibblehub.com Accessed Janauary 2022

340. Authority Merriam-Webster.com https://www.Merriam-Webster.com Accessed January 2022

341. "Exousia" Greek word for Authority https://www.bi-blehub.com Accessed January 2022

342. The Amplified Study Bible by Zondervan @2017 Accessed January 2022

343. Unbeliever Merriam-webster.com https://www.Merriam-Webster.com Accessed January 2022

344. "Apistos" Greek word for Unbeliever https://www.bi-blehub.com Accessed January 2022

345. Energized Merriam-Webster.com Https://www.Merriam-Webster.com Accessed January 2022

346. "Energes" Greek word for Energized https://www.bi-blehub.com Accessed January 2022

347. Superabundantly Merriam-webster.com https://www.Merriam-Webster.com Accessed January 2022

348. "Hyperrkperissou" Greek word for Superabundantly https://www.biblehub.com Accessed January 2022

349. Sealed Merriam-Webster.com https://www.Merriam-Webster.com Accessed January 2022

350. "Sphragzo" Greek word for Sealed https://www.bible-hub.com Accessed January 2022

351. Blessing Merriam-Webster.com https://www.Merriam-Webster.com Accessed January 2022

352. "Makarios" Greek Word for Blessing https://www.bi-blehub.com Accessed January 2022

353. Reverent Merriam-Webster.com https://www.Merriam-Webster.com Accessed January 2022

354. "Eulabeia" Greek for Reverent https://www.biblehub.com Accessed January 2022

355. Guidance merriam-Webster.com https://www.Merriam-Webster.com Accessed January 2022

356.   "Hodegeo" Greek word for Guidance https://www.biblehub.com Accessed January 2022

357.   Oppose Merriam-Webster.com Https://www.Merriam-Webster.com Accessed January 2022

358.   "Anthistemi" Greek word for Oppose https://www.biblehub.com Accessed January 2022

359.   God-Breathed https://www.biblehub.com Accessed January 2022

360.   "Theopheastes" Greek for God breathed https://www.biblehub.com Accessed January 2022

361.   God Merriam-Webster.com https://www.Merriam-Webster.com Accessed January 2022

362.   "Theos" Greek word for God https://www.biblehub.com Accessed January 2022

363.   Peace Merriam-Webster.com Https://www.Merriam-Webster.com Accessed January 2022

364.   "Eirene" Greek word for Peace https://www.Biblehub.com Accessed January 2022

365.   Matthew Henry's Concise Commentary Accessed January 2022

366.   Resurrection Merriam-Webster.com https://www.Merriam-Werbster.com Accessed January 2022

367.   "Anastasis" Greek word for Resurrection https://www,biblehub.com Accessed January 2022

368.   Ellicott's Commentary for English Readers' https://www.biblehub.com Accessed January 2022

369.   Lord Merriam-Webster.com https://www.Merriam-Webster.com Accessed January 2022

370.   "Kuriakos" Gree word for Lord https://www.biblehub.com Accessed January 2022

371. Hiding Merriam-Webster.com https://www.Merriam-Webster.com Accessed January 2022

372. "Kruptos" Greek word for Hiding https://www.biblehub.com Accessed January 2022

373. Longingly Merriam-Webster.com https://www.Merriam-Webster.com Accessed January 2022

374. "Orego" Greek for the Word Longingly https://www.biblehub.com Accessed January 2022

375. Matthew Henry's Concise Commentary https://www.biblehub.com Accessed January 2022

376. Devoted Merriam-Webster.com https://www.Merriam-Webster.com Accessed January 2022

377. "Proskartereo" Greek word for Devoted https://www-biblehub.com Accessed January 2022

378. Matthew Henry's Concise Commentary https://www.Biblehub.com Accessed January 2022

379. Prophesy Merriam-Webster.com Https://www.Merriam-Webster.com Accessed January 2022

380. "Propeteia" Greek for Prophesy https://www.Biblehub.com Accessed January 2022

381. Resist Merriam-Webster.com https://www.biblehub.com Accessed January 2022

382. "Anthistemi" Greek word for Resist https://www.biblehub.com Accessed January 2022

383. Law of the Lord https://www.lovegodgreatly.com Accessed January 2022

384. "Nomos" Greek word for Law of the Lord https://www.biblehub.com Accessed January 2022

385. Wisdom Merriam-Webster.com https://www.Merriam-Webster.com Accessed January 2022

386. "Sophia" Greek word for Wisdom https://www.bible-hub.com Accessed January 2022

387. Reverent Merriam-Webster.com Https://www.Merri-am-Webster.com Accessed January 2022

388. "Eulabeia" Greek word for Reverent https://www.bi-blehub.com Accessed January 2022

389. Wicked Merriam-Webster.com https://www.Merriam-Webster.com Accessed January 2022

390. "Poneros" Greek word for Wicked https://www.bi-blestudytool.com Accessed January 2022

391. Matthew Henry's Concise Commentary https://www.biblehub.com Accessed January 2022

392. Ointment Merriam-Webster.com https://www.Merri-am-Webster.com Accessed January 2022

393. "Muron" Greek word for Ointment https://www.bible-hub.com Accessed January 2022

394. Strength Merriam-Webster.com https://www.Merri-am-Webster.com Accessed January 2022

395. "Ichus" Greek word for Strength https://www.bible-hub.com Accessed January 2022

396. Fear Merriam-Webster.com https://www.Merriam-Webster.com Accessed January 2022

397. "Phobos" Greek word for fear https://www.biblehub.com Accessed January 2022

398. Matthew Henry's Concise Commentary https://www.biblehub.com Accessed January 2022

399. Rest Merriam-Webster.com https://www.Merriam-Webster.com Accessed January 2022

400. "Anapauo" Greek word for Rest https://www.biblehub.com Accessed January 2022

401. Power Merriam-Webster.com https://www.Merriam-Webster.com Accessed January 2022

402. "Dunamis" Greek word for Power https://www.bible-hub.com Accessed January 2022

403. Enriched Merriam-Webster.com https://www.Merriam-Webster.com Accessed January 2022

404. "Kukloo" Greek word for Enriched https://www.bible-hub.com Accessed January 2022

405. Forfeit Merriam-Webster.com https://www.Merriam-Webster.com Accessed January 2022

406. "Zemioo" Greek word for Forfeit https://www.bible-hub.com Accessed January 2022

407. Barnes Noted of the Bible, https://www.biblehub.com Accessed January 2022

408. Grace Merriam-Webster.com Https://www.Merriam-Webster.com Accessed January 2022

409. "Charis" Greek for Grace https://www.biblehub.com Accessed January 2022

410. Sovereign Merriam-Webster.com https://www.Merriam-Webster.com Accessed January 2022

411. "Pantokrator" Greek word for Sovereign https://www.biblehub.com Accessed January 2022'

412. Critical Merriam-Webster.com Https://www.Merriam-Webster.com Accessed January 2022

413. "Kritikos" Greek word for Critical https://www.bible-hub.com Accessed January 2022

414. Matthew Henry's Concise Commentary https://www.biblehub.com Accessed January 2022

415. Earth Merriam-Webster.com https://www.Merriam-Webster.com Accessed January 2022

416.   " Ge" Greek word for Earth https://www.biblehub.com Accessed January 2022

417.   The Amplified Study Bible by Zondervan @ 2017 Accessed January 2022

418.   Misusing Merriam-Webster.com https://www.Merriam-Webster.com Accessed January 2022

419.   "Apochresis" Greek word for Misuse https://www.biblehub.com Accessed January 2022

420.   Humanity Merriam-Webster.com https:/www.Merriam-Webster.com Accessed January 2022

421.   "Anthroos" Greek word for Humanity Https://www.biblehub.com Accessed January 2022

422.   Temporarily Merriam-Webster.com https://www.Merriam-Webster.com Accessed January 2022

423.   "Proskairos" Greek word for Temporarily https://www.biblehub.com Accessed January 2022

424.   Matthew Henry's Concise Commentary https://www.biblehub.com Accessed January 2022

425.   Anxiously Merriam-Webster.com https://www.Merriam-Webster.com Accessed January 2022

426.   "Merimnao" Greek word for Anxious https://www.biblehub.com Accessed January 2022

427.   Timidity Merriam-Webster.com https://www.Merriam-Webster.com Accessed January 2022

428.   "Delia" Greek word for Timidity Https://www.biblehub.com Accessed January 2022

429.   Disciples Merriam-Webster.com https://www.Merriam-Webster.com Accessed January 2022

430.   "Mathetes" Greek word for Disciples https://www.biblehub.com Accessed January 2022

431.   The Amplified Study Bible by Zondervan @ 2017 Accessed January 2022

432.   Allotted Merriam-Webster.com https://www.Merriam-Webster.com Accessed January 2022

433.   "Proskleroo" Greek Word for Allotted https://www.biblehub.com Accessed January 2022

434.   Angry Merriam-Webster.com Https://www.Merriam-Webster.com Accessed January 2022

435.   "Orge" Greek word for Angry https://www.biblehub.com Accessed January 2022

436.   Scarlet Merriam-Webster.com https://www.Merriam-Webster.com Accessed January 2022

437.   "Kokkinos" Greek word for Scarlet https://www.biblehub.com Accessed January 2022

438.   The Amplified Study Bible by Zondervan @ 2017 Accessed January 2022

439.   Expectantly Merriam-Webster.com https://www.Merriam-Webster.com Accessed January 2022'

440.   "Apekdechomai" Greek word for Expectantly https://www.biblehub.com Accessed January 2022

441.   Rescue Merriam-Webster.com https://www.Merriam-Webster.com Accessed January 2022

442.   "Rhuomai" Greek word for Rescue https://www.biblehub.com Accessed January 2022

443.   Decree Merriam-Webster.com https://www.Merriam-Webster.com Accessed January 2022

444.   "Dogma" Greek word for Decree https://www.biblehub.com Accessed January 2022

445.   Genuine Merriam-Webster.com Https://www.Merriam-Webster.com Accessed January 2022

446. "Alethinos" Greek Word for Genuine https://www.biblehub.com Accessed January 2022

447. Courageous Merriam-webster.com https://www.Merriam-Webster.com Accessed January 2022

448. "Tharseo" Greek word for Courageous https://www.biblehub.com Accessed January 2022

449. Regret Merriam-Webster.com https://www.Merriam-Webster.com Accessed January 2022

450. "Metamelomai" Greek word for Regret https://www.biblehub.com Accessed January 2022

Index

future, 100, 103, 124, 192, 233, 242, 305, 308, 318, 336, 346, 416

G

garment, 187, 340

generation, 213, 395

Gentiles, 37, 201

gift, 15, 39, 42, 54, 55, 56, 57, 107, 127, 128, 155, 190, 333, 345, 374, 376, 397

glory, 14, 20, 26, 33, 38, 51, 70, 99, 100, 107, 122, 138, 143, 147, 161, 174, 179, 184, 211, 259, 288, 289, 313, 315, 320, 337, 364, 372, 373, 395

God, 1, 2, 3, 5, 6, 7, 8, 11, 12, 13, 14, 15, 16, 17, 18, 19, 20, 21, 22, 23, 24, 25, 26, 27, 28, 29, 30, 31, 33, 34, 36, 37, 38, 40, 42, 44, 45, 46, 47, 48, 50, 51, 52, 53, 54, 55, 56, 57, 58, 59, 60, 61, 64, 66, 67, 68, 69, 70, 71, 72, 73, 75, 76, 79, 80, 81, 82, 84, 85, 86, 88, 90, 91, 92, 93, 94, 95, 96, 97, 98, 99, 100, 103, 104, 105, 106, 107, 108, 109, 111, 113, 114, 115, 117, 120, 121, 122, 123, 124, 125, 126, 127, 128, 130, 132, 133, 134, 135, 136, 137, 138, 140, 141, 142, 143, 144, 145, 146, 147, 149, 150, 151, 152, 153, 154, 155, 156, 157, 158, 159, 160, 161, 162, 163, 164, 165, 166, 167, 168, 169, 170, 171, 172, 173, 174, 175, 176, 177, 178, 179, 180, 181, 182, 183, 184, 185, 186, 187, 188, 189, 190, 191, 192, 194, 195, 196, 197, 198, 199, 200, 201, 202, 203, 204, 205, 206, 207, 208, 210, 211, 212, 213, 214, 215, 217, 218, 219, 220, 221, 222, 223, 224, 225, 226, 227, 228, 229, 230, 231, 232, 233, 234, 235, 236, 237, 238, 239, 240, 241, 242, 243, 244, 245, 246, 248, 249, 251, 252, 253, 254, 255, 256, 257, 258, 259, 260, 261, 263, 264, 265, 266, 267, 268, 269, 270, 271, 272, 273, 274, 275, 276,

M

milk, 108, 206, 233

minions, 246

ministers, 137, 138

ministry, 5, 7, 8, 27, 34, 48, 117, 201, 261, 303, 337, 347, 364, 395, 410, 417

miracles, 4, 6, 13, 14, 15, 20, 52, 291, 389

misery, 251

misfortune, 89

mistreated, 58, 59, 103, 166

money, 10, 11, 22, 122, 236, 267, 281, 282, 353

moons, 93

moral, 133, 216, 217, 281, 309, 327

morning, 51, 68, 95, 184, 272, 342, 391

Moses, 102, 325, 326, 376, 417

mountain, 310, 318

mountains, 34, 108, 111

mourners, 389

mouth, 29, 34, 38, 45, 55, 82, 92, 102, 103, 122, 167, 168, 171, 194, 246, 247, 261, 288, 295, 347, 354, 355, 407, 410

mouthpiece, 213

mustard seed, 52

mysteries, 69, 70

N

narrow path, 274

nations, 33, 143, 186, 208, 226, 236, 238, 394

nature, 155, 260, 277, 281, 311, 330, 339, 368

naysayers, 410

Nehemiah, 81, 82

school, 3

scorpions, 309, 310

scriptures, 1, 26, 36, 37, 38, 61, 67, 76, 84, 85, 104, 157, 185, 201, 230, 250, 305, 328, 332, 349, 400

season, 92, 185, 236, 249, 304, 367, 386

secrets, 158, 171, 172, 211

security, 131, 378

seed, 33, 93, 111, 112, 121, 122, 225, 228, 233, 265, 268, 270, 387

self-control, 220, 318, 355, 391, 400

serpents, 309, 310

servants, 13, 48, 70, 87, 106, 231, 359

shame, 25, 27, 321

shelter, 164, 339

shield, 142, 157, 158, 264, 276

sick, 4, 5, 20, 21, 73, 140, 309, 358

Silas, 22, 23, 24

sin, 5, 24, 28, 38, 39, 40, 41, 42, 43, 57, 72, 76, 103, 117, 125, 126, 127, 130, 131, 133, 134, 165, 168, 179, 194, 206, 222, 223, 234, 240, 248, 250, 273, 275, 293, 294, 302, 303, 304, 310, 311, 317, 347, 348, 351, 368, 369, 374, 375, 387, 399, 402, 403, 412

sinful, 29, 131, 155, 275, 311, 379, 412

sisters, 192, 193, 223, 287

skepticism, 36

slave, 134

slavery, 72, 75, 248

sleep, 68, 131, 378

slothful, 82

snares, 82

social media, 172

Z

Zerubbabel, 413, 414

www.ingramcontent.com/pod-product-compliance
Lightning Source LLC
Chambersburg PA
CBHW070857120626
46546CB00001B/34